Anonymous

**King and commonwealth**

A history of the great rebellion

Anonymous

**King and commonwealth**
*A history of the great rebellion*

ISBN/EAN: 9783337204075

Printed in Europe, USA, Canada, Australia, Japan

Cover: Foto ©ninafisch / pixelio.de

More available books at **www.hansebooks.com**

# KING AND COMMONWEALTH

A HISTORY

OF

THE GREAT REBELLION.

Nor set down aught in malice.

LONDON
SEELEY, JACKSON, AND HALLIDAY
1874

# KING AND COMMONWEALTH.

## CHAPTER I.
CONSTITUTIONAL INTRODUCTION.—GOVERNMENTS OF ELIZA-
BETH AND JAMES I.

No people ever was and remained free, but because it was determined to be
so; because neither its rulers nor any other party in the nation could
compel it to be otherwise. If a people—especially one whose freedom has
not yet become prescriptive—does not value it sufficiently to fight for it
and maintain it against any force which can be mustered *within* the
country, it is only a question in how few years or months that people will
be enslaved.—MILL, DISSERTATIONS AND DISCUSSIONS.

A PEOPLE, to be free, must take part in, or possess control over, the three powers of government, Legislative, Executive, Judicial. As to the first, if they are to be masters of their persons and properties, neither laws must be made nor taxes imposed without their consent; secondly, ministers of the executive, whether councillors of state, tax-collectors, military or police officers, must be personally responsible to the law courts, or they may infringe with impunity the laws the people have secured; lastly, though persons and properties be protected by laws, and though ministers be liable to prosecution, this protection is nominal only, unless the judges who interpret the laws, are sufficiently independent of the executive. {Three functions of government, I. Legislative, II. Executive, III. Judicial.}

I. Englishmen of the seventeenth century shared in the legislative power with the sovereign, who could make no laws without consent of the two Houses of Parliament. Their properties were protected from arbitrary seizure, their persons from arbitrary imprisonment, by two statutes, the Magna Charta, first granted by King John, and the Confirmatio Chartarum, first granted by Edward I. {I. Legislative. Liberties of Englishmen in 16th and 17th centuries.}

These together provide, first, that no person shall be put in prison without legal warrant, or kept there without being brought to trial according to the laws of the land; that is, that the question of law shall be decided by the established judge of the law; secondly, that the question of fact, whether a man accused at the suit of the crown, has, or has not, committed the crime laid to his charge, shall be decided by a jury of twelve of his countrymen; and lastly, that no taxes of any sort shall be imposed without consent of Parliament.

**Classes represented in Parliament.** Several classes of the nation shared indirectly in the government by being represented in Parliament. In the Upper House sat the temporal and spiritual lords of the realm in their own right. To the Lower House all the fifty-two counties of England and Wales, with the exception of Durham, returned two members each, elected by freeholders possessed of lands or tenements to the annual value of 40s.* The term **Freeholders including feudal tenants and yeomen.** freeholder included two classes, holders of land by knight's service, and holders of land by free socage.† The first class was composed of feudal tenants, gentlemen by birth, who had originally held land in return for military service, and whose tenure was still subject to several irksome burdens. The second class was composed of yeomen, men of ignoble blood, but with a tenure dating from feudal times. The Normans of the conquest would have thought it beneath them to hold land by any other than a military tenure. But in many cases they permitted the despised Saxons to remain in possession of their lands, sometimes on condition of performing agricultural services which soon took the form of a fixed annual rent; sometimes on condition merely of taking an oath of fealty and paying occasional fines. Thus in England there sprang up in quite early times an independent class who were owners of the soil, and though not of gentle birth, sat on juries, voted at county elections, and attended the courts in which freeholders met together to transact the business of their county.

* Money was about three times its present value, that is, one shilling then could purchase as much food or other necessaries of life as three shillings now; so this would now represent land which would bring in £6 a year as rent and cost say £150 to buy.

† Socage is probably derived from Saxon *soc*, "liberty," "privilege," "franchise." *Socagers* were bound to attend the court of the lord to whose *soc* or "right" of justice they belonged.

Besides county representatives, the House of Commons contained over four hundred members, returned according to usage by certain privileged towns. These were the classes possessed of political rights. Below these were the whole mass of the unenfranchised—hired labourers, tenants at will, and copyholders.* These were the descendants of those Saxons whom the Normans had reduced to a state of serfdom; and, unlike freeholders, were incapable either of sitting on juries or voting at elections. For the last hundred years, however, they had nearly all been free, and were protected in person and property by the same laws as freeholders.

All classes being thus possessed of the same liberties, their common freedom gave them common interests, and caused them to unite in spite of social distinctions, and oppose the establishment of arbitrary government.

In France the political condition of the people was inferior to that of the English, and this mainly from want of union and fellow-feeling between the different ranks into which French society was divided. There was no class answering to the English yeomanry; the feudal tenants were a noble and privileged class, and were divided by this barrier of privilege from their unfortunate inferiors in rank, on whom the main burden of direct taxation fell; as the inequalities of taxation increased, the different classes became more and more isolated, and thus the kings, never meeting with combined resistance from the whole body of their subjects, came by degrees to usurp absolute power, to impose taxes at will, and to govern without the aid of any national assembly.

II. A people are little benefited by the possession of good laws, unless those laws are respected and obeyed by those who are entrusted with the execution of them. The executive power was then, as now, exercised by ministers of the crown. But in the course of two centuries the position of these ministers has been totally changed. The queen's ministers are now in such close harmony with the Parliament, that they have been defined as a committee of the

*Burgesses.*

*Copyholders and hired labourers unrepresented.*

*No privileged class.*

*II. Executive Power now exercised by a committee of the legislature.*

---

* The *copyholder* held land of the lord of the manor, subject to certain restrictions and agricultural services enumerated in the *copy* of the roll of the estate. So long as he performed those services he might not be dispossessed.

legislature.* Chosen out of the predominant party in Parliament, they conduct the government only so long as they can command a majority of votes in the Lower House. If their measures are outvoted, they have no choice but to resign office, or by obtaining a dissolution, to appeal to a new Parliament for renewal of the support which is their only claim to power.

<small>Executive in 16th century exercised by the crown.</small> In the sixteenth century, on the contrary, the executive power lay entirely in the hands of the king, who settled all questions of administration, made peace and war, appointed and dismissed officers of state, and expended the revenue, uncontrolled by the representatives of the people. Yet, great as was the power thus exercised by the crown, two safeguards were provided against its abuse. The first was <small>Two safeguards. (1) No army in England.</small> negative, the absence of a standing army in England. In France absolute power was upheld by an army, recruited in part by foreigners, and officered solely by nobles; this army the king found no difficulty in maintaining, as he imposed taxes at pleasure. No such right, however, belonged to English monarchs, who were without the funds necessary for the support of a standing army; and it was only by means of a standing army, possessed with an 'esprit de corps' of its own, and divided in interest from the people, that arbitrary government could be permanently established. The House of Commons always originated money bills; they held, therefore, the purse-strings of the nation, and were careful only to grant supplies sufficient for the ordinary purposes of government.

* Though this is substantially true as a contrast to the position of the ministry in the 16th century, it would be a great mistake to disregard the influence of the *forms* under which the constitution works. (I.) Even now the control of the Commons is not so great as it seems. The ministers are not mere delegates, for Parliament controls rather than directs; it has no right to tell the Queen's ministers what to do, though it can veto their proposals, and censure them for their acts when done; the initiative remains with the cabinet. (II.) The influence of the crown is more than it seems. (i.) It has a voice in discussing despatches which settle foreign policy. (ii.) Though it cannot exclude from office a man who has made himself indispensable to the nation, it has, no doubt, a negative voice in the selection of the less conspicuous members of the cabinet, and thus exercises a real, though imperceptible, influence on the attitude of rising politicians.

The *form* is always of vast importance in constitutional questions. The popular influence, which seems to be the substantial power, is the wind that fills the sails and gives the motion; but the exact direction of the motion must still depend in a large measure on the helmsman. The shipwreck of the 17th century came from an attempt to sail in the teeth of the wind. A skilful helmsman may do much by gaining and losing tacks, but the Stuarts were not skilful.

CONSTITUTION.] SAFEGUARDS—DANGER OF ABUSE. 5

The principles of the constitution contained a second and positive safeguard against the abuse of the regal power. (2) Responsibility of the king's ministers. Great lawyers had long since declared that the king, like his subjects, was bound to respect the laws. "The king," Bracton wrote as early as the thirteenth century, "also hath a superior, namely God, and also the law, by which he was made a king." It was not likely, however, that the subject would have either the power or the desire to arraign sovereigns themselves before courts of law. A fiction of the lawyers intervened and gave a better means of securing the same end. This fiction was that the "king could do no wrong." From this it followed that if wrong was done, the ministers, and not the king, must have advised and executed the wrong; ministers could not screen themselves behind the king's name; if they broke the laws in the performance of their functions, though it was at the king's bidding, they were still liable to be sued by the injured parties in a court of justice.

Still these safeguards had not been found sufficient to prevent the executive from violating the law. In the first place, several powers, sometimes simply oppressive, sometimes actually illegal, were regarded as belonging to the crown in right of the royal prerogative. By these both the subject's property and liberty were endangered. Thus the king, though he dared not tax without consent of Parliament, used to borrow large sums under the name of loans, which were seldom repaid. Both the king and his council imprisoned without showing legal cause. Ordinances were made by the King in Council, which, though regarded as temporary measures only, were in matter of fact laws, and sometimes had penalties attached to them for disobedience. So again, though the use of torture was not lawful by the common law, and contrary to several statutes, State prisoners were constantly put to the rack on the strength of warrants signed by the king. Liberties not secure. (1) Illegal powers exercised by crown.

In the second place, though the law allowed the subject to seek redress, the redress was rarely attainable. Few dared to incur the king's displeasure by attacking the conduct of his servants, and if they did, juries were often intimidated,* judges were often corrupt. The strength of the chain is the (2) Judges dependent upon crown.

---

* Under the Tudors, juries had been fined and imprisoned for deciding against the crown. If they decided for the crown, though unjustly, they could not be punished, because they could not have been tampered with by the sovereign!

strength of its weakest point. The weak point of the English constitution lay in the dependence of the judges upon the crown; unless the interpreters of the laws were independent, no law could ever effectually secure the liberties of the people.

(3) Arbitrary courts. And in the third place, besides the common law courts, other courts of justice existed, in which the accused was neither tried by jury nor sentenced according to known laws.

III. Judicial. Omitting the Court of Chancery, which had no jurisdiction in political cases, there were then, as now, three chief courts of justice, the King's Bench, the Common Pleas, and the Exchequer, all of which sat at Westminster; four or five judges belonged to each, who in all cases were bound to give judgment, not according to their own pleasure, or the will of the king, but according to the law of the realm, whether statute or common law.*

Since the Act of Settlement in 1702 the common law judges hold office for life, receive salaries fixed by law, and can only be dismissed from office if convicted of some offence, or in consequence of an address of the two Houses of Parliament. But in the seventeenth century they only held office at the pleasure of the king, and being dependent in part upon his bounty for their salaries, were regarded as the servants of the court.†

But these courts at any rate acknowledged the known laws, and tried prisoners by jury. Of a very different character was the Court of Star Chamber, so called because its sittings were held in a room leading out of Westminster Hall, of which the walls were decorated with stars. The germ of this court lay in a jurisdiction exercised from the time of Edward III. by the king's Common Council, which was accustomed to call to account offenders too powerful to be brought to submit to the ordinary courts of law. Then came a second stage. An Act of Parliament was passed in the reign of Henry VII. (1491), forming a court of justice, composed of certain members of the

* The common law consists of customs handed down from Norman times, and of the judgments of judges founded upon those customs; statute law of acts of Parliament.

† Thus in James' time the Admiralty judge acknowledges the receipt of instructions, "by which I understand his Majesty's resolution to continue Sir John Eliot in prison. I am glad I did forbear to deliver my opinion of the state of his cause, lost perhaps it might have differed somewhat."—Forster's Eliot, i. ii. 4.

council, and entrusted with powers of judging cases of riots, the bribing of juries, and other specified offences. This second stage gave a parliamentary sanction to the court, but limited its powers and specified its persons. It was out of this chrysalis that the Court of Star Chamber emerged. By the end of Henry the Eighth's reign, it had reached its third, or final stage, in which it boasted parliamentary sanction, at the same time that it repudiated the conditions under which that sanction had been given. The limits of persons and of offences had both disappeared. The powers formerly vested only in the members of the court of Henry VII. had silently passed into the hands of the whole body of the Common Council,* while its jurisdiction had been extended beyond the offences specified by the statute to cases of breach of trust, fraud, and libel.

Besides the Court of Star Chamber, there was a second court, the Court of High Commission, which deprived the subject of the protection granted him by the common law, and of trial by jury. After Henry VIII. quarrelled with Pope Clement VII. about a divorce from Catherine of Arragon, Parliament passed an Act of Supremacy, declaring the king the supreme head of the Church. This was re-enacted when Elizabeth came to the throne (1558), and an addition made to it, granting the queen power to appoint persons to exercise jurisdiction in ecclesiastical affairs, as, for instance, in the reformation of heresies and abuses. Elizabeth, therefore, was acting within her powers when, in 1583, she erected a permanent commission, consisting of twelve bishops, privy councillors, and others; but she undoubtedly was straining her power when she gave this court an authority—not granted her by the statute—to try suspected persons by juries, or *by any other means they could devise*, and to punish by fine and imprisonment. Thus, while the Court of Star Chamber, by judging cases of libel, deprived the subject of liberty of speech, the Court of High Commission deprived him of liberty of conscience. Both alike, therefore, soon came to be hated by the people; both were distinctly contrary to Magna Charta, for in neither was the accused tried by jury or by the laws of the land; both were contrary to the first axioms of jus-

* The king had two councils: his Privy Council, which advised with him in all State matters, and his Common Council. In the Common Council sat, not only all members of the Privy Council, but also some of the common law judges, and others added at the pleasure of the king.

tice, the separation of accuser and judge, for in these courts the ministers of the crown first prosecuted a man in their capacity of councillors, and then themselves passed sentence upon him as judges.

Queen Elizabeth was not disposed to yield up any powers, legal or illegal, that had been exercised by her predecessors on the throne. She, however, was careful not to strain them beyond what the temper of the nation would bear. Though she *Caution with which Elizabeth exercised her power.* often violated the rights of individuals, she never attacked those of large numbers at once, and always kept on good terms with her parliaments, by making concessions at times when a refusal would have caused ill-feeling. But notwithstanding the tact with which her government was conducted, as the people increased in knowledge and wealth, they grew more and more sensitive to infringements of their rights, and gave signs that through their representative, the House of Commons, they would soon call upon the crown to resign the powers it had usurped to the great detriment of the subject's liberty.

That the legislature should make laws, and the executive break them, was a sufficient cause in itself to produce a rupture between the two powers. The probability, however, of such a rupture was greatly increased by the fact that a second cause of quarrel existed between the crown and the Parliament—religious *The Reformation directed by the English kings.* differences. In England, the Reformation had been, no doubt, a popular movement, as it had been abroad; but it was controlled and directed by a monarchy which had but a partial sympathy with its aims. The consequence was an exceeding moderation. The king was made head of the Church in place of the pope; the monasteries were dissolved; the clergy were allowed to marry; the doctrine of purgatory was denied, as was that of a physical change in the elements at the sacrament; images and crosses were removed from churches; the people were allowed to read the Bible in their own tongue; an English liturgy was composed; and the English sovereigns, heads of the Church, said, as it were, to the people, 'Thus far shall ye go, and no farther.' But no sooner had the princes finished their work, than a new set of reformers arose, preaching another, fuller, more popular reformation.

The main principle of the reformers was to get rid of those

superstitious observances which marred the freedom of the worshipper's communicating with his Maker; they did not believe in the necessity of priestly intervention, nor in the special sanctity of prayers in a foreign tongue. On the continent, this principle had been carried much further than in England; and when exiles, who had fled the country during the persecutions of Mary's reign, returned home from Flanders, Strasburg, or Geneva, they regarded the English Church as hardly deserving the name of reformed. 'How many signs of Romish superstition,' they said, 'are left in the prayer-book, and the services! What abuses yet remain in administration! Look at the plurality of benefices. How can one man be in a dozen places at a time? Are the clergy still to flaunt the priestly surplice and gaudy popish vestments, foolish and abominable apparel, in which the Catholic priests pretend to make mere water holy, to achieve a miraculous transformation of bread and wine, or to conjure the devil out of persons and places possessed? Is the communion-table not to stand, table-like, in the body of the church, but to be set up in the chancel like the altar of the papists? Shall the sign of the cross in baptism, the bowing at the name of Jesus, the ring in marriage, the keeping of saints' days, all these remains of popish superstitions, be observed in a church that calls itself reformed! Surely the snake is only scotched, not killed.'

Elizabeth, on the contrary, while she regarded the authority of her bishops as a support to the power of the crown, also hoped, by disallowing further change in church ceremonies, to conciliate Catholics. Her ecclesiastical power was absolute. She, therefore, refused to give the Puritans satisfaction even in matters of form. If the Puritan minister would officiate at the services of the Church, he must wear vestments he abhorred; if he would baptize a child, he must make the sign of the cross; if he would join two people in marriage, he must use the ring; in all points, he must conform exactly to the minutiæ of the rubric.

The Act of Supremacy was a double-edged sword, cruel to Puritans and Catholics alike. All clergymen holding benefices, all laymen holding office in the State, who refused to take an oath, when tendered, recognizing the queen as head of the Church, were to be deprived of their benefices or

Act of Uniformity. offices (1558). The Act of Uniformity forbade ministers, beneficed or not, to use any other than the established liturgy; for the first offence, they forfeited all their goods and chattels; for the second, they suffered a year's imprisonment; for the third, imprisonment for life; while fines were imposed upon laymen who stayed away from their parish church on Sundays or holidays (1559).

But persecution, instead of suppressing the reformers, only increased their numbers and animosity. From attacking ceremonies, they went on to attack the authority of the bishops. If the Holy Scriptures, they said, contain all things necessary for salvation, then where in them is to be found mention of that proud hierarchy of archbishops, bishops, and priests, by which the English Church is governed? Turning their eyes towards Scotland, they there saw established a church on a Presbyterian model, governed by assemblies of ministers and lay elders on less hierarchical principles than the Episcopal. For this model they claimed the authority of a Divine Right, as being the original form of church government established by the will of God in the time of the apostles.

Reformers desire establishment of Presbyterian Church.

To the queen, this new programme of reform, attacking, as it did, not only episcopal authority, but her own prerogative as head of the Church, was still more distasteful than that which had required merely a reform of ceremonies.

An established church may be either self-governed or governed by the State. The Episcopal Church was a State church in the fullest sense of the term; archbishops and bishops, like ministers of state, were appointed by the sovereign; no laws to regulate the conduct of the laity in spiritual matters could emanate from any source but the queen in Parliament; and, in fact, there was no spiritual authority distinct from the State. On the other hand, the Presbyterian Church prided itself on being self-governed. According to this system, every parish had its minister, its deacon, and its lay elder, together forming a little court of justice, or kirk session, which called parishioners to account for spiritual and moral offences, such as drunkenness, scolding, or Sabbath-breaking; and punished by censures, fines, or imprisonment. So many parishes formed a presbytery; so

Episcopal Church dependent upon the State.

Presbyterian Church independent of State control.

many presbyteries formed a province, and both presbytery and province possessed a distinct judicial assembly, composed of lay elders and ministers. Lastly, there was a general assembly of the church, composed of all the ministers of parishes, together with a sprinkling of lay elders, and to this body appeals were made from the judicial decisions of the lesser assemblies. The orders and regulations made by the general assembly of the church were binding upon the whole nation, clergy and laity. This church had been established in Scotland by rebellion, and its ministers did not hesitate to set up their own authority in opposition to that of king and State. "Disregard not our threatening," they said to James VI., "for there was never yet one in this realm, in the place where your grace is, who prospered after the ministers began to threaten him."

Of these two systems, the Episcopal form of church government, though less popular, was also less tyrannical than the Presbyterian. The powers of English bishops were far more limited than those of Scottish assemblies. The Church of Scotland, however, which gave power to the ministers of the people, instead of to courtly prelates, suited the enthusiasm of the age, and naturally recommended itself to the more earnest reformers on this side the border. Rejoiced to find that Elizabeth regarded the Presbyterians as rebellious fanatics, the bishops on their side now set up a counter claim of Divine Right in favour of the Episcopal Church as administered by the queen; and, in return for the privilege of fining, imprisoning, and ejecting nonconformists, taught the people that kings rule by Divine Right, as the vicegerents of God upon earth, and that opposition to the commands of princes is disobedience to the commands of God. *Episcopal Church less tyrannical than the Presbyterian.* *Bishops support the power of the crown.*

But Puritan ministers, though deprived of their livings, could not be silenced. They thought the whole state of society and religion in England needed to be penetrated with a new spirit. Themselves eager readers of their Bibles, zealous preachers, active reformers, filled with true missionary zeal, they found that the court and nobility cared little for serious matters, and that noblemen and gentlemen spent their time in gaming, in dancing, in attending grand shows, or in fighting on the continent. They aimed at a social as well as a religious *Puritans cannot be suppressed.*

reform. Printing had largely increased the numbers of readers and writers, and had at the same time extended the range not only of serious but also of profane literature. It was an age of poets. There were two hundred living in the last part of the century, Spenser and Shakespeare amongst them. The middle classes followed the same kind of amusements as their superiors, frequenting the bear-garden, the bowling-green, the gaming-house, and the theatre. The country people had their wakes and fairs and festivals. Amidst so much rioting and pleasuring the Puritans saw few ministers competent to lead the people to more serious paths. The clergy, so far from checking the freedom of society, were as eager in the pursuit of amusement as their parishioners: before the Reformation their incapacity had been the reproach of the Catholic Church; it was now equally the reproach of the newly established Church. Many Catholics, rather than lose their livings, had taken the oaths required of them—were they reformed? While they passed their time in taverns, gaming and drinking, they were not likely to acquire the new art of preaching. "Dumb dogs," said the Puritans, are "left to guard the Church, while we are turned out." In many villages no sermon was heard "from year's end to year's end." Such a church seemed to invite reform; and the Presbyterians were ready for the task. Persecution not going far enough to extirpate the reformers, only attracted the minds of others to the consideration of the questions in dispute, and discussion led to more advanced views on reform. Episcopacy was generally the religion of the upper classes. Presbyterian opinions prevailed amongst the middle ranks; and now the very poorest of the nation began also to have their special ideas on religious questions. Men, women, and children, poor people who had nothing to support them but their handicrafts and trades, would in summer-time meet in the fields outside London at five o'clock in the morning, and in winter in private houses, in order to worship after their own fashion. Every congregation, they maintained, however small, ought to be left free to settle its own affairs, without interference from either bishops or assemblies. Amongst these latest reformers were several distinct sects, which, without holding the same doctrines, agreed in their general view of church government; and being taught by weakness to combine together in spite of minor differences of opinion, were the

*Sectarians.*

first to raise the flag of 'liberty of conscience.' More cruelly used than Presbyterians, many of these sectarians fled the country for Holland, where they established churches on their own principles. Those who stayed in England ran the risk of imprisonment for life.

In spite, however, of persecution, the reformers were devotedly loyal to the queen. For though, through political motives, she persecuted Puritans at home, abroad she supported the Protestants in the fierce conflict they were waging with Catholicism. On one side were arrayed the pope, the King of Spain, the Emperor of Austria, the Catholic princes of Germany; on the other, Sweden, Denmark, Holland, and the Protestant German princes; and it was chiefly owing to the support of England that this side was able to maintain its ground against the Catholics. *Elizabeth supports Protestant cause on continent.*

The popes had long desired to force back into their fold the country that was thus recognized as the head of Protestant States. Pius V. had said he wished he could shed his blood in an expedition against England; and now Gregory XIII. urged on Philip II. of Spain to attempt the conquest of the heretic kingdom. He could not have found a prince or nation more suited for his purpose. The Spaniards and English hated one another with a national as well as a religious hatred. A love of enterprize and discovery had spread rapidly amongst all classes during Elizabeth's long reign. Adventurers, led often by noblemen and gentlemen, sailed to America and the West Indies, making fruitless efforts to discover gold mines, or to found colonies. On these expeditions they burnt the settlements and seized the treasure ships of the Spaniards, who, being already possessed of Mexico, Peru, and much of the West Indies, regarded themselves as sole lords of the New World, and were quite prepared for a war to the knife with the intruders. *Enmity between Spain and England.*

It was thus to fight the battle at once of the pope and of the nation that the Invincible Armada sailed from Spain. It sailed to take vengeance on a heretic queen, who, while supporting the Dutch in rebellion, disputed the claims of Philip to the possession of two continents. It came threatening England with conquest and Protestantism with destruction. But storms and winds and the courage of English seamen shattered and destroyed the Armada (1588). The triumph of England was the salvation of the Protestant cause. The invaded now becoming the invaders, burned Spanish galleons in the very harbours of Spain.

*Her foreign policy a chief cause of Elizabeth's popularity.* With the people success will go far to justify even a tyrannical government. Hence it was that, although storms were rising, and the political atmosphere was charged with electricity, no violent contention ever arose between Elizabeth and her subjects. The occasional illegal acts committed by her government, the cruel sentences passed upon Puritans by the courts of High Commission and Star Chamber, were forgiven because she pursued a foreign policy that accorded with the wishes of the nation, and caused England to be feared and respected. The bonds of loyalty seemed strong because they had not been tried too severely. It is a principle in mechanics that girders should not be strained beyond the limits of perfect recovery. An excessive tension may not only cause danger for the moment, but may be a source of permanent weakness. Such a tension came when the nation was ruled by monarchs who had neither the capacity to lead their Parliaments nor the temper to follow them.

*James I., his character.* On the death of Elizabeth the great Tudor line was extinct.* James VI. of Scotland, who outwardly united the two kingdoms, failed to unite his subjects to himself. He was thought cowardly, conceited, pretentious. It was believed that flattery was the readiest road to his favour; he certainly suffered himself to fall under the control of unworthy favourites, so that his court received the character of being the head-quarters of riot and vice, if not of far darker crimes.

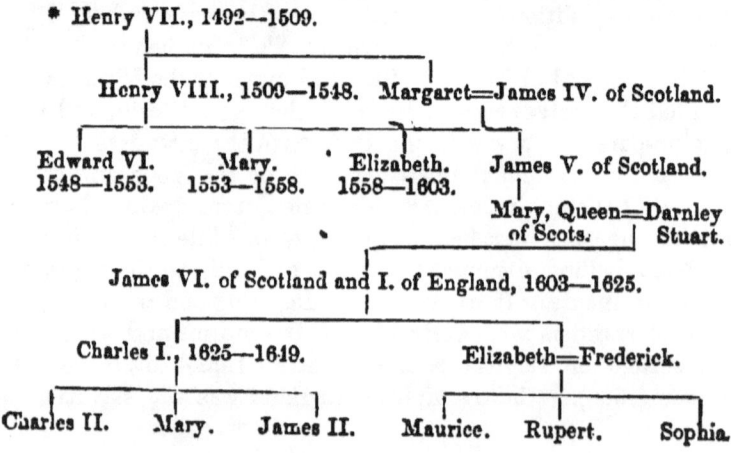

* Henry VII., 1492—1509.

The members of the Commons refused to grant the money of the nation to be lavished on such favourites or wasted in such riot. James, therefore, did not trouble himself with often meeting the representatives of the people. Holding the theory that he was possessed of absolute power, he ventured to try to carry that theory into practice. A few instances will show the manner in which the liberties of the subject were violated by his government.

His first Parliament granted him for life duties on exports and imports, called tonnage and poundage (1604). These duties were fixed at a certain rate; for instance, there was a duty of 2s. 6d. on every hundred-weight of currants imported into the country. James, of his sole authority, trebled this duty, and afterwards, without asking the consent of Parliament, imposed heavy taxes upon almost all merchandise. In principle there is no distinction between the illegal levying of a direct or an indirect tax. The ignorant, however, are much more struck by that which comes plainly before them. Hence, had James attempted to raise a direct tax, such as the subsidies granted in Parliament, which were levied on land and articles of personal property, he would have aroused far more indignation than he did by the imposition of illegal customs. The subsidy must have been paid directly into the hands of the tax-gatherer, whereas the illegal duties were paid in the first instance by the merchants, and the fact that these merchants repaid themselves out of the profits of the consumer by raising prices, was not obvious to the vulgar. The people, however, really suffered in purse as well as in right, and Parliament would have been wanting in its duty, if it had not protested against this interference with the property of the subject.

*James imposes illegal taxes.*

The person of the subject was no safer than his property. It is contrary to the common law of England to force any man to criminate himself. The Courts of High Commission and Star Chamber, however, did not follow the procedure of the common law courts, and were in the habit of tendering the prisoner an oath, technically called the oath *ex officio*, to answer truly all questions put to him. Two Puritans, for refusing to take this oath, were imprisoned by the Court of High Commission. The common law allowed every man committed to prison upon a criminal charge, to apply to the court of King's Bench for a so-called writ of *habeas corpus*, directing the

*Illegal commitments.*

gaoler to produce his prisoner and the warrant upon which he was committed, before the court on a stated day.* The judge, upon view of the warrant, discharged the prisoner, released him on bail, or sent him back to prison to await his trial, according as the charge against him was no offence in the eye of the law, or a bailable offence, or one for which no bail could be received.

The two Puritans in question were brought before the judges of the King's Bench on a writ of *habeas corpus*. Fuller, their counsel, argued that they ought to be released, because the High Commissioners had not been empowered *by law* to imprison, or fine, or administer the oath *ex officio*. This argument struck at the root of the authority of the High Commission, and Fuller was himself summoned before the court, on the ground that he had slandered the king's authority. He refused, like his clients, to take the oath, "to answer truly all questions put to him," and applied to the Court of King's Bench for a prohibition to stay the proceedings. It was by means of such prohibitions that the common law courts were accustomed to prevent the ecclesiastical courts from meddling with cases which properly came under the cognizance of the common law. The judges sent the prohibition, but at the same time signified that they should not interfere, if the High Commissioners charged the prisoner with heresy and schism. The Puritan advocate was accordingly convicted of heresy, fined £200, and committed to prison. The common law judges would not interfere in his favour, though he appealed again to them, and he seems, eventually, to have regained his liberty only by submitting, and paying the fine.†

{Arbitrary procedure of Court of High Commission.}

The Courts of Star Chamber and High Commission, however illegally their jurisdiction was acquired and conducted, at least brought definite charges against the accused, and allowed him a

* *Habeas corpus ad subjiciendum* are the first words of the writ to the gaoler, meaning that he is to *have the person* (of the prisoner) to produce before the court (so *habeas corpus ad testificandum* are the first words of a writ for producing a prisoner to give evidence). The writ was anciently called *corpus cum causâ*, because it required the return of the *cause* of detention, as well as of the *body* imprisoned. The principle of the writ was contained in the Magna Charta of King John, which enacted that "no freeman should be imprisoned but by lawful judgment of his peers or by the law of the land." It was used between subject and subject in the time of Henry VI., and against the crown in that of Henry VII., so that it was fully recognized as law long before the re-enactments in the reign of Charles I., and the *Habeas Corpus Act* of Charles II., 1679.

† Gardiner, Hist. of Eng. (1603—1616), i. 445.

form of trial. The King's Council went even further than this, and constantly committed political opponents of the government, without bringing any charge against them, or allowing them the benefit of a trial. The imprisonment extended from weeks, or months, to years, and the writ of *habeas corpus*, which ought to have protected any subject from such an outrage, was rarely obtainable. In the case of Arabella Stuart, the causeless displeasure of the king formed the ground of a life-long imprisonment. This lady, who was first cousin to James, married, through pure affection, a distant relation, William Seymour, a descendant of Mary, the youngest daughter of Henry VII. James, jealous of the union of two relations, both of whom had a distant claim to the crown, confined Seymour in the Tower, and placed Arabella in confinement at Lambeth. Both made their escape, with the intention of meeting at Leigh, near Blackwall, on board a French vessel, which was engaged to carry them across the Channel. Arabella arrived before her husband, and, in spite of her entreaties, her attendants, in fear of pursuit, forced the captain to sail. Seymour, on his arrival, finding the French vessel gone, hired a collier, and was landed in safety at Ostend. Arabella was not so fortunate. When within sight of Calais, a vessel, sent from Dover in pursuit, overtook the fugitive, and carried her back to England. On her arrival, she was immediately committed to the Tower, whence she wrote to the two chief justices, imploring them to secure her a trial by the usual writ of *habeas corpus*: "And if your lordships may not, or will not, grant unto me the ordinary relief of a distressed subject, then, I beseech you, become humble intercessors to his Majesty, that I may receive such benefit of justice as both his Majesty by his oath hath promised, and the laws of this realm afford to all others, those of his blood not excepted. And though, unfortunate woman! I can obtain neither, yet, I beseech your lordships, retain me in your good opinion, and judge charitably, till I be proved to have committed any offence, either against God or his Majesty, deserving so long restraint or separation from my lawful husband." Arabella's just demand remained ungranted. Her marriage was no crime at law, and had she been brought before the judges, they could hardly have done less than order her release. The idea of attempting to change the succession would have been ludicrous, if true, but there was no ground for suspicion of political motive in the marriage to give a shadow of excuse for her restraint. Separated from her husband, and broken-hearted, Arabella lost her reason, and, after some four years of confinement, at last died in the Tower.

The Countess of Shrewsbury, Arabella's aunt, was brought up before the council, on the charge of being an accomplice in her niece's escape. Refusing to implicate herself, by answering in any way to a charge so unknown to the law, she bravely replied, that, if the council had a charge against her, she would be ready to answer before her peers. Such an appeal to the hated liberties of the subject was not suffered to pass unpunished, and for several years her name appears in the list of unhappy inmates of the Tower.

It was not only the king's animosity which was to be dreaded, but the greed of the court. The interests of the nation were bought and sold by courtiers and ministers. Several of James' council were in receipt of salaries from the King of Spain. Others were in a nefarious league with the pirates who then preyed on our shipping. The story of Sir John Eliot and Captain Nutt sheds a flood of light on various judicial and executive anomalies of the reign. In 1623 Eliot was Vice-admiral of Devon. Amongst his duties were those of boarding pirate vessels, and deciding upon the lawfulness of prizes. Captain Nutt, an English pirate, who, at the head of several ships, had for three years past ranged the seas between the coasts of England and America, was notorious alike for audacity and cruelty. Sailing to Torbay and landing in force whenever he came ashore, he dared the vice-admiral to seize him, and boasted of the pardons he had already obtained. Armed with a copy of one of these pardons, conditional on the captain's surrendering himself within a certain time, Eliot risked his life and went on board the pirate vessel. There was little doubt that the time within which the pardon was valid was already past, but Nutt, acting probably on the supposition that Eliot could only be influenced by mercenary motives, agreed to surrender himself, and to pay a fine of £500, together with six packs of calves' skins. If the pardon were good, the fine would be shared between the vice-admiral, Eliot, and the lord-admiral, Buckingham. Directly the man was ashore, Eliot placed him under arrest, and then wrote an account of the whole transaction to the council. He took occasion to point out how the pirate, even while treating, had audaciously seized a Colchester brig, laden with woods and sugar to the value of some £4000, but left the question of the validity of the pardon entirely to their lordships' decision. The first result of this was, that Eliot received a letter from Conway, the under-secretary of state, highly commending him for his good service, and intimating that he should before long receive the honour of kissing the king's hand. Within a few days Eliot repaired to London, not, however, to kiss the king's hand, but to become a prisoner in the Marshalsea, and answer in the Court of Admiralty charges preferred against him by the Council Board. The pirate, Nutt, to give his court friends an excuse for shielding him, had the audacity to come forward as the accuser of his captor, alleging that Eliot, both by letter and message, had urged him to sail to Dartmouth and make prizes of divers ships that were there, laden with goods and money out of Spain; and that it was not until thus encouraged that he had ventured on seizing the Colchester brig. The letter Nutt was unable to produce; the charges were denied both by Eliot and his officers. The judge of the Admiralty, in his reports to the council, did not venture to express an opinion in regard to Eliot, but pointed out how the lord-admiral's interests might be neglected, if the vice-admiral were kept long absent from his post in Devon. But while Buckingham at the time was in Spain, Eliot's enemy, and Nutt's friend, Sir John Calvert, the principal secretary of state, was in England. It was through his influence that the council had proceeded against Eliot. The pirate had rendered him some service in the establishment of a colony in Newfoundland, and if his word may be believed, this was his sole motive for seeking to blacken the character of the vice-admiral, and obtain a pardon from the king for that "unlucky fellow, Captain Nutt." It was no wonder Eliot felt angry and used stronger language in writing to Secretary Conway than he usually employed. "I cannot so much yet undervalue my integrity, to doubt that the words of a malicious assassin, now standing for his life, shall have reputation equal to the credit of a gentleman." Nutt, however, by means of his powerful friend, obtained his pardon and, in addition, a grant of £100 out of the ship and goods seized at Torbay. The duration of Eliot's imprisonment is uncertain; probably he remained in the Marshalsea until the following October, at which time Charles and Buckingham returned from Spain. In the following month he was canvassing for a seat in the last of James' parliaments.*

While person and property were thus dealt with, it was hardly likely that there should be any recognition of the later rights of freedom of speech and freedom of thought. Presbyterians and sectarians were forced to fly the country, in order to escape imprisonment. Puritan preachers were ejected from their livings. Puritan writers were prosecuted in the Star Chamber. James himself made a jest of the fines inflicted on them;—"it were no reason that those that will refuse the airy sign of the cross after baptism should have their purses stuffed with any more solid and substantial crosses."† But persecution that does not go far enough to extirpate its victims defeats its own ends. Sympathy was felt for the Puritans, their opinions spread, and the division between the two parties grew wider and wider. Clergymen who found favour at court adopted doctrines approaching to those of Rome, and supported the power of the crown by teaching the duty of passive obedience, and the doctrine of the Divine Right of kings. Clergymen who found favour with the people taught that in the plain words of Scripture is to be found all that the Christian needs for his guidance; and denounced to their hearers, as sinful and displeasing to God, popish ceremonies and doctrines, and the worldly court-life, with its drinking, swearing, acting, fine dressing, and dancing.

Thus, at the end of James' reign, men of very various opinions were all alike designated Puritans. There was the sectarian, who desired that each separate congregation should be allowed its own special form of worship; the Presbyterian, who desired to see a church similar to that of Scotland established in England; the churchman, who objected to popish ceremonies and doctrines; the patriot, who, from opposing tyranny in the State, came to mistrust a church that taught the duty of passive obedience to kings' commands; and, lastly, the earnest man, who, by merely leading, in his own person, a pure life, seemed to reprove

*Puritans persecuted.*

*Word Puritan designates men of various opinions.*

---

\* Forster: Life of Sir J. Eliot, i. 2.
† Ellis Orig. Letters, iii. 450: Coins were called crosses from the stamp of the cross on the reverse, as sovereigns from the king's head on the obverse.

the manners of the court; all these became alike objects of the scoffs and jeers of the king's friends, and were classed together as factious hypocrites and Puritans.

But neither James' pretensions to absolute power, nor his actual infringement of the constitution, nor the persecution of Puritans, nor the vices of his court, did so much to alienate the affection of his subjects, as did the conduct of his foreign policy. The Thirty Years' War had now begun. Matthias, Emperor of Germany, King of Austria, Hungary, and Bohemia, was childless. To secure the succession, he caused his cousin Ferdinand, archduke of Styria, to be crowned as next king of his great kingdoms of Bohemia and Hungary.* This prince had been brought up by the Jesuits, and was so ardent a Catholic that he said he would sooner beg his bread from door to door, than that the Catholic Church should suffer injury. He had long since driven the Protestants out of his own duchy of Styria. Sooner than accept such a fanatic as their king, the Bohemians, of whom the majority were Protestants, rose in rebellion, and offered the crown to one of their own persuasion, Frederick, prince of the Palatinate,† who

*James' foreign policy cause of division between himself and his subjects.*

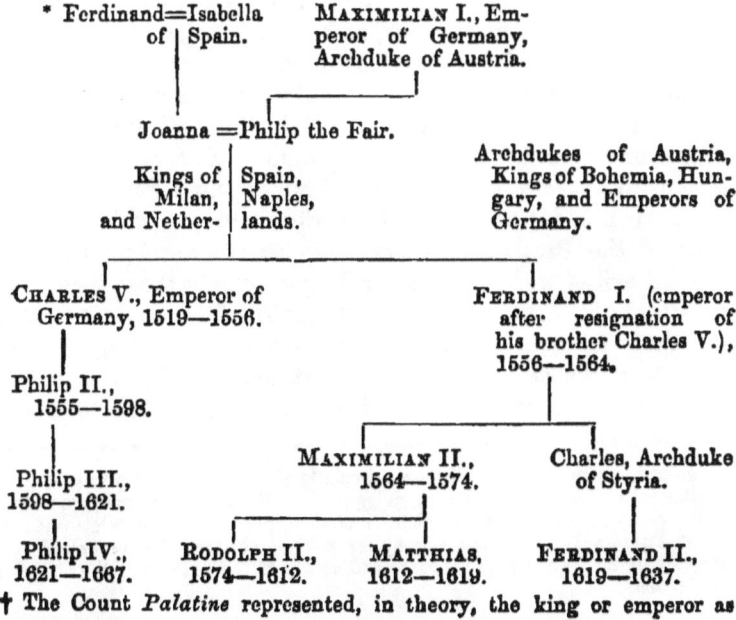

* Ferdinand=Isabella of Spain.   MAXIMILIAN I., Emperor of Germany, Archduke of Austria.

Joanna =Philip the Fair.

Kings of Milan, and Netherlands. | Spain, Naples, lands.

Archdukes of Austria, Kings of Bohemia, Hungary, and Emperors of Germany.

CHARLES V., Emperor of Germany, 1519—1556.

FERDINAND I. (emperor after resignation of his brother Charles V.), 1556—1564.

Philip II., 1555—1598.

Philip III., 1598—1621.

MAXIMILIAN II., 1564—1574.

Charles, Archduke of Styria.

Philip IV., 1621—1667.

RODOLPH II., 1574—1612.

MATTHIAS, 1612—1619.

FERDINAND II., 1619—1637.

† The Count *Palatine* represented, in theory, the king or emperor as

accepted the dangerous gift, and was crowned King of Bohemia (August, 1619).

**Thirty Years' War.** This was the origin of the great religious struggle between Catholics and Protestants, which is called the Thirty Years' War. Frederick, the Protestant champion, had for his enemies, Ferdinand, elected Emperor of Germany on the death of Matthias (1619); the Catholic princes of the German empire; and Philip III. of Spain.

The Austrian Emperors of Germany, and the Kings of Spain, Milan, and the Netherlands, being near relations, always acted in one another's interests. Jealousy of the united power of Spain and Austria inclined France to prefer political to religious considerations, so that it usually supported the Protestant princes in withstanding the encroachments of the emperors; but it was useless at the present time for Frederick to look for help to a country torn by civil dissensions, and governed by a minor.

From James, his Protestant father-in-law, whose daughter, Elizabeth, he had married amidst the rejoicings of the English (1613), as well as from his fellow Protestant princes of the empire, he might, not without reason, hope for support, in a war nominally undertaken in the interests of the Protestant cause.

James, however, hating war, had made peace, on his accession, with the old Catholic enemy, Spain, and declared his intention to the French ambassador, of "avoiding war as his own damnation." But, on the breaking out of the Thirty Years' War, the king found himself placed in a dilemma. For he must either give up his theory of non-intervention, or suffer England to fall from the proud position to which Elizabeth had raised her, as head of the Protestant States. Even now, when we recognize the full evil of war, it seems hardly generous in those themselves possessed of liberty to refuse assistance to a free people maintaining their freedom against foreign armies. To English Protestants, in whose minds the remembrance of the Armada was still fresh, it seemed at once both base and foolish to look on

---

judge in his own *palace*. Barons, especially those of frontier provinces, had similar royal judicial privileges delegated to them. Such provinces were called palatine. In Germany there was an upper and lower Palatinate; the lower *Palatinate* comprised the upper part of the rich Rhine valley, with Heidelberg for its capital, and conferred a vote at the election of the emperors of Germany.

with indifference, while a Protestant people were deprived of liberty of conscience by armies composed of foreigners and Catholics. Protestant Europe was one country, and a blow struck at one Protestant State was regarded as a blow struck at the interests of all Protestant States.

James, however, acting in opposition to the wishes of his subjects, refused to support his son-in-law. In the first place, he desired to avoid hostilities with Spain, in the interests of a match that he had been negotiating for the past six years between the Prince of Wales and Philip the Third's daughter, to whose dowry he cannily looked as a means of paying his debts, without applying to Parliament for aid. He had just executed England's greatest captain, Sir Walter Raleigh, to please Philip. In the second place, he disliked the idea of assisting subjects in rebellion against their prince. In favour of the first motive, there was nothing to be said. Who could uphold a King of England in relying on foreign gold for the support of his government, rather than on the goodwill of his subjects? In favour of the second more might be urged, though not from James' point of view. The Bohemian nobles, the authors of the rebellion, were rapacious and lawless, and without the moral qualities necessary for the conduct of a revolution and the establishment of a free government. A state of anarchy in Germany was foreseen as the probable result of their success, and even several Protestant princes refused to assist Frederick in weakening the imperial power, by which alone some sort of law was maintained between the different States that composed the empire. Accordingly, neither England nor France took part in the struggle; the Protestant princes made peace for themselves (July, 1620); and Frederick was defeated and driven out of Bohemia (Nov., 1620). When the armies of Spain and Austria proceeded to invade the Palatinate, Frederick's hereditary dominions, James summoned a Parliament, with a half-formed resolve of breaking with Spain, and taking an active part in the war (1620).

It was impracticable for England to maintain a large army in the Palatinate, and even the attempt would have required supplies far larger than the country was disposed to grant. James was aware of these facts, and therefore the slower to enter upon hostilities. It must be allowed that the Commons acted unreasonably. The country gentlemen, who came up to Westminster once in five or six years, were not enlightened by newspapers, and had no means of acquainting themselves with the intricate course of foreign politics, or of forming any correct estimate of the probable cost of a war. Now, while knowledge of their own incapacity prevented them from pretending to direct operations, their Protestant zeal caused them to press James to assist his son-in-law, and their ignorance to suppose that this could be done at comparatively a small expense to the country. Elizabeth had always had the skill so to direct the blow that it should inflict the greatest injury to her adversary at the least possible cost to herself. She would have seen that the sea was England's field of fame, and would never have marched an army to Heidelberg. Had she still sat on the throne, perhaps a dash upon some Spanish port might have rendered the Protestants a material assistance, by drawing Philip's armies off from Germany. But her foreign policy, when not marred by misplaced parsimony or favouritism, had been marked by her exceptional genius, and it was unreasonable to expect her commonplace successor to strike out a line of action at once spirited, effective, and economical. It was probably fortunate for Enggland that he never heartily made the attempt.

*Commons press James to enter on spirited policy, but slow to grant necessary funds.*

The Parliament was asked for money sufficient to maintain for the winter some regiments of English volunteers, engaged in defending Heidelberg, the capital of the Palatinate. But the Commons, before voting money, desired to see the king commit himself to a decided policy, and prepared a petition, begging him to marry his son to a Protestant princess, and to make war on Spain. James, hearing beforehand of the contents of the petition, wrote a letter, forbidding the House to meddle with his son's match; and adding, as a warning to those who should disregard the royal command, that, "as for liberty of speech, he was free to punish any man's misdemeanours in Parliament, both during and after their sitting." In meddling with matters of peace and war, the Commons were not so sure of their ground, but liberty of speech* they regarded as a precious inheritance from their

*Commons petition James to marry his son to a Protestant princess.*

---

* Even in Edward the Third's time, the Commons seem to have been allowed to debate on many things concerning the king's prerogative; and

earliest ancestors. A second petition was at once prepared, begging his Majesty, "such a wise and just king, to recognise liberty of speech, their ancient and undoubted right." James replied by saying "he would not infringe their privileges, only he did not like their style of speaking—how could any privileges be their undoubted right and inheritance, when these were all derived from the grace and permission of his ancestors and himself?"

The Commons, too wise to let such doctrine as this pass unchallenged, entered a protest in their journals (18 Dec., 1621), to the effect that, 'Their liberties and privileges were the undoubted birthright of the subjects of England; the State, the defence of the realm, the Church, the laws and grievances were proper matters for them to debate; members have liberty of speech, and freedom from all imprisonment for speaking on any matters touching Parliament business.' James, in the full assembly of his council, and in presence of the judges, caused the journal-book to be brought before him, and, with his own hand, erased this protestation, declaring it to be invalid, void, and of none effect. *Commons enter in their journals declaration of their privileges.*

The dissatisfaction of the nation at the king, and his Spanish Catholic match, was greatly increased after the dissolution of this Parliament (6 Jan., 1622). Abroad, the Protestants were being defeated, persecuted, crushed. Frederick was driven, not only out of Bohemia, but out of *Protestants defeated.*

---

Henry IV. promised to take no notice of any reports made to him of their proceedings before such matters were brought before him by the advice and assent of *all* the Commons. A Parliament, or "speaking-house," would be a poor guardian of liberties without itself having liberty of utterance. The principle was well stated nearly half a century after this (1667): "No man can doubt but whatever is once enacted is lawful; but nothing can come into an Act of Parliament but it must be first affirmed or propounded by somebody; so that if the Act can wrong nobody, no more can the first propounding. The members must be as free as the Houses; an Act of Parliament cannot disturb the State; therefore the debate that tends to it cannot; for it must be propounded and debated before it can be enacted."—May's Parl. Practice, 102.

Besides freedom of speech on subjects of Parliamentary debate, the principal privileges of Parliament were:

The right of both Houses of judging and punishing their own members for any misdemeanour committed in Parliament.

The right of the Commons of determining any disputed election.

The right of members of both Houses to enjoy freedom from arrest, and exemption from all legal process, while Parliament was sitting, except on charges of treason, felony, and breach of the peace.

his hereditary dominions, the Palatinate, and forced, with his family, to take refuge in Holland, and live on the alms of the Prince of Orange. Protestants were banished from Austria Proper. In Bohemia, the Protestant faith and civil liberty disappeared together. In the Palatinate, the Protestant worship was suppressed. In France, the government was in arms against the Huguenots, and succeeded in wresting one stronghold from them after another. Spain seized the hopeful opportunity to renew the war with Holland.

<small>Spanish marriage spoken, written, preached against.</small> The Puritan pulpits "rang against the Spanish marriage." In vain James told the bishops to prevent the clergy from preaching on such topics; in vain he issued proclamations, forbidding the people to talk; their voices could no more be restrained than a "mountain torrent." Pamphlets were written and published which risked the ears, if not the lives of their authors. Most malignant of all, <small>Tom Tell-Truth.</small> "Tom Tell-Truth" attacked the king and his government on every side.

"I, a poor unknown subject," says the pamphleteer, "who hear the people talk, will undertake that discontinued but noble office of telling your Majesty the truth. Some there are that find fault with your government, even to wishing Elizabeth were alive again, for we have lost by change of sex. Great Britain, say they, is a great deal less than little England was wont to be. The excess of peace hath long since turned virtue into vice, and health into sickness.

"The Spaniards and the Duke of Bavaria play with your Majesty as men do with little children, at handy-dandy, which hand will you have? and give them nothing. The very losers at cards fall a cursing and swearing at the loss of the Palatinate; and, when told of your Majesty's proclamation not to talk about State affairs, answer in a chafe, 'You must give losers leave to speak.'

"You sent my Lord of Doncaster into France to mediate peace. It would have been better had the money spent on that embassage been given to the poor Huguenots; they may well call England the 'Land of Promise.' The princes that serve the Pope send arms; you—that should fight the battles of the Lord—ambassadors.

"No need for your Majesty to fear the Puritan religion; if a king will be absolute and dissolute, it is a wonder he will suffer any other; for it may be observed in some parts of Christendom\* that let a king ruling over a Protestant people be never so wicked in his person, nor so enormous in his government, let him stamp vice with his example, let him remove the ancient bounds of sovereignty, and make every day new yokes and new scourges for

\* *I.e.*, in England.

his poor people, let him take rewards and punishments out of the hand of justice, and distribute them without regard to right or wrong ; in short, let him so excel in mischief, ruin, and oppression, as Nero compared with him may be held a very father of the people. Yet, when he hath done all that can be imagined to procure hate and contempt, he may go boldly in and out to his sports, clothed in his quilted garments, stiletto-proof, he shall not need to take either the less drink when he goes to bed, or the more thought when he riseth.

"His minions, a pack of ravenous curs, think all other subjects beasts, and only made for them to prey upon ; they may revel and laugh, when all the kingdom mourns. His poor Protestant subjects shall only think he is given them of God for the punishment of their sins, for the preachers shall praise him and make the pulpit a stage of flattery, He ought to be obeyed, not because he is good but because he is their king. The subject is tied to such wonderful patience and obedience as doth almost verify that bold speech of Machiavel, when he said, ' Christianity made men cowards.'"\*

James, after quarrelling with his Parliament, eagerly renewed the Marriage Treaty with Spain. He hankered more than ever after the Infanta's dower, and hoped, by means of Philip's interest with the Emperor, to secure the restoration of the Palatinate to Frederick. The Spaniards, on their side, were ready for a treaty which would secure them from a war with England while fighting in Germany. Following the suggestion of the Spanish ambassador, Charles undertook a secret journey to Spain, intending to conclude the treaty in person, and return home with his bride by his side (Feb., 1623). He was accompanied only by his father's favourite, George Villiers, Marquis (afterwards Duke) of Buckingham. *Charles and Buckingham go to Spain.*

Philip IV. took advantage of this foolish act to raise his demands, and obtained the consent of both James and Charles to secret articles, in which they engaged never to put the laws against Catholics into force, and to obtain the consent of Parliament to their repeal within three years. The promise was worthless ; for James well knew the Parliament would never consent.

Wearied by the delays caused by the Spaniards, Charles returned home (Oct., 1623) before the time agreed on for the performance of the marriage ceremony, and afterwards wrote to the Earl of Bristol, with whom he had left his proxy, that there was to be neither marriage nor friendship, unless Philip consented to restore the Palatinate to Frederick by force of arms. This demand broke off the *Marriage Treaty with Spain broken off.*

\* Somers' Tracts, II. 487—9.

treaty; for whatever delusive hopes Philip had held out to James, he had never undertaken to do more than endeavour, by his interest with the Emperor, to effect a peace favourable to Frederick. "We have a maxim of State," said a Spanish minister, for once speaking the truth, "that the King of Spain must never fight the Emperor."

*Money voted by Parliament to carry on war with Spain.* Buckingham, who had quarrelled with the Spaniards, was now eager for war. James found his favourite would leave him no peace till he summoned a Parliament, which he did sorely against his will, and then Buckingham, with Charles by his side to confirm his story, gave the two Houses a false account of what had taken place in Spain, declaring that the Spaniards broke off the match because the prince would not become a Catholic. James' court was not a good school for training a young prince in the duties of veracity; and it was certainly unfortunate for Charles' character that the circumstance of his first introduction to Parliament should have been of so ambiguous a nature. However, the story thus supported was believed for the time, and the question of peace and war with Spain being submitted to the Commons' consideration, they voted a subsidy of £300,000 for the recovery of the Palatinates. The same year four regiments crossed the Channel to assist the Dutch in fighting the Spaniards in the Netherlands (1624).

*French Marriage Treaty.* While the nation desired a Protestant alliance, the king only thought of a dowry. James now proposed to marry his son to another Catholic princess, Henrietta, sister of Louis XIII., King of France. He died, however, before the marriage took place, after a reign of twenty-three years (25th March, 1625). Though a French marriage was hailed as a deliverance after the Spanish project, yet the history of the next twenty years will perhaps seem to justify the Commons' antipathy to any Catholic marriage.

## CHAPTER II.

CHARLES' FIRST PARLIAMENTS.—IMPEACHMENT OF BUCKING-
HAM.—PETITION OF RIGHT.—(1625-1629).

What shall we do for money for these wars ?
RICHARD II.

LITTLE was known of the new king, who was only twenty-three years old when he came to the throne, and had seldom appeared in public. His manners were grave and cold ; he loved order and propriety. " I will have no drunkards in my bedchamber," he said, and turned out of office one of Buckingham's own brothers. The courtiers followed the lead of their master, and led outwardly decorous lives.*

But all hopes that were entertained of good agreement between king and people were doomed to a speedy end. Charles, who from his earliest years had heard taught at his father's court the doctrine of the Divine Right of kings, regarded it as the duty of Parliament submissively to vote supplies and carry out the wishes of the monarch, without questioning his government or bargaining for redress of grievances. His subjects, on the other hand, still smarting at James' disregard of the laws of the land and the privilege of Parliament, were determined to make the new king acknowledge the limits which the laws set to the prerogative of the Crown.  *Certainty of quarrel between King and Parliament.*

An immediate cause of quarrel between Charles and the nation lay in the ascendancy of Buckingham, whose popularity had faded almost as soon as born. For if he had broken off the Spanish match on the grounds alleged by himself, he had since brought about the king's marriage with another Catholic, Henrietta Maria, sister of Louis XIII. It is rare for a favourite to

* Birch, I. 12 ;—Hutch. Mem.

remain supreme during the life of one master; still more rare for him to gain the affection of a second. Disappointment that Buckingham had not been ruined on the death of James now intensified the hatred felt by all classes towards him. Almost every officer employed by the Government was his creature, and at his command. "He on whom the duke smiled, was advanced; he on whom he frowned, cast down."* The highest nobles in the land found that, to stand well in the eyes of the king, they must court the favour of this haughty minion —this upstart country squire. Buckingham himself was ill-fitted to exercise power. Handsome, of fascinating manners, courageous and not implacable, he was yet vain withal, insolent, reckless, no genius, and utterly selfish; a man who would embroil his country in war to salve a wound of vanity, and then, after pledging his country's word, break it again to satisfy a change of whim. Such was the adviser with whom Charles met his first Parliament—a Parliament he soon summoned, as he was preparing a fleet for an expedition carefully kept secret from the country, and found himself in urgent need of money to fit this out. (18th June.)

*Buckingham hated; his character.*

*Charles' first Parliament.*

A dreadful plague was raging in London, of which the people were dying by thousands a week, so that the Houses were anxious to finish their business quickly and end the session. A bill for two subsidies,† amounting to something short of £200,000, was brought into the Lower House, and the members understanding from a message sent by the king

---

\* Strafford, Letters and Despatches, I. 28.

† A subsidy was an income tax of 4s. in the pound upon the annual value of lands, and a property-tax of 2s. 8d. in the pound upon the actual value of goods. Those whose lands were not worth 20s. a year, or whose personal property was less than £3 in value, were not taxed. These subsidies were levied by commissioners, appointed by the Chancellor of the Exchequer from amongst the inhabitants of the county or borough. The assessment was made according to an old valuation, so that, owing to a constant rise in the money-value of lands, and goods (the price of wheat, for instance, doubling in Elizabeth's reign), the real rate of the subsidy was very much less than the nominal. A tenth or a fifteenth was generally voted in addition to the subsidy. These were originally the real tenth or fifteenth of all the movables or personal property of the subject. Each county or borough was responsible for a certain sum, which was levied by commissioners, appointed by its representatives in the Commons. Since the last valuation had been made in the reign of Edward III., in that of Charles I., when the purchasing power of money had decreased five times, the tenths and fifteenths instead of being taxes of 2s. and of 1s. 4d., were more like taxes of 5d. and 3d., in the £ respectively.

that he was satisfied with the amount, and would allow them to re-assemble at some more convenient season, began to disperse in large numbers to their homes. The House was already emptied of two-thirds of its members, when the Bill of Tonnage and Poundage, granting the king the custom duties, came before it.

Although the usual practice since the reign of Henry V. had been to grant the customs for life, the Commons, owing to the thinness of their House, and their wish for time to regulate the scale of duties, only granted them to Charles for a year, delaying to make him a life grant until the next session of Parliament. The bill passed the Upper House;* but Charles, taking the contents as an insult, refused to give it his consent. The Parliament, however, might have adjourned without greater causes of discontent than the favour shown to Catholics and the rejection of the Tonnage and Poundage Bill, had not Buckingham deliberately fomented a quarrel. *[margin: Charles refuses his consent to Bill of Tonnage and Poundage.]*

At the calling of James' last Parliament, when the match with Spain was broken off, the duke had allied himself with the popular leaders. Now, wishing to be entirely free of their control, especially in the conduct of the fleet, he determined to bring about a rupture with the Parliament and so effect a dissolution. Accordingly, on the day when the two Houses adjourned, and the king's assent was given to the bill for two subsidies, the members heard, to their dismay, that they were required, within a fortnight's time, to meet again at Oxford, a town where the plague had already appeared. (10th July.) *[margin: Buckingham desires a dissolution.]*

Short as the interval was between the two sessions, events were not wanting to breed suspicion and distrust. Dr. Montague, a clergyman, censured by the Commons for publishing books upholding the Divine Right of kings, and teaching confession, the use of images, and other Roman doctrines, had been appointed chaplain to the king. Charles had agreed in the French Marriage Treaty not to put the laws against Catholics into force; and these conditions, kept secret at the time, were now beginning to be divulged. The customs were still levied, though the king had no legal claim to them, having refused his assent to the Bill for Tonnage and Poundage. The national fleet was not allowed to defend the nation ; reserved for the king's high purposes, which were still unrevealed, it might not move to *[margin: Causes of discontent.]*

---

* This has been proved by Forster's Life of Sir John Eliot, i. v. 6.

clear the channel of the Turkish pirates, now ravaging the coasts, plundering merchant vessels, and carrying off captives by hundreds. There was an ugly story abroad, that eight ships had been actually lent the French king to assist him in blocking up the Huguenots, brother Protestants, in Rochelle. And now, as a crowning cause of discontent, the Parliament was re-assembled, at an unusual place, at the hottest time of a plague-smitten season (Aug. 1st), and asked for a paltry sum that might just as well have been included in the previous grant. Long journeys were no light matter in those days, when roads were so bad that a coach and four could often go little more than four miles an hour. The members regarded the demand now made upon them almost as an insult, and felt convinced that there was some other motive for this patent disregard of their convenience than the lack of a paltry £40,000. Thus, instead of granting a second supply, the House began to debate upon the abuses of the administration, and to point at the duke as the cause of them.

"Strange, the adjournment for only a few days, and that meeting there in Oxford! As it could not be that the king should have such mutability in himself, was not the real cause manifest to them? To have the whole kingdom hurried in such haste for the will and pleasure of *one subject!* All this was beyond example and comparison."*

*Parliament dissolved.* On this, Charles carried out Buckingham's intention, and dissolved the Parliament at once (12th Aug.). There had been good cause for the caution displayed by the Commons in granting the king's supplies. Charles and Buckingham, keeping their purpose concealed even from the Privy Council, pressed seven merchant vessels, and sent them with a ship of war under Captain Pennington's command, to be employed by *Charles lends Louis ships to use against Rochelle.* Louis XIII. in blocking up the Huguenots in Rochelle. The sailors, however, showed their spirit. Learning at Dieppe their destined service, masters and men persisted in sailing back to the Downs, swearing that they would be hanged or thrown overboard before they would fight; while Pennington, who fully shared the feelings of the crews, wrote to the king, asking to be removed from command. In re-reply, however, he was only peremptorily ordered back to the French coast, and received a royal warrant authorizing him to

* See Forster's Life of Sir John Eliot, i. vi. 4.

compel obedience, "even unto the sinking of the ships." The men, being now told that the civil war in France was at an end, and that they were to be employed against Genoa, an ally of Spain, were with difficulty a second time persuaded to sail. At Dieppe, however, the truth could no longer be concealed. One vessel sailed back to the Downs, and the rest of the crews deserted their ships, leaving them to be manned by Frenchmen. A gunner—the only Englishman who took part in the service—was killed by a shot before Rochelle. *Sailors desert the vessels.*

This story was the common talk of the nation at the time of the dissolution of Parliament. An expedition so unpopular was especially unfortunate when the king was bent on going to war with Spain. No English king could hope to carry on war without obtaining large parliamentary grants, unless he was prepared to resort to illegal means of raising money. James had disliked Parliaments, and therefore, with good reason, clung to peace. Peace was still open to Charles, for war had not been declared; but he preferred breaking the law to breaking his resolution. Money was raised in the form of loans.

By these means, a fleet of ninety vessels was collected. It sailed in the autumn (4th Oct.). Buckingham, though lord-admiral, was too wise to command in person. Sir Edward Cecil, created Viscount Wimbleton for the occasion, was sent as deputy, to take the blame in case of failure. Success those who knew the state of the fleet hardly ventured to hope for. The agents the duke employed in manning, provisioning, and furnishing the vessels, had shamefully embezzled the funds, so that victuals were bad, men sick, and ships leaky, even at starting. Wimbleton received secret instructions to seize shipping and stores in the Spanish harbours, and to capture a fleet of richly laden merchantmen, returning home from the West Indies. Charles had great hopes that his exchequer would be replenished with Spanish bullion. *Fleet sails against Spain.*

Wimbleton, however, after entering the harbour of Cadiz and surprising a fort, found his troops disorderly, and finally returned to England without having fought an enemy or made a prize (Nov., Dec.). Disease broke out on the voyage home; hundreds perished at sea; hundreds were landed in a dying condition, solely, as it was said, through the bad food supplied for both soldiers and sailors. Upon the success of *Returns home disgraced.*

3

this expedition Buckingham's reputation was staked. It had been planned by him, by his advice its destination had been kept secret from Parliament, and he was justly regarded as the real author of the disgrace.

*Charles summons a Second Parliament.* Meantime the loans had fallen short; the seamen came up to London clamouring for their pay; the royal exchequer was empty. There was no escape, and Charles had to summon a second Parliament, which met only some six months after the dissolution of the first (6th Feb., 1626).

The illegal methods of raising money, the employment of English ships for crushing French Protestants, the fiasco of the fleet, were all set down to Buckingham.

*Buckingham advised to conciliate the country.* The duke received hints of what was coming. "The office of high-admiral," wrote a friendly counsellor, "requires one whole man to execute it. Your grace hath another sea of business to wade through, and the voluntary resigning of this office would fill all men, yea, even your enemies, with affection." Buckingham, Lord High-Admiral of England and Ireland, Governor-General of seas and navy, Master of the Horse, Warden of the Cinque Ports, refused to resign one of these or his other titles to popular clamour.

But while Charles asked for a subsidy, the Commons appointed a committee to search into grievances. The committee soon satisfied themselves that all evils found their head and source in Buckingham. On this the king tried threats. "I must let you know," he wrote in a letter to the House, "that I will not allow any of my servants to be questioned amongst you, much less such as are of eminent place and near unto me. The old question was, What shall be done to the man whom the king will honour? But now it hath been the labour of some to seek what may be done against him whom the king thinks fit to honour. .... I wish you would hasten my supply, or else it will be worse for yourselves, for if any ill happen, I think I shall be the last that shall feel it."

*Buckingham impeached.* The Commons, undaunted, impeached the duke for high crimes and misdemeanours (22nd April). In cases of parliamentary impeachment, the House of Commons is accuser, the House of Lords judge. The earliest case occurred towards the end of Edward the Third's reign (1376). From the time of Henry VI. there was no impeachment for nearly two centuries (1449—1621), till the practice was revived in the reign of James I., when two of the king's ministers were impeached for bribery and corruption—Bacon, lord chancellor, in 1621 ; the Earl of Middlesex, lord treasurer, in 1624. In times when the Parliament and the crown, the law and the prerogative, were struggling for mastery, and when the crown dismissed and appointed at pleasure both judges and ministers of State, such a power was a most useful weapon in the hands of the Commons. Now, since the trials of Warren Hastings (1791) and Lord Melville (1805), the right of impeachment has ceased to be exercised, because the relation of all parties has changed. The law has gained the victory over the prerogative. Courts of justice are independent, and ministers of the crown only hold office at the pleasure of the Commons.

The reverse of all this might have been affirmed at the time when Buckingham was impeached. The special allegations against him were his holding many offices at the same time, selling places of judicature, lending ships to Louis to be used against Rochelle, with various other offences, in all thirteen. But the Commons did not, in fact, impeach Buckingham for any particular crime. Their quarrel with him was that he alone possessed the royal ear, and that he counselled Charles to commit illegal acts at home, and pursue a wavering course of foreign policy, detrimental to the interests of the Protestants. The English nation has always been intolerant of tyranny at second hand. It seemed to them now monstrous that the wishes of people and Parliament should be over-ruled by the fancies of one unworthy favourite. They determined, therefore, to impeach the duke, as the only constitutional means then possessed of securing the change of ministry they desired.

*True charge against Buckingham.*

"What vast treasures he has gotten," said Sir John Eliot, conducting the impeachment before the Lords, " what infinite sums of money, and what a mass of lands ! If your lordships please to calculate, you will find it all amounting to little less than the whole of the subsidies which the king has had within that time. A lamentable example of the subjects' bounties so to be employed ! His profuse expenses, his superfluous feasts, his magnificent buildings, his riots, his excesses, what are they but the visible evidences of an express exhausting of the State, a chronicle of the immensity of his waste of the revenues of the crown ? No wonder, then, our king is now in want, this man abounding so. And as long as he abounds, the king must still be wanting. . . .

*Speech of Sir John Eliot.*

"Of all the precedents I can find, none so near resembles him as doth Sejanus, and him Tacitus describes thus: that he was *audax, sui obtegens, in alios criminator: juxta adulatio et superbia.*\* If your lordships please to measure him by this, pray see in what they vary. He is *bold*, and of such a boldness, I dare be bold to say, as is seldom heard of. He is *secret* in his purposes, and more, that we have showed already. Is he a *slanderer?* Is he an *accuser?* I wish this Parliament had not felt it, nor that which was before. As for his *pride and flattery*, what man can judge the greater? . . And now, my lords, I will conclude with a particular censure given on the Bishop of Ely in the time of Richard I. That prelate had the king's treasures at his command, and had luxuriously abused them. His obscure kindred were married to earls, barons, and others of great rank and place. No man's business could be done without his help. He would not suffer the king's council to advise in the highest affairs of state. He gave *ignotis personis et obscuris* the custody of castles and great trusts. He ascended to such a height of insolence and pride, that he ceased to be fit for characters of mercy. And therefore, says the record, of which I now hold the original, *per totam insulam publicè proclametur;*—PEREAT QUI PERDERE CUNCTA PESTINAT; OPPRIMATUR NE OMNES OPPRIMAT"† (10th May).

*Charles visits the House of Lords,* When Charles heard that Eliot had compared the duke to Sejanus, he exclaimed, "He must intend me for Tiberius!" and with the defendant by his side, went to the Upper House, and tried to overawe the duke's judges by informing the Lords that he had given orders for punishment of some insolent speeches spoken to them yesterday, and that he could himself be a witness to clear the duke of every charge *and imprisons two members of the Commons.* brought against him (11th May). He was as good as his word, and the same day committed to the Tower two of the managers of the impeachment, Sir Dudley Digges and Sir John Eliot. The Lords, of whom many were concealed enemies of the favourite, let the king speak and depart in silence. The Commons agreed to do no business until their members were restored to the House.

*Charles angrily dissolves the Parliament.* Charles might have ended the struggle by a dissolution, but as he still hoped to obtain a supply, he preferred to release the two members. Finding, however, that the Commons would not grant money, unless the duke was first removed from office, he determined to put a stop to the impeachment, by dissolving the Parliament. "No, not a minute!" he said to the Lords, who came in person to petition him to stay the

\* Tac. Ann. iv. 1.      † Forster's Life of Sir J. Eliot, i. vii. 6.

dissolution, and the next day he carried out his purpose (15th June).

The people had been anxiously watching the course of events within the House. "This is the king's last Parliament," they said, aware of Charles' indignation at the impeachment of his minister. "And now that the Parliament is dissolved, and the duke still in power, what will follow next?" "Is it not time to pray? Unless God show us the way out, we are but in an ill case."* {Fears entertained in the country.}

Charles did not keep his subjects long in doubt of his intentions. In fact, a series of measures followed, attacking more classes and more interests within a shorter period than had been ever known in English history.

Although Charles was already engaged in war with Spain, and had not received a penny from his last Parliament, he had still the temerity to enter into war with France. Several causes of quarrel existed between himself and his brother-in-law, Louis XIII. Shortly before the death of James, Cardinal Richelieu, Louis' chief minister, had effected a league between France and the Protestant powers (1624). The French were to fight the armies of Austria and Spain, while the King of Denmark, Christian IV., assisted by men from England, and money from France, was to lead the Protestant forces of Germany for the recovery of the Palatinate. {Coalition of Protestant powers against Spain and Austria.} The fleets of England and Holland were to attack Spain, while the Turks were engaged to fall upon Hungary. But as soon as Louis had reduced the Huguenots in Rochelle by the aid of the ships borrowed from Charles, he deserted his allies, and made peace with Spain (March, 1626). The reason of this sudden change in French policy was that the Huguenots, regardless of the interests of their co-religionists, seized the moment when France was about to engage in foreign war, to rise in arms against the government. The English contingent had already been fitted out with the money granted in James' last Parliament. But Louis now refused permission for these troops to pass through France on their way to join the German army, so that they were obliged to take a long sea passage to Zealand. Disease broke

---

* Ellis. 3rd Series, 227, 228.

out, and 5000 men out of the 14,000 men perished before they
saw the face of a foe.*

Christian IV., thus left unsupported, was defeated at Lutter
(27th August, 1626), and the armies of the emperor, Ferdinand
II., were soon overrunning the north of Germany (1627-8).
Charles, who had agreed in his marriage treaty not to put the
laws against Catholics into force, and had afterwards lent Louis
ships, expecting, in return, to receive aid for the recovery of the
Palatinate, naturally felt aggrieved at the conduct of the French
government. Moreover, Buckingham had some personal dis-
agreement with Richelieu, which was believed to be his only
motive for breaking the peace between the two nations.

War with France. The war was unpopular in England, because the
French, through their well-known jealousy of Spain
and Austria, were regarded as the natural allies of the German
Protestants. But Charles and Buckingham were ill advised
enough to hope that, by merely declaring themselves friends of the
Huguenots, they would be carried along on a flood-tide of popularity, and thus be able to raise money enough by illegal means for
the support of two wars at once. A general loan was
Money raised by il- demanded; every man, rich or poor, was required to
legal means. give in the same proportion as he had been rated in
the last subsidy granted by Parliament. This so-called loan was
in fact nothing less than a tax laid on land and property, without
consent of Parliament. Henry VIII., the most absolute of the
Tudor sovereigns, once endeavoured to raise money by means of
a general loan; but even in his time the attempt produced wide-
spread discontent; a serious insurrection broke out in Suffolk,
and the imposition was withdrawn (1525). Since that time a
steady increase in wealth and knowledge had for more than a
century been strengthening the middle classes, and confirming their attachment to their liberties. Leaders were now
to be found in the House of Commons, ready boldly to point
the attention of the nation to acts of arbitrary power, and
to brave the consequences of the royal displeasure. It was

* Vessels were not then required, as they happily are now, to have on
board a sufficient supply of lime juice, or other preventives against consequences of a salt diet. Hence the fatal ravages of scurvy in those times. The
symptoms of this disease are described as—discoloured spots, swelled legs,
extraordinary lassitude and dejection, sudden death resulting on the least
motion or exertion of strength. See G. Anson's Voyage, L x.

hardly likely, therefore, that an act from which Henry VIII. and Cardinal Wolsey had shrunk, should fail to rouse indignation when attempted by Charles and his detested favourite.

Opposition arose on all sides from rich and poor. The prisons were full of gentlemen who refused to lend. Lincolnshire "almost rebelled;" Shropshire "utterly denied." Several gentlemen, on being brought before the Council Chamber, refused to kneel, for fear of seeming to acknowledge that they were in any way responsible for a legitimate refusal of an illegitimate demand. In London, only two or three in a parish would pay, and that though goods were seized, and the duke threatened, saying, "Sirrah, take heed what you do; did not you speak treason at such a time?" Charles himself was reported to be so inflamed against refusers, that he was "vowing a perpetual remembrance, as well as a present punishment."* {Opposition to loan offered by all classes.}

Five gentlemen, imprisoned for refusing the loan, applied to the Court of King's Bench for a writ of *habeas corpus*.† The judge sent a writ to the gaoler, commanding him to produce his prisoners before the court, with the warrant on which they had been imprisoned. The gaoler replied that they were committed by a warrant from the king's council, by the special command of his Majesty, but that no special cause of imprisoment was mentioned. Accordingly, the question was pleaded before the judges of the King's Bench, whether or not the king had power to commit his subjects to prison without alleging any crime against them. The court was crowded, and shouts of applause were raised at the arguments of the prisoners' counsel. The judges, however, gave judgment in favour of the king, and the five gentlemen were remanded to prison. {Judgment of Court of King's Bench concerning personal liberty of subject.}

The poor, who refused the loans, were pressed into the service of the army and navy. On some districts an extra imposition was laid, called "coat and conduct money," for fitting out the soldiers. The rich had soldiers quartered on them, who acted as though the king's soldiers were as much above the law as their master. Not content with killing and carrying off oxen and sheep from the owners' grounds, they murdered and robbed upon the highways, "nay, in fairs and markets, for to meet a poor man coming from the market {Disorderly conduct of soldiers.}

* Straff. Letters, I. 38; Birch. 190, 154, 157, 164. † See p. 16.

## DEFEAT AT ROCHELLE. [1627.

with a pair of shoes, and take them from him, was but a sport and merriment." The highways became so insecure, that, to suppress disorders, Charles issued commissions to execute martial law. The ordinary course of justice was then set aside, and the commissioners tried and sentenced the soldiers under forms more summary than those of the common law. In spite, however, of the crimes committed, the remedy seemed to the nation worse than the disease. Standing armies and courts-martial being alike unknown to English statute or common law, Charles had no more legal power to issue commissions to try soldiers by martial law than he had to try civilians.* To increase the general indignation, the clergy received orders to preach up the duty of passive obedience and the divine right of kings. Those who looked out for promotion complied, but the preachers were regarded as mere lacqueys of the court. It was adding insult to injury, first to take the people's properties illegally, and then to tell them that submission was a duty, pleasing to God.

*Commissions issued for execution of martial law.*

*Clergy preach duty of passive obedience.*

At last, at the expense of so much bitterness between king and commons, a fleet of 100 vessels was fitted out, and sailed for France (27th June). Buckingham took the command himself; a landing was effected on the Isle of Rhé, and the Huguenots in Rochelle were persuaded to trust to the honour of the English, and try the event of war against Louis XIII. once more. But, after two months had been spent in an unsuccessful siege of the fortified town of St. Martin,† Buckingham made a disastrous retreat along a narrow causeway, beset on either side with salt pits and ditches. So many officers and soldiers were slain, so many taken prisoners, that not above half the number of those who sailed returned to their homes. Beside the cries of private mourning

*Expedition of Buckingham to Rochelle.*

---

\* Kings of England had indeed always exercised the right of issuing ordinances of war for the regulation of their armies. But this military law had been confined to military offences committed on actual service, while these ' soldiers, mariners, and other dissolute persons,' were (1) not on actual service, and (2) had committed offences which were cognizable at the courts of common law; hence fears were naturally entertained that so tempting a method of procedure would be extended to civilians. Since England has had a standing army, a Mutiny Act is annually passed, allowing courts-martial for punishment of military offences, and reserving the crown power to frame further articles in case of actual war.

† For map, see p. 46.

were heard those of public indignation. Buckingham was believed to have gone to Rochelle in a pet, merely to gratify his spleen against Louis, without caring either for the Huguenots or his troops; and the people, in whose minds the remembrance of Elizabeth's triumphs was still fresh, went back to King John's time to find a parallel disgrace, describing it as "the shamefullest overthrow the English have received since we lost Normandy."

A clamour was raised for a Parliament. The coasts were infested; pirates entered the harbours, and sailed up the rivers; the very fishermen were afraid to put out; trade was decaying, for merchants refused to build vessels only to be pressed into the king's service; the sailors came round about the palace at Whitehall, crying out for pay. Charles had pledged himself to relieve Rochelle, the siege of which, by Louis, was the only outcome of his intervention; but how he was to carry on two wars, in the face of all these difficulties, was a question to puzzle the wisest head. The lords of the council were afraid to try forced loans again, and Charles, though, as he truly said, he did "abominate the name," consented to follow their advice, and send out the summons for another Parliament. *Charles summons a third Parliament.*

The House was filled with patriots, elected against court candidates by overwhelming majorities. Eliot, Pym, Coke, Selden, Wentworth, were all there; and Oliver Cromwell, a young man of twenty-nine, took his seat for the first time as member for the town of Huntingdon. *Enemies of court in large majority.* Charles opened this, his third Parliament, with threats (17th March). "If you," he said, "should not do your duties in contributing what the State at this time needs, I must, in discharge of my conscience, use those other means which God hath put into my hands." The threat only made the Commons more determined to put an end to the loans, billeting of soldiers, and imprisonments, "those other means" which had caused such just and bitter resentment.

Debates on granting the king a supply, and on finding a remedy for grievances, advanced hand in hand. The decision of the judges, that the king might not commit a subject to prison, *except at his pleasure,** was thought a wanton outrage on the intelligence of the nation. According to this theory, the laws were only binding on the king so long as he graciously chose not

* Forster's Life of Sir J. Eliot, ii. ix. 2.

to act in right of his royal prerogative, so that Acts of Parliament, regarded for centuries as the bulwarks of public liberty, were rendered absolutely meaningless.

<small>Judgment of King's Bench canvassed in Commons.</small> "To have my body pent up in a gaol," exclaimed an indignant patriot, "without remedy of law, and to be so adjudged . . If this be law, why do we talk of liberties? Why do we trouble ourselves with a dispute about law, franchises, property of goods, and the like? What may a man call his own, if not the liberty of his person? I am weary of treading these ways."

A security was needed that the old laws should be kept in force, and the king's prerogative be prevented from trampling them under foot. "We must vindicate—what?" said Wentworth, "new things? No! our ancient, lawful, and vital liberties! We must reinforce the laws made by our ancestors. We must set such a stamp upon them as no licentious spirit shall dare hereafter to invade them."

The Commons, however, still believed the king would feel bound in conscience to respect a law which he passed himself; <small>Petition of Right.</small> and, under this impression, drew up a bill, in the form of a Petition of Right, to serve as a new guarantee for the preservation of liberty. They called their bill the Petition of Right, because it was but a confirmation of old laws, of rights already possessed. The Petition demanded:

1st. That no freeman be required to give any gift, loan, benevolence, or tax without common consent by Act of Parliament.

2nd. That no freeman be imprisoned or detained contrary to the laws of the land.

3rd. That soldiers and mariners be not billeted in private houses.

4th. That commissions to punish soldiers and sailors by martial law be revoked, and no more issued.

The Upper House, which the king had partially packed by the creation of several new lords, proposed to add to the petition the following saving clause:—"We humbly present this petition to your Majesty, with due regard to leave entire that sovereign power wherewith your Majesty is entrusted for the protection of your people." The Commons, however, refused to ac- <small>Saving clause proposed by Lords, rejected by Commons.</small> cept the amendment, which conceded the very point at issue. "All our petition," said Pym, "is for the laws of England; this power seems to be another power distinct from the power of the law. We cannot leave him a sovereign power, for he was never possessed of it." After several conferences between the two Houses, the Lords yielded and passed the petition in the form desired by the Commons (27th May). Charles, being in want of money, did not venture in any direct manner to refuse his consent, but when the petition was read before assembled King, Lords, and Commons, the lord keeper read out, instead of the usual words by which the royal assent is signified, a new form, "that the king wished that right should be done, and that he held himself in conscience as much obliged to maintain their just rights and liberties as his own prerogative" (2nd June). The Commons were engaged in preparing a remonstrance against the evil advisers by whose counsel this worthless answer had been given, when a message came from the king, forbidding the House to meddle with affairs of State (5th June). There followed a prolonged silence. Not to meddle with affairs of State, meant that they must endure the ascendancy of the duke, and see the name of England despised abroad from a policy which was at once meddlesome, feeble, and fickle; while at home outrages were done to the dearest liberties of their country, which it was their bounden duty to defend. Some members sat down in tears, dumb through grief; others mingled their speech with tears; some hundred wept in all, they felt so much was at stake. "Let us palliate no longer," cried the old lawyer, Sir Edward Coke, "if we do, God will not prosper us. I think the Duke of Buckingham is the cause of all our miseries—that man is the grievance of grievances; it is not the king but the duke"—(a great cry of "'Tis he, 'tis he!" "Yea, yea!" "Well moved, well spoken")— "that saith, 'We require you not to meddle with State government or the ministers thereof'" (5th June).

*Charles' first answer to Petition of Right.*

*Charles forbids House of Commons to meddle with affairs of State*

Two days later, Charles yielded, the Petition of Right was read a second time, and the reply given in the usual form: "*Soit droit fait comme il est désiré*" (7th June).

*King's second answer to Petition of Right.*

The Commons, on their side, passed a bill for five subsidies, after which Parliament was prorogued (26th June).

While Parliament was sitting, another fleet which was sent to Rochelle, returned without raising the siege. "What wonder!" said the people; "was not the commander Buckingham's brother-in-law?" No allowance had been made for the shallowness of that sandy coast: Lord Denbigh, finding his ships drew too much water to approach the city, seemed only too glad of an excuse for sailing away at once. It was believed that the expedition had been got up, not to save Rochelle, but merely to blind the eyes of Parliament. One of the duke's household, called Dr. Lamb, was set upon by the rabble in the streets of London, and so brutally knocked about that he died the same night. The city magistrates could not, or would not, find the offenders. The people sang,

"Let Charles and George do what they can,
The duke shall die like Dr. Lamb."

*Felton murders Buckingham.* Felton, described as a gentleman of low stature, few words, and melancholy spirit, after pondering over a remonstrance of the Commons, declaring Buckingham the cause of all the evils under which the kingdom suffered, conceived it his duty to rid his country of an enemy. The duke was at Portsmouth, preparing to set sail immediately in command of another fleet for the relief of Rochelle. He was in company with several officers, French and English, when, in passing through a dark lobby leading from a breakfast-room into a hall, he was stabbed to the heart. "The villain hath killed me!" he cried, pulled out the knife, staggered to a table, and fell dead in the arms of the bystanders (23rd Aug.). No one had seen the blow struck, and suspicion was falling on the Frenchmen, when Felton stepped forward out of the crowd and said, "I am the man who did the deed, let no one suffer who is innocent." The people could not restrain their joy; healths were drunk to the murderer, verses written in his honour. Crowds gathered to see him on his way to London and the Tower, greeting him as the slayer of the Philistine. "Now, God bless thee, little David," "The Lord be merciful unto thee," "The Lord comfort thee," were the cries that reached his ears.

*Judges declare use of torture against the common law.* On being brought before the council and threatened by Bishop Laud with the rack, unless he revealed the names of his associates, he replied that he alone was author of the deed, and that as for the rack, he could not say whether torture might make him accuse his lordship, or which of their lordships. The threat was not put into execution. The judges unanimously declared the use of torture was contrary to the common law of England, and the king did not think it prudent to override their decision. Felton was hanged at Tyburn. To the last he felt little remorse for the murder. Though he confessed he had done wrong in shedding blood, he could not be brought to doubt but that good would result to Church and State from his act.

The duke was only thirty-five. Charles called him "his martyr," and never forgave those who opposed him during life, or spoke ill of him after death. His fate shows the truth of the common maxim that those who are above the law are above the protection of law; but the crime was the crime of a fanatic. Not a shadow of suspicion rests on the popular leaders. They were at once too far-sighted and too honourable. Acts of treachery and violence, whatever the immediate advantage gained, are sure in the long run to recoil to the injury of the side that practises them. Sooner or later, violence is condemned by public opinion, for in a constitutional struggle, the mass of the nation have really more the feelings of a jury than of parties to a case. It is only by winning a favourable judgment from the large and wavering masses, that any party, which has no armed force behind it, can obtain a sure and final triumph. Violent partisans are always to be found ready to approve and employ all means without distinction to advance their ends; but the English leaders knew that the statue of Wingless Victory can only stand in the shrine of law and right. *Popular leaders not implicated in the crime.*

The fleet, which now sailed under Lord Lindsay, was as unsuccessful as though Buckingham himself had lived to command it. While Charles delayed, Richelieu's genius and energy were at work. The city was gradually shut in on the land side by a line of circumvallation extending nine miles, while a vast mole of nearly a mile in length was raised across the roadstead. After two unsuccessful attempts to force their way through the mole, the English returned without having placed a morsel of food within reach of the starving inhabitants. The town had a strong position between the sea and the marshes on the rocky promontory from which it got its name of the "little rock." Originally a colony of serfs, who had fled from the oppressions of their feudal lords, it had a tradition of political as well as of religious freedom. Once a fief of the English kings, and now much dearer as a stronghold of Protestantism, the English were deeply interested in its heroic resistance, and regarded themselves and their country as irretrievably disgraced, when, after 16,000 were said to have died of famine, the city at last surrendered at discretion (8th Oct., 1628).

Fall of Rochelle. The fall was a fatal blow to the cause of the Huguenots. Liberty of conscience was still left them, but their fortresses were destroyed, their assemblies, their privileges, their organization by churches abolished. Instead of being a power within the state, they became a sect.*

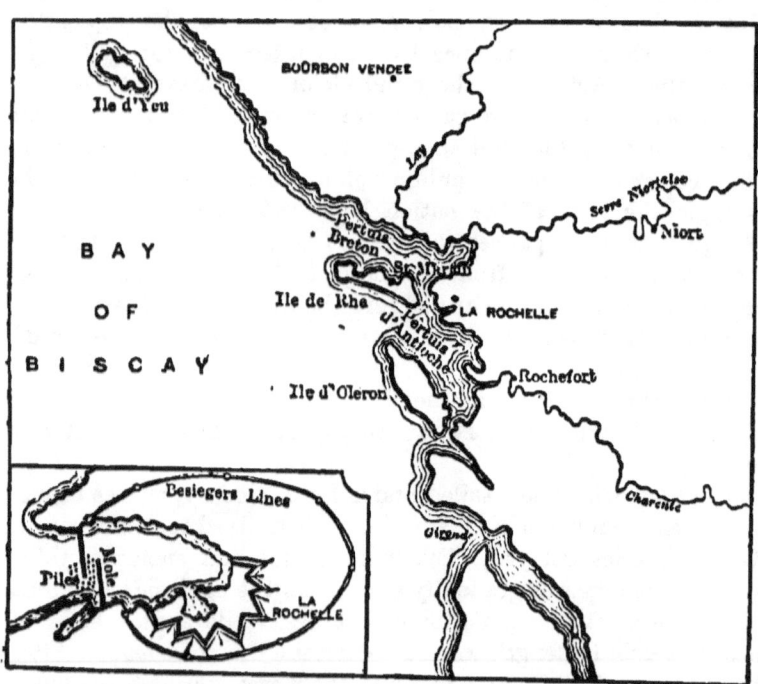

The English, after this defeat of their religion, could not console themselves for long with the victory they had obtained over the government in the Petition of Right. At first the people in London rung bells and made bonfires, believing their liberties to be now secured; but their mistake was soon proved. Notwith-

* Lavallée, Hist. de France.

standing the king's distinct promise to respect the rights enumerated in the Petition, the customs were still levied. A merchant, a member of the Commons, who refused to pay £200 duty, had his goods seized to the value of £5000. "If all the Parliament were in you, we would take your goods," said the custom-house officers. Men who ventured on speaking or writing against the introduction of Catholic ceremonies and doctrines into a Protestant church, were brought before the Star Chamber on charges of libel, fined, cast into prison, and, in some cases, mutilated. Bishop Laud, a cruel persecutor of Puritans, was translated to the see of London (July). Clergymen, tried and censured by the last Parliament for publishing books and sermons maintaining the right of the king to take his subjects' goods without their own consent, were now rewarded with bishoprics or rich livings. Charles did not seem to realize the alteration he had made in his position by giving his consent to the Petition of Right. Previously, no special tie bound him to act by law. No special charge of deceit, therefore, could be brought against him if, like his father, he tried to exalt his position into that of a French king, free arbitrarily to tax and imprison his subjects. But now a victory had been fairly won by patriots armed only with the legal weapons of the constitution, and by confirming the old charters by a new statute, he had pledged his word to their observance; by infringement now, he would lose the confidence as well as the affection of his subjects.

*Petition of Right broken by ministers.*

Meantime the place of Buckingham was filled. The name of Sir Thomas Wentworth had hitherto been counted among the chief leaders of the opposition. But his subsequent conduct seemed to show that his actions had been dictated by pride rather than by patriotism. Haughty and ambitious, scorning to hold a second place, he had chosen to rise to influence as an enemy of the court, rather than lower himself and sue for favour to Buckingham. Promotion, however, is sure to be offered to a dangerous opponent, who will sacrifice principles to place. A month before Buckingham's death, Wentworth was already a minister. Thus when Felton made the first place vacant, Charles had already enlisted in his service a man, whose great abilities and commanding nature rendered him far more competent to be his adviser in the exercise of arbitrary government than the vain

*Sir Thomas Wentworth fills Buckingham's place in council.*

and frivolous favourite he had lost. Wentworth made no conditions as to the policy to be pursued; thus he left his party, not to forward their views in office, but simply to gratify his inordinate ambition. He appointed a meeting with his old friend and companion, Pym, at Greenwich, and there discoursed to him "of the dangers they were like to run by the courses they were in, and what advantages they might have, if they would listen to some offers which would probably be made to them from court." "You need not use all this art," replied Pym, "to tell me that you have a mind to leave us. But remember what I tell you. You are going to be undone. And remember also, that though you leave us now, I will never leave you, while your head is upon your shoulders."

*Second session of Charles' Third Parliament.* Thus Wentworth, created Lord Wentworth, and a member of the Privy Council, at the next session of Parliament sat amongst the king's ministers in the Lower House, ready to throw all the weight of his abilities and eloquence upon the side of arbitrary power (20th Jan.).

The Commons immediately began to debate upon their grievances. 'The goods of merchants had been seized for refusing to pay illegal customs. Further, though no man ought to lose life or limb but by the law, the Star Chamber sentenced men to lose their ears.' "Next it will be our arms, and then our legs, and so our lives." Charles, not content with thus breaking his royal promise, had descended to duplicity. Though by the king's own orders the Petition of Right, with the proper answer, had been entered in the journals of the House, yet copies had subsequently been dispersed over the country, with the first evasive answer annexed. An inquiry was held : it was found that the printer had received royal orders to suppress the true copies, and make a new impression. 'Noblesse oblige,' but such double dealing would have brought obloquy on an attorney. The strength of loyalty lies in sentiment, and this was a fatal omen of the future for king and commons.

*Commons inquire into illegal acts of ministers and officers of executive.* Meantime Charles sent message after message bidding the House pass a bill, granting him the customs, for this was in fact the only purpose for which he had called the Parliament. "Let the merchants have their goods restored," said the Commons, "before the bill is passed." "Kings," said one, "ought not, by the law of God, thus to oppress their subjects. I know we have a good king, and this is the advice of his wicked ministers, but there is nothing can be more dishonourable unto him." They proceeded to question those ministers; they demanded of the king's attorney-general by whose warrant he had discharged Catholic priests; they demanded of the farmers of the customs on what warrants they had seized the goods of merchants who refused to pay illegal duties; they demanded of the judges on what grounds they had refused to let the merchants have their cause tried at law. No acts could have given more dire offence to Charles. Other Houses of Commons had attacked some single minister of state, but none had ever ventured on questioning the conduct of the king's servants at large. An immediate dissolution being fully expected, the popular leaders determined not to separate, without first passing a vote against the illegal levying of the customs. On the 2nd of March Eliot rose to address the House. The Speaker, Finch, a thorough courtier, rose also, and saying that he had the king's orders for an immediate adjournment, left his chair. Two members, Denzil Hollis and Valentine, standing on either side, forced him back to his seat, and held him down, whilst Eliot made a short speech, in which he declared it to be the duty of the House to maintain religion and the rights of the subject, and brought forward a declaration to that effect, which he desired the Speaker to put to the vote. But Finch, with tears, refused to receive it or put it to the vote, declaring that he had the king's command to the contrary. Again he tried to rise from his chair, and again was forced down by Hollis and Valentine. "God's wounds," said Hollis, "he should sit there until it pleased them to rise." "You are the disgrace of your country, and the blot of a noble family," cried one of his own kinsmen. The king's councillors, coming forward to rescue the Speaker, were forcibly driven back to their seats. Blows were given, and sword hilts handled. "Let all," said Strode, "who desire the declaration read and put to the vote, stand up." Whereupon the majority of the House started to their feet, and Eliot flung down the paper before them. At this moment a messenger from the king came to the door, with orders to the sergeant to withdraw with the mace, which, by custom, always

*The Speaker refuses to put Eliot's declaration to the vote.*

*Tumult in the House. King's messenger refused admittance.*

lies on the Commons' table, while the House is proceeding with business. No sooner, however, had the sergeant laid his hand upon the mace, than a cry was raised to lock the door, and Sir Miles Hobert turned the lock, and put the key in his pocket. Eliot then read a protest against any who should levy or pay customs. "And for myself," he said, "I protest further, as I am a gentleman, if my fortune be ever again to meet in this honourable assembly, where I now leave, I will begin again." While he was speaking, the gentleman usher of the black rod, sent by Charles to pronounce a dissolution, vainly knocked at the door for admittance. And now Hollis, standing by the Speaker's chair, with a paper containing three resolutions in his hand, called out, that he put the question, "that they were traitors who should introduce Popery; that they were traitors who should levy the customs, ungranted by Parliament; that they were traitors who should voluntarily pay them." "Ay, ay," was shouted on all sides. The door was unlocked, and the members rushed out, carrying away in the stream a third messenger waiting outside from the king (2nd March).

The next day Charles signed a proclamation for a dissolution. The Commons "had," he said, "tried to erect an universal overwhelming power to themselves, which belongs only to us, and not to them." They had in fact tried to gain control over the executive power. So far the charge was true. The nation was weary of entering upon wars without its own approval or consent; of giving money for one object, and seeing it spent on another; of seeing good laws not only violated by ministers of the crown, but rendered nugatory by the quibbles of time-serving judges. The Petition of Right was already a dead letter. Judges, ministers, custom-house officers, all acted as though the king's consent to such a law had never been given. The Commons saw that it was but a vain guarantee against tyranny to 'have a king's word to the contrary.' They were on the right track when they sought to make the officers of the executive personally responsible, as according to the principles of the constitution they had always been. Charles, on his side, published a proclamation against Parliament, threatening "certain vipers of the Commonwealth" with condign punishment, and declaring it "presumption for any one to prescribe to him any time for the calling of that assembly."

## CHAPTER III.

### ELEVEN YEARS OF ARBITRARY GOVERNMENT.—1629—1640.

ΚΡΕΩΝ. ἄλλῳ γὰρ ἤ μοι χρή γε τῆσδ᾽ ἄρχειν χθονός;
ΑΙΜΩΝ. πόλις γὰρ οὐκ ἔσθ᾽ ἥτις ἀνδρός ἐσθ᾽ ἑνός.
ΚΡΕΩΝ. οὐ τοῦ κρατοῦντος ἡ πόλις νομίζεται;
ΑΙΜΩΝ. καλῶς ἐρήμης γ᾽ ἄν σὺ γῆς ἄρχοις μόνος.
CREON. Who else save I hath right to rule this land?
HAEMON. It is no state where all belongs to one.
CREON. Is not the state the sovereign's property?
HAEMON. A manless state how grand to rule—alone!—Soph. Ant. 739.

CHARLES had now made up his mind to govern without the aid of Parliament, and thus raise himself into the position of an absolute monarch. His education and his character had alike tended to blind his mind to the fact that, from the subjects' point of view, such an intention was criminal. Princes rarely converse with their fellows on an equal footing, or hear their own opinions and actions freely criticized. They are, therefore, apt to grow up prejudiced. Charles was especially unfortunate in this respect. In James' court, no man could maintain a footing who was not obsequious enough to let his own opinion follow that of his Majesty. The divine right by which kings rule, the superiority of the prerogative to the law, the subject's duty of passive obedience, were household words to the young prince. His social training was as bad as his political; the companions amongst whom he was thrown, were not only obsequious but immoral, and when he became king, his father's influence lived on in one of the most worthless of his favourites. Edward I., indeed, a king whose only thought was for his people's "security under fixed laws and customs" yet failed in inspiring his son with any such noble aims, though he banished the evil companions who were bent on marring that son's mind. But Charles was in all points a prince far superior to Edward II. Had he been trained by a father endowed with the noble qualities of Edward I., he might have run a peaceful course and lived and

*Charles' education and character.*

4—2

died in accord with his subjects. Charles' virtues, in fact, were his own, and displayed themselves in spite of his education. His manners and his tastes were refined, and his enemies were never able to deny that he was both a good husband and a good father. On the other hand, nature had bestowed on him no special gifts to counteract the evil effects of his political training. His character was cold and unbending, and he was without any generous sympathies, that might have brought him to recognize good in cause or man opposed to his own fixed ideas. Obstinate and opinionated when he came to the throne at twenty-four, so he remained to the last day of his life; no amount of experience proved sufficient to teach him the necessity of yielding to public opinion, or even of listening with patience to arguments that offended his high notions of what was due to himself as a king. With such an education and such a character, he was born in an evil time for himself. He had found a minister who could put his wishes into act, for Wentworth set himself, with all the energy of his nature, to the support of arbitrary government. Having shared in the counsels of the patriots, and knowing their deep-rooted love of liberty, this clear-sighted counsellor never deceived himself into thinking that any half measures were sufficient for success. On the Continent, many instances had proved that a standing army was the surest support to an arbitrary throne. With a fleet only and without such an army, Wentworth would *Advice of Wentworth too good for Charles.* say, a government had but 'one leg to stand upon.' To secure an army he must have money. At present much of the monies taken from the pockets of the people passed into those of courtiers and their dependents, instead of enriching the royal exchequer. It was easier to save money than to get it, and Wentworth, therefore, advocated economy in administration, in fact, the true financial policy of getting money's worth for money given. But Wentworth's advice was too good and his energy too great for his master. The minister was to be like the dwarf in the fairy tale, he was not to prescribe prudence but to save his employer from the results of imprudence. Advancing Wentworth as he did, Charles shrank from opposing the wishes of his wife and curtailing the perquisites of his friends. Under these conditions, the king's government might be violent, it could never be strong.

Wentworth speedily concluded peace with France (April, 1629) and Spain (Nov., 1630). Experience had already proved that it was impossible to carry on war without applying to Parliament for aid. To provide for the expenses of the court and government was no easy matter, even when the country was at peace.

Charles' vain and passionate wife, Henrietta Maria, who in an ill-temper could dash her hands through the panes of a window, or turn a whole company out of her presence with one of her royal scowls, was not a queen to be easily guided by a minister. With some, however, her smiles were as potent as her frowns, and she soon won an ascendancy over her husband equal to that which Buckingham once exercised. To her, happiness meant a gay life at Whitehall, with a constant series of balls and masques, so that the expenses of the court rose rapidly, and soon reached sums far larger than those considered enormous in the time of James. Delighting, as she did, in the exercise of power and patronage, it was to the queen, and not to the king, or to Wentworth, that courtiers and their dependents applied, in order to obtain lucrative monopolies, offices, or pensions. The court offices were, indeed, regarded as a sort of booty. Fixed salaries there were none; but fees and perquisites were numerous, and every man's hand was open to a bribe. There was no shame felt in the matter. The Earl of Dorset, a member of council, and a judge in the Star Chamber, openly declared that he thought it no crime for a courtier to receive a reward from one for whom he procured a favour.

<sub>Character of Henrietta Maria.</sub>

<sub>Charles' court and government corrupt.</sub>

Out of the royal revenue* had to be provided, not only money sufficient to satisfy the desires of the court, but also to keep up the navy, to provide for the repairs of castles and forts, the expenses of ambassadors, and the salaries of officers of the executive.

* The king's ordinary revenue consisted—
(1.) Of fines paid by feudal tenants.
(2.) Of rents accruing from lands belonging to the crown.
(3.) Of fines and fees paid in courts of justice.
(4.) Of forfeitures of lands and goods for offences.
(5.) Of the first-fruits and tenths of all spiritual preferments in the kingdom. The first-fruits or annates were the first year's whole profits by a valuation made in the thirteenth century (1288—1292). The decimæ were the tenth part of the annual profit of every living by the same valuation. These taxes, originally paid to the pope, were annexed to the crown by an act passed in the twenty-sixth year of Henry VIII. (By a statute of 2nd and 3rd Anne, the revenue of first-fruits and tenths has been vested in trustees for ever, to form a perpetual fund for the augmentation of poor livings.)
(6.) Of the customduties, when granted to the king for life. To these however, Charles had no legal claim. See p. 31.

Since Parliamentary grants were out of the question and the ordinary revenue did not nearly meet the demand, a raid was made upon the property of all classes of society.

The nobility and gentry suffered as much as any. Holders of land on the borders of royal forests were accused of having encroached on the king's domains; the judges received orders to ferret out the weak points of titles, and when the cases came into court, to intimidate jurors into giving verdicts in the king's favour. Adverse verdicts entailed fines of ruinous amounts, and the legal rule that no prescription holds good against the crown was carried so far that even lands held by a title of three hundred years were reclaimed as royal property. By these means, the bounds of Rockingham Forest were increased from six miles to sixty. But 'depression of the nobility,' says Bacon, 'may make a king more absolute, but less safe.' These, and similar encroachments, only helped to cement the alliance between peers and commoners.

*Money raised by illegal means.*

There was an old feudal custom, long fallen into disuse, that on the accession of a new king, all who held land of him by knights' service, worth above the paltry sum of £20 per annum, should receive the order of knighthood, or pay a fine. Fines were now exacted from noblemen and gentlemen in all parts of the country, for having neglected to be knighted when Charles came to the throne. The fines levied were three or four times the amount at which the delinquents would have been rated for subsidies. The Catholics in return for their support were allowed to compound at an easier rate.*

The poor were also attacked. A statute, passed during the reign of Elizabeth, requiring that cottagers should have four acres of ground attached to their dwellings, had probably never been enforced, had certainly long since fallen into disuse; the poor householders were now held responsible, and complained that they were "mightily vexed," for commissioners were sent twenty miles round London to search out and fine those who had disobeyed the statute. The commissioners employed were "needy men of no fame, prisoners out of the Fleet," whose services, of course, could be cheaply bought; the money they collected mostly went to enrich two lords, who had received as a favour from the king, leave to put the commission into execution.

*Old laws raked up.*

\* Ellis, Orig. Letters, ii. cclxxi.

If no old law could be raked up, Charles would act by proclamation. For instance, he forbade by proclamation the building of new houses, in or about London. Builders either bought licences, or else ran the risk of being called to account and punished for disregarding the proclamation.* Thus one man was fined £1000, and ordered to pull down forty-two dwelling-houses, stables, and coach-houses, by a certain time, on pain of paying a second £1000. Any classes who refused such black mail were severely dealt with. The innkeepers of London were inhibited from dressing any meat, because they declined to pay an excise duty on wine, when levied by the sole authority of the Council. They were soon glad to compound.

As a further means of raising money, the king granted or sold patents for the exclusive sale or manufacture of certain articles. The monopolists formed companies, of which all traders or manufacturers were forced to become members and obey the regulations. By these means taxes were laid on articles of every-day use and consumption, such as salt, corn, lace, tobacco, barrels, linen, cloth ; but most of the money so raised, while impoverishing the nation by raising the price of all necessaries, enriched, not the king, but his courtiers and their dependents. For instance, out of every £12 raised by the monopoly of wine, only £1 reached the exchequer, the other £11 stopping by the way amongst the vintners and the owners of the patent. If the companies sold bad articles, there was no redress. The poor women in London complained that the soap made by the company burnt the linen, scalded their fingers, and was full of tallow and lime. The soap-boilers were Catholics, and got the queen's laundress to subscribe to the goodness of the soap, but "she tells her Majesty she does not wash her linen with any other than Castile soap, and the truth is, most of the ladies that have subscribed have their linen washed with Castile soap." The Lord Mayor, whom the women followed about in the streets,

*Marginal note: Monopolies.*

---
\* Lawful proclamations were those—
(1) Issued by the crown in its purely executive capacity.
(2) Prohibiting acts already prohibited by law, or calling on the subject to perform some duty to which he was bound by law.
Unlawful proclamations were those usurping the legislative power, which the crown by right could only exercise in common with the two Houses of Parliament, as for instance, those granting individuals privileges against the rights of others, imposing duties not imposed by law, prohibiting under penalties acts which the law did not recognize as offences.

clamorously petitioning against the new soap, received a sharp reproof at the Council Board for giving too soft answers. The monopolies alienated London, which might have supplied the sinews of war to the king, as it eventually did for the Parliament. It was noted that "discontinuance of Parliaments brings up this kind of grain, which commonly is blasted when they come."

Besides being extortionate and arbitrary, the government was often cruel; and the common law judges, instead of administering justice impartially between subject and sovereign, allowed themselves to be made the instruments of oppression. Upon the dissolution of the last Parliament, several members of the Commons were imprisoned on warrants signed by the king, charging Members of late Parliament committed illegally to prison. them with having stirred up sedition. Their counsel argued that sedition was a bailable offence, and that, therefore, they ought to be let free on bail. The judges, however, following the king's instructions, required the prisoners, not only to find bail for the present charge, but securities for their good behaviour in the future. As they refused to comply with these demands, which would have kept them under the thumb of the court and its judges, they were ordered back into prison.

These country leaders, who led the opposition in Parliament, risked much—property, liberty, life. Sir John Eliot, being of too noble a nature to be wrought upon either by corruption or intimidation, naturally became the victim of a government that always required submission before it relaxed its hold. He had long since been obliged to give away his property in trust for his children, to preserve himself and his family from ruin. An information in the King's Bench was now brought against Hollis and Valentine for raising a tumult in the Commons on the last day of the session, and against Eliot, for words spoken in the House. The three pleaded that the offences with which they were Judgment of King's Bench on Eliot, Hollis, Valentine. charged, being committed in Parliament, were not punishable in any other place. The most important of all privileges of Parliament, freedom of speech concerning matters of Parliamentary debate, was here called into question; and the prisoners' counsel brought forward many precedents to show that the liberties and privileges of Parliament could only be determined in Parliament, and not by any inferior court. The King's Bench, however, decided that it had a right to judge the alleged offences, though committed in Parliament, and condemned the defendants to be imprisoned during the king's pleasure ; Eliot to pay a fine to the king of £2000, Hollis 1000 marks,* Valentine £500 (Feb. 12, 1630).†

In the course of twelve months' time, the other prisoners either consented to find sureties for good behaviour, or paid their fines, or were allowed to go at large on some excuse or other. Sir John Eliot alone refused to make any concession of principle, and was still closely confined in the Tower. Consumption attacked him, and his doctors prescribed air and exercise, but he was not allowed to pass out of the walls of his prison. "I am now," he writes, "where candlelight may be suffered, but scarce fire ;" and this, though his lodgings had been changed to a dark gloomy chamber. He sent a petition to the king, informing him that he had fallen into a dangerous disease, and praying to be allowed to take some fresh air. Charles replied that the petition was not humble enough. Sir John sent a second by the hand of his son. "I am heartily sorry," he wrote, "I have displeased your Majesty, and beseech you once again to command your judges to set me at liberty, that when I have recovered my health, I may return back to my prison." But no order for release came : and the Lieutenant of the Tower offered to present a third petition with his own hand, and made no doubt but that Charles would grant it if Sir John would only write so as to acknowledge his fault, and humbly pray for pardon. "I thank you, sir," replied Eliot, "for your friendly advice, but my spirits are grown feeble and faint, which when it shall please God to restore unto their former vigour, I will take it into consideration." He did not mean to use the language of a culprit, and purchase his own life by betraying the cause of the nation. Death soon released him while still in the prime of his life (æt. 40). His son sent a petition to the king, begging that his father's body might be buried in his own county of Cornwall. Charles wrote under

*End of Sir John Eliot.*

* 1 mark = 13s. 4d. ; therefore, 1000 marks, £666 13s. 4d.
† In 1667, only seven years after the Restoration, the Commons resolved that the judgment now given against Eliot, Hollis, and Valentine, though right as regarded the imputed riot, was illegal in extending to words spoken in Parliament; the Lords concurred in the vote and reversed the judgment. This decision established, once for all, the privilege of freedom of speech in Parliament, unlimited by any authority except that of the House itself.

the petition these words : " 'Let Sir John Eliot's body be buried in the church of that parish where he died.' And so he was buried in the Tower." Such was the fate of one of the purest-hearted of patriots (1632).

His history shows in an eminent degree the nobleness of the leaders of the opposition and the constitutional rectitude of their aims : with a true loyalty to his king, whom he tried in vain to urge into right courses, he won the leadership of the Commons, not more by his vivid eloquence than by the single-minded devotion of his character. There was a true pathos in his stoical bearing under suffering. In the solitude of his prison he bade his friends, 'for their own sakes forbear coming to visit him.' Dying in the Tower he appealed to his son at college not to let him 'receive by any misconduct of his that wound which no enemy could give—sorrow and affliction of the mind.' The limit he gently put to the intercessions of the friendly governor reminds us of the scene in Plato when Socrates put Crito's appeal aside by telling him that he heard the laws of his land remonstrating with him 'to think of right first, and of life and children afterwards.' Thus, unlike the Royalist victim of the Revolution, he departed 'as a sufferer and not a doer of evil.'* His country did not lose by his adherence to principle. In later times when the cause of liberty was in peril its defenders thought of Eliot and fought on.†

*Illegal courts. Court of the North.* Illegal judgments were now the curse of the nation. Where the common law courts could find no crime, the illegal courts came into action. North of the Humber, the Court of the North, of which Wentworth was president, took the place of the Star Chamber in the south. Its origin was even more questionable. Henry VIII., after an insurrection in 1536, issued a commission to the Archbishop of York and several gentlemen of the north, to examine into the grounds of the disorder, and to punish offenders in riots and conspiracies. But long after all traces of the insurrection had disappeared, the court remained, and its authority was gradually extended. The people dwelling north of the Humber complained that they were shut out from the protection of the common law courts at Westminster, and that their personal liberty and property were at the mercy of arbitrary judges, who sentenced according to their

* See p. 98, and Plato, "Crito," 54.
† See p. 105.

discretion. While the Court of the North was thus accused of encroaching even upon the civil jurisdiction of the Westminster courts, the Star Chamber was chiefly concerned with criminal cases, such as forgery, perjury, riot, libel, conspiracy, and every kind of misdemeanour. It adjudged any punishment short of death, as pillory, whipping, branding, cutting off the ears, fine, and imprisonment.

The customs were levied with rigour, though they had never been granted to Charles by statute.

Chambers, one of several merchants whose goods had been seized for refusing to pay illegal duties, vented his in- dignation by saying before the Council Board, "that the merchants in no part of the world were so screwed and wrung as in England ; that in Turkey they had more encouragement." The judges of the common law courts could have found no law by which to inflict a heavy punishment for a few hasty words. The judges of the Star Chamber, guided in their judgment by their discretion, declared the expressions used were likely to make the people believe that Charles' happy government was a Turkish tyranny, and sentenced Chambers to pay a fine of £2000, and to sign a submission. Chambers wrote under the submission these words: "I do utterly abhor and detest the contents of this submission, and never, till death, will acknowledge any part thereof." He was refused by the judges his habeas corpus, and remained a prisoner many years. <small>Sentence of Star Chamber on Chambers.</small>

Wentworth, as the councillor who possessed most influence in the government, incurred the hatred of all lovers of liberty, without gaining the friendship of the queen or the court. Regardless of the interests of courtiers and their dependents, he resolutely endeavoured, as far as he could obtain Charles' support, to govern with a view to increase the power of the crown. This administration required the surrender of illicit gains, and the punishment of criminals, however close their connection with men in high places. While, therefore, its vices incurred the odium of the country, its virtues incurred the odium of the court. However much a Somerset or a Buckingham may have been hated by rival aspirants to royal favour, it was the men who were hated and not their régime. Under them, so long as the interests of the favourite remained untouched, free licence was given to all to make their fortunes by the first means <small>Administration of Wentworth and Laud.</small>

that came to hand. The court and government of James had been thoroughly corrupt. The corruption of the courtiers under James had continued under Charles. But, where free rein was given him, Wentworth thus, not unaptly, describes the character of his administration : " Where I found a crown, a church, and a people spoiled, I could not imagine to redeem them from under the pressure with gracious smiles and gentle looks ; it would cost warmer water than so . . . . True it was, indeed, I knew no other rule to govern by but by reward and punishment ; and I must profess that where I found a person well and entirely set for the service of my master, I should lay my hand under his foot, and add to his respect and power all I might ; and that where I found the contrary, I should not dandle him in my arms, or soothe him in his untoward humour, but if he came in my reach, so far as honour and justice would warrant me, I must knock him soundly over the knuckles."* In Yorkshire, as president of the Court of the North, by preventing the proceeds of his trenchant measures from being filched by petty tax-gatherers, he succeeded in raising the royal revenue in the four northern counties to four or five times its previous amount. In London, Laud was also a zealous servant of the crown, and though ruthlessly trampling on recalcitrant merchants who refused to pay illegal customs, would try to remedy abuses and give ear to complaints, if trade were in any way injured for the advantage of a courtier.

In the year 1632 Wentworth was appointed Lord Deputy of Ireland. During the reigns of Elizabeth and James I., Ireland had for the first time been brought into complete subjection to English rule. English laws and English customs had been introduced into every province, and the Protestant Church established in place of the Catholic. The population was divided into three parts : 1st, the native Irish ; 2nd, the old English settlers in Dublin and the neighbouring counties of Kildare, Louth, and the two Meaths, which constituted 'the English pale'; 3rd, new English and Scotch settlers who had been planted upon lands taken from Irish rebels by Elizabeth and James.

*Wentworth, Lord Deputy of Ireland.*

*State of Ireland.* The Irish and old English settlers, forming a large majority of the population, were Catholics ; the new settlers Protestants. Though the Acts of Supremacy and Uni-

* Straff. Letters and Despatches, ii. 20.

formity had been enacted by an Irish Parliament, they were not fully put into force, because it was hardly possible to fine nonconformists, when 'in six parishes scarce six came to church.' Those, however, who refused to take the oath of supremacy when tendered, were shut out from holding any office in the State, or even from practising as lawyers. The people were ignorant and untaught. The Protestant clergy could not speak the same language as their flocks, and, while living with idle hands in a false position, had won for themselves an indifferent character. The Catholic bishops exercised far more power than the Protestant; the great lords, whether English or Irish, oppressed their tenants; the ministers of justice took bribes; the officers employed by the government, and the Protestant clergy, extorted large fees on every possible pretext; an undisciplined army was scattered over the country, living at free quarters; pirates from Dunkirk, Algiers, Spain, the Bay of Biscay, so infested the coasts, that the people were plundered in every creek; while the captains of the king's ships refused to move against them, alleging want of victuals, though the crews—'mere rabbles of disorderly people'—did the country more injury than the pirates themselves; meantime merchant vessels were run aground, rifled and burnt in sight of Dublin Castle; there was little trade; the taxes did not pay the expenses of the government, so that there was a debt of £100,000 owing by the crown.\*

Wentworth was probably sent there because fair promises had been made to the Irish, which it was disagreeable to fulfil. The king hoped Wentworth's genius would keep Ireland quiet; he could not yet have hoped it would forge Ireland into a weapon to use against English liberty.† Wentworth set himself to work to rule despotically, but after he had put first his master's interest, he showed some regard for that of the people entrusted to him. No corruption was allowed; the fees received by the officers, high and low, in the government employ, were inquired into; judges were not allowed to act as mere instruments of great lords' oppression: the army was remodelled; discipline enforced; Wentworth saw every single man himself, though it numbered nearly 4000; the soldier paid for all he took; captains were made to understand that for the future they must perform garrison duty, must drill their troops, and provide them

<sub>Wentworth's administration.</sub>

\* Straff. Letters and Despatches. † See p. 89.

with good arms and horses, instead of appropriating the funds for their own uses. They soon found that the lord deputy was not the sort of man to jest with; they had either to do as they were told, or leave the service. The navy was unfortunately independent of his control. In Wentworth's own words, it grieved his heart that he had no power over the Admiralty. His grief indeed was no matter for wonder. The ship that was conveying over from England his wardrobe, furniture, and plate, was seized on the passage by that same Captain Nutt whom James I. and Secretary Calvert in 1623 let loose a second time upon the world.* As it was, to protect Dublin harbour from pirates, he fitted out a vessel at his own charge. He encouraged trade, but only so far as he thought the increase of Irish trade not detrimental to that of England. Thus in order to ensure to English manufacturers a readier sale for their cloths from the absence of Irish competition, he actually destroyed the woollen trade in Ireland. At the same time he introduced into Ulster the manufacture of linen from flax, erected looms, brought workmen from France and Flanders, and sent the first cargo of linen to Spain at his own risk. For this prohibitive policy in the supposed interest of England, Wentworth deserves no special blame. It is a blot attaching quite as much to the character of English parliaments as to that of English kings. What was special in that policy now, was the length to which it was carried. No deputy before Wentworth had been in possession at once of the necessary energy, determination, and disregard of human suffering, to uproot one branch of industry in the vain hope of seeing another spring up in its place. Notwithstanding this suicidal act, the vigour of the government soon produced striking results; the debts of the crown were paid off, and in four years the customs were raised from £1200 to £40,000 and were still on the increase.

Yet the Irish felt no gratitude to the deputy, for if he protected them from the oppression of the government officers, and of their own aristocracy, he laid their property open to the rapacity of the king, and their personal freedom to his own vengeance.

The Irish had been required by Elizabeth and James to surrender their lands, in order to receive them back to hold by feudal tenure. The grants, by which the land had been restored, ought to have been enrolled in the Court of Chancery. But though the Irish of Connaught had paid £3000 for the purpose,

* See p. 18.

the enrolment had in many cases been neglected, and James' council had advised him on this pretext to forfeit the whole province, and to plant English Protestants on the lands thus taken from their rightful owners. When Charles came to the throne, the Irish, in terror of this project, proposed to support an army of 5000 men for three years, in return for fifty-three royal concessions or "graces." Of these the most important were, that the inhabitants of Connaught should be allowed to enrol their grants; that the crown should lay claim to no estates that had been held for sixty years; and that an Irish Parliament should be held to confirm these graces. Charles had agreed, signed the graces, and promised that a Parliament should be summoned to confirm them.

This Parliament was at last summoned by Wentworth, after the army had been supported for four, instead of for three years, the time originally agreed upon. It would seem hardly credible that neither the king nor his deputy, after having received the money, should have had the smallest intention of performing their part of the compact. Yet such was the case; it was only with great reluctance that Charles allowed a Parliament, "that hydra, cunning as malicious," to be summoned at all. Wentworth, however, was confident that he should be able to manage it, by playing off the jealousies of Protestants against Catholics, and of Catholics against Protestants, and succeeded so well, that he persuaded the Parliament to grant the king six subsidies, giving the members to understand that after they had proved themselves such dutiful subjects, the king would be sure to grant them their desires. Never were men more deceived. The perfidious deputy, when sure of the money, turned round and told the Commons that most of the graces were prejudicial to the crown, and that it was his duty to beseech his Majesty not to grant them. They were helpless. A law called Poyning's Law had been passed in 1495, by which no bills could be introduced into the Irish Parliament except such as had been first allowed by the king and the English council. Hence the Irish House of Commons was not nearly so independent in action as the English, and the Parliament was dissolved without the most important graces having been passed into law.

*Wentworth obtains a subsidy from Irish Parliament.*

The consequences were soon experienced. Wentworth travelled west into Connaught, and inquired into defective titles (1635). The Council Chamber, an *Lands in Connaught forfeited to crown.*

arbitrary court, answering the same purpose as the Star Chamber in England, fined the first jurors who declared against the crown £4000 each. After this example, little resistance was made. Some lands were declared to belong to the crown, that had been held for 300 years, and land-owners were glad to be allowed to pay a rent to the king for part of their lands, and to give up the rest for him to bestow on new Protestant settlers. This attack upon their property was far from being all that the Irish suffered. The deputy's pride and vindictiveness were unparalleled. Any who offended he marked out for destruction, and hunted down. Lord Mountnorris, vice-treasurer in Ireland, and a captain in the navy, was suddenly summoned, with several other officers in Dublin, to attend the deputy at a council of war (12th Dec., 1635). Mountnorris found himself accused of having said, six months before, at a dinner table, that a gentleman, struck by Wentworth, "had a brother that would not have taken such a blow." The court, composed mainly of councillors, then and there, in the presence of the deputy, sentenced the victim to be deprived of all office, and to be shot dead. The latter part of the sentence Wentworth only intended to be passed, not executed; the former he caused to be put in force, and prided himself on thus having humbled a man towards whom he had for a long time felt ill will.

Laws against Catholics not enforced. His ecclesiastical policy was somewhat less severe. Though the endowments of churches had been given to Protestant bishops and clergymen, every parish was allowed its priest and its mass-house, simply because Wentworth did not feel himself strong enough to put the Act of Uniformity into full force. When the English should be more thickly settled, when there should be in the country an army composed entirely of Protestants, strong enough to crush rebellion, he looked forward to forcing every Papist to conform to the Protestant worship.

Meantime the success of his Irish government did not lessen the number of the deputy's enemies at home. The queen and her tribe looked upon Ireland as a country where offices ought to be bestowed, as in England, upon her Majesty's recommendation. Wentworth begged the king that no office might be given away without the deputy's consent. Charles agreed, but ungenerously objected to make the denials himself. "You," he wrote, "must take upon you the refusing part." The disappointed courtiers displayed their spite by exclaiming against the deputy's pride and tyranny. True, they said, he refused to take bribes, but he was none the worse off, for he never gave any, as others refused his presents. If Wentworth's enemies in London might be believed, Mountnorris was actually shot, and people could even tell where the bullets had entered his body.

In spite of the great financial success of the Irish administration, the revenue raised in that country could not possibly be made to provide for the expenses of the English government. Hence although Wentworth carefully husbanded his surplus funds, and although so many illegal modes of taxation were resorted to in England, poverty prevented Charles from rendering the Protestant cause on the continent any effectual support either by arms or by negotiation.

The Thirty Years' War was still raging. The Emperor Ferdinand II., after his armies had overrun the north of Germany, nourished hopes, not only of rooting the Protestant doctrines out of Germany, but also of reducing the Catholic princes to dependence upon Austria (1628—1630). But at the moment when his power seemed greatest, the Protestants were saved by the break up of the Catholic camp. The Catholic princes of Germany feared they might lose their own independence if they suffered the emperor to overpower their Protestant fellows. The pope himself, Urban VIII., alarmed at the interference of Austria in Italy, joined the side of the French, and thus indirectly aided the Protestants. Finally Richelieu, still the chief minister of Louis XIII., eager as his successors for a divided Germany, called on Gustavus Adolphus, King of Sweden, to help in restoring the German princes to their ancient rights, by overthrowing the tyranny of the emperor.

*Thirty Years' War.*

Gustavus, with a small army of 30,000 men, defeated the Imperial general, Tilly, at Leipzig (Sept., 1631), and penetrated into the heart of Bavaria. At Lutzen he defeated the celebrated Wallenstein, and lost his own life (Nov., 1632). After his death every nation engaged was fighting for some special interest, and the war continued for seventeen years with varied success. Frederic, prince of the palatinate, died in 1632, still an exile from his dominions, but leaving his son to continue his claims.

The course of Gustavus was followed in England with deep interest. English and Scotch volunteers, after serving in the Swedish armies, returned home to note with grief that while they had been fighting in defence of the Protestant faith and political rights, their own country was falling subject to the sway of a religion that differed little from the Romish, and of a tyranny in the State that threatened to make government by Parliaments a thing of the past. Wentworth's influence, however, foiled the war-party; "Good my lord," he wrote to Laud in 1637, "if it be not too late, use your best to divert us from this war [with Austria]; it will necessarily put the king into all high ways possible, else will he not be able to subsist under the charge of it, and if these fail the next will be but the sacrificing those who have been his ministers."

*Coasts of Britain infested by pirates.* Not only, however, was Charles too poor to aid the Protestant cause, he could not even defend the coasts of his own kingdom. Dutch and French fishing vessels encroached on the English fisheries, refusing even to 'vail their flags' to the king's ships, while pirates from Algiers made descents upon the coasts of both England and Ireland, and carried off captives to be slaves to the Mussulman.

*Ship-money.* To raise a fleet, Charles ventured on a great strain of his prerogative. A lawyer, Noy, had found in the Tower some old writs, calling on the ports and maritime counties to provide ships for the public service. It was suggested by Finch, chief justice of the Common Pleas, that the same demand should now be made, not only on ports and maritime counties, but also on inland counties, and that instead of causing each county to provide so many ships, a general tax under the name of ship-money, should be levied on land and property, in the same manner as a subsidy granted in Parliament.

People wondered, and even dependents of Wentworth ventured to express their dislike to the new imposition. "I would rather," one wrote, "pay ten subsidies in Parliament, than ten shillings this new-old-way of dead Noy's." None, however, had yet resisted illegal demands with impunity, and no immediate opposition being offered, Charles gained yearly a sum of about £200,000 by this tax. He employed some of the money on the object for which it was nominally raised. The Dutch fishers were driven off the coast, and Rainsborough led an expedition against Salee on the coast of Algiers, whence he brought back from slavery 370 Englishmen and Irishmen (1637). The rest of the money went to the king's coffers, and the court gloried in the success of this high-handed policy. Privy councillors would laugh when the expression 'Liberty of the subject' was used before them; they said that the taxes and monopolies in England were nothing compared with those endured by other king- doms, and that the people ought to be thankful for the happiness of England, which grew rich in long years of peace while cruel wars devastated the continent and its inhabitants perished from famine. The facts were true enough, but it offers no satisfaction to sufferers to be told that others suffer more. The English people, who prided themselves on the free constitution of their country, felt as though an insult were offered them when their condition was compared with that of the slavish peasant of France, who could call nothing his own.* Gentlemen, freeholders, artisans, would talk and argue about their rights, and regret their old government by Parliaments. The students at the Inns of Court were noted for their loyalty, but even they, in getting up a masque in the queen's honour, could not forbear having a sly cut at the government. After the well-mounted masquers, with their gold and silver lace, their cloth of tissue, their silver spangles, followed the antimasquers, cripples, and beggars, on "poor lean jades;" amongst them a fellow with a bunch of carrots upon his head, and a capon upon his fist, who begged a patent of monopoly as the first inventor of the art to feed capons fat with carrots; after him came riding a man on a little horse with a great bit, who begged a patent that none might use any bits but such as were made by him. The crowd in the streets applauded, understanding a covert reproach at the monopolies, which raised the prices of the commonest necessaries of life.

*Discontent general in country.*

\* During the reign of Henri IV. the prisons of Normandy were full of prisoners unable to pay the tax on salt. So many died, that 120 corpses were taken out at a time. The Parliament of Rouen begged his Majesty to take pity on his people; but the king, who had been informed that the tax was very productive, said he wished it to be continued, and seemed as though he would make a joke of the rest—' Semblait qu'il voulût tourner le reste en risée.'—Lavallée, iii. 57.

Judgment of Court of Exchequer in Hampden's case.
John Hampden, a gentleman of Buckinghamshire, was among the first to endanger his property and liberty in support of his country's rights. He refused to pay the forty shillings at which a piece of his land was rated for ship-money. Charles consented to allow the case to be tried at law. He thought himself sure of the judges, for he had already obtained the signatures of all twelve to an extrajudicial opinion, publicly read in the Star Chamber, 'that his Majesty might command all his subjects to provide and furnish such number of ships with men, munition, and victuals, and for such time as he should think fit, for the defence and safeguard of the kingdom, and that he was the sole judge both of the danger, and when and how the same was to be prevented and avoided.'

The cause of Hampden was pleaded for thirteen days before all the twelve judges of the Westminster courts, who by virtue of the Star Chamber opinion, stood in the same relation to the parties, as though previous to a trial for murder they had in a public and notorious manner declared their belief in the innocence of the accused. The whole nation, poor and rich, Puritans and Episcopalians, alike waited eagerly for the judgment.

Hampden's counsel brought forward what seemed an overwhelming weight of evidence. They could point to the various statutes from Magna Charta to the Petition of Right, that declared taxation, without consent of Parliament, illegal. Even if precedents to the contrary were to be found in times when "the government was more of force than of law," such, they argued, must give way before the authority of statute law. This was in fact unanswerable. But the crown lawyers maintained that absolute power —power to act without consent of Parliament — was innate in the person of the King of England. Some of the judges in giving sentence treated all constitutional statutes as waste paper. "Where Mr. Holborne," said Justice Berkeley, "supposed a fundamental policy in the creation of the frame of this kingdom—that in case the monarch of England should be inclined to exact from his subjects at his pleasure, he should be restrained, for he could have nothing from them but upon a common consent in Parliament—he is utterly mistaken herein. The law knows no such king-yoking policy. The law is itself an old and trusty servant of the king's; it is his instrument or means which he useth to govern his people by. I never read nor heard that lex was rex, but it is common and most true that rex is lex." "The king," said another, "may dispense with any law in cases of necessity." Out of the twelve judges only four pronounced in favour of Hampden; one of these had intended to give his judgment on the side of the crown, but changed his mind through the persuasion of his wife, who bade him not to fear danger for himself or his family, for she would sooner suffer any want or misery with him, than that he should act against his conscience (1637).

But at the moment when the victory of the king seemed complete and courtiers were most exultant, danger was nearer than they thought. The decision gave universal discontent. It is hard to have your property taken from you illegally, but harder still to be told that that illegality is law. It was a Cadmean victory Charles had won; the levying of ship-money was more difficult after the verdict than before, and he could not put thousands into prison for expressing discontent. Wentworth, wiser than his master, had not approved of the trial at all—"Hampden," like other opposers of tyranny, "had better have been whipped into his right senses;" "if the rod be so used that it smarts not, I am the more sorry."

The nation hated the government of the State as arbitrary, corrupt, and cruel; it hated, however, still more the connivance at Popery, which characterized the government of the Church. During the reign of Elizabeth, several severe laws had been passed against Catholics, condemning priests and Jesuits to suffer death as traitors, forbidding the exercise of the Catholic worship, and ordering recusants who refused to attend service in the parish church, to pay a fine of £20 a month. But now these laws were not put into force; fines were not regularly levied: if priests were arrested, they were at once discharged on warrants signed by the king or his secretaries. A Catholic chapel, built at Somerset House for Queen Henrietta's use, was publicly consecrated with three days' ceremonies, masses, and singing of litanies. Agents from the court of Rome actually resided in London; they were known to everybody; their carriages rolled down the streets without any one daring to say a word against them. Many of the courtiers, some of the king's council, and even some of the bishops, were open or concealed Catholics; court ladies constantly went over to Rome, and

*Government of the Church.*

the queen's Capuchin friars boasted that not a week passed but there were two or three conversions.

The king, however, all the time, had no thoughts of weakening his own prerogative by making the Church of England dependent on a foreign see. He was courting Rome to procure the pope's interest for the restoration of the palatinate to Charles, the eldest son of his sister, Elizabeth. The pope, on his side, was willing to keep on good terms with the heretical government, in order to save English Catholics from persecution. In itself this toleration was laudable. The motives, however, that influenced Charles to exercise it, were no enlarged views of religious toleration. He forbore to put the laws against Catholics in force, because the Catholics supported his pretensions to arbitrary power. The public law was set aside by a private agreement. At the same time, to make the contrast more bitter, Puritans, often guiltless of any crime at law, were suffered to pine away in prison under sentences of the courts of High Commission and Star Chamber.

Various causes afford excuse for the bitter and intolerant spirit with which the Puritan regarded his Catholic fellow-countrymen. Many still lived who could recall to mind the events of 1588, when the Armada threatened the shores of England. Thousands still lived who remembered the discovery of the Gunpowder Plot. Jesuits had taught the doctrine, that heretic princes might be dethroned and murdered. Several attempts had been made upon Elizabeth's life. William the Silent, the heroic maintainer of Dutch liberty, had perished by the hand of a fanatic. The same fate had befallen the great Henri IV. of France. Diversity in the Church was thought incompatible with unity in the State. On the continent, not only did Catholics persecute Protestants, and Protestants Catholics, but one Protestant sect could not tolerate another; in England Presbyterians approved of the persecution of sectarians. In fact the principles of toleration had hardly as yet been enunciated, much less had they received a fair trial. It is experience alone that gives confidence, and few are bold enough to enter upon an untried course of action. The ordinary Englishman regarded the free toleration of Catholics as a crime both against his God and his country; as a Protestant he considered it a direct encouragement to the spread of idolatry and superstition; as a patriot, an opening for

*Excuse for intolerance of Puritans.*

Catholic priests to usurp political power, and bring England again into dependence upon a foreign jurisdiction.

There were, indeed, grounds for the fear, entertained by many, that a union would finally be effected between the Established Church of England and of Rome. Altars and images were restored to churches; popish ceremonies were revived, popish doctrines taught; the work of the Reformation was in part undone; the worshipper was required to believe that all his church taught him was true and necessary for salvation, even though her teaching found no foundation in the Bible; and again, in order to hold communion with God, he must seek the aid of priests and assist in ceremonies he regarded as superstitious. <small>Character of the Puritans.</small>

But though a Puritan, even if a Presbyterian or sectarian, could be forced to conform and attend his parish church, he could not be prevented from spreading his opinions and making them felt by others. For his manners and his conduct betrayed him, and they were such as to command approval. Morality was inculcated by the ministers of the Church, as much as by the more popular preachers, but practice is more than profession, and that Church was supported by a court which treated vice lightly and made a scoff of virtue. The genuine Puritan, on the contrary, was distinguished by his strict observance of the moral virtues. He sought in the Bible, but more especially in the books of the Old Testament, for the rules by which to guide his actions; he gained a vivid conception of a personal God, with whom his own soul could enter into direct communion, and beneath whose displeasure it was fatal to fall; and he felt with the Hebrew of the Old Testament, "he that keepeth the law, happy is he; its ways are ways of pleasantness and all its paths are peace; if thou hadst walked in its ways, thou shouldst have dwelt in peace for ever."

Imbued with such feelings, a certain seriousness of demeanour characterized the Puritan, and he not unnaturally preferred to pass his time in listening to sermons, in prayer, and in attending to the business of his calling, than in seeking amusement at the theatre, the fair, or the dance, where he was sure to hear coarse and profane language spoken, and to fall into the society of drunkards. Confident that his conduct was approved by God, he could look down upon the unregenerate, and regard their scoffs with contempt. Amongst uneducated tradesmen and artisans, there were many fanatics, who refused to take part in any amusements, however innocent, and who almost seemed to court ridicule by their austere mode of life, their ostentatiously plain dress, their close-cut hair, and their frequent use of the words of scripture.

At the head of the Church stood Laud, Archbishop of Canterbury. A man more unsuited to assuage the religious passions of the times could hardly have held the position. However great a virtue in itself, sincere zeal, when untempered by charity, has produced the cruellest of persecutors. Some by nature are possessed of a largeness of mind that enables them to sympathize with the thoughts and feelings of others ; while to some experience and education teach the duty, or at least the necessity of tolerating what they fail themselves to understand. Laud was sincere in his views, but nature had not generously gifted him with the quality of mercy. He came into power untutored by the experience won by working with others of different opinions. His abilities were only ordinary, and though his education was good for his time, it gave him learning rather than wisdom, and never succeeded in making up for the deficiencies of his heart. The new opinions seething around were nothing to him but a troublesome and dangerous fanaticism that required to be suppressed. Such sincere bigots placed in power have often wrought their country untold harm. They may by force succeed in stifling the new movement for years, perhaps for centuries ; but, in either case, it is sure at last to break forth, possibly in some new form, and always with dangerous violence. Philip II., acting in the full belief that his work was sacred, drove freedom of thought out of Spain ; hence, to this very day, the tyranny of extremes retards his country's advance and prosperity. Happily for England, Laud's success was of short duration. The reaction came in his lifetime, and he paid a heavy penalty for his rash attempt to force conformity upon a people panting for spiritual freedom.

The courts held by bishops, as well as the Court of High Commission, called to account ministers and laymen who did not attend church, or who failed to perform every ceremony exactly as ordained in the Prayer-book, or, indeed, as prescribed by Laud on his sole authority. A minister of Durham, for speaking in a sermon against the use of pictures and images, was degraded by the Court of High Commission, fined £500, and placed in prison, where he waited eleven years for the hour of release. The Court of Star Chamber, in which Laud himself sat as a judge, was always ready to support the cause of the Church. Three professional men, Prynne, a lawyer; Burton, a London minister; and Bastwick, a doctor, had written books inveighing against the bishops. On being brought before the Star Chamber, they were charged with felony, for having tried to stir up sedition, and sentenced to pay fines of £5000 each, to stand in the pillory in Palace Yard, Westminster, to have their ears cut off, and to be imprisoned for life. Sentences of Star Chamber on Burton, Bastwick, Prynne.

"So far," said Bastwick, addressing the crowd, surging round the pillories, "am I from base fear, or caring for anything that they can do, that had I as much blood as would swell the Thames, I would shed it every drop in this cause. Therefore, be not any of you discouraged, be not daunted at their power." "Had we," said Prynne, "respected (regarded) our liberties we had not stood here at this time." "Sir," said a woman to Burton, "there are many hundreds which, by God's assistance, would willingly suffer for the cause you suffer for this day." A mournful cry arose from the crowd, as the prisoners' ears were cropped, and many pressed forward to dip handkerchiefs into the blood streaming down the scaffold.

John Lilburne, a young man about twenty years old, was brought before the Star Chamber on a charge of being concerned in bringing seditious books over from Holland. He was required to swear, laying his hand upon the Gospels, to answer truly all questions put to him. He refused. "The oath," he said, "is of the same nature as the High Commission oath, which oath I know to be unlawful, and withal I find no warrant in the word of God for an oath of inquiry, and therefore, my lords, I dare not take it."* In accordance with his sentence, Lilburne was tied to a cart's tail and whipped from the Fleet prison to Westminster Yard, at every two or three steps receiving on his bare back a blow from a knotted treble-corded whip. The young enthusiast never flinched, but all the way quoted texts of Scripture, exhorting the crowd to resist the bishops. At Westminster Yard he bowed to his judges, whom he saw looking out at him from the Court of Star Chamber win- Lilburne refuses illegal oath.

* State Trials, 1.

dow, and then sitting in the bent painful attitude required by the pillory, continued his exhortations. "I will never take the oath, though I be pulled to pieces by wild horses; neither shall I think that man a faithful subject of Christ's kingdom, that shall at any time hereafter take it. My brethren, we are all at this present in a very dangerous and fearful condition, in regard we have turned traitors unto our God, in seeing His almighty great name and His heavenly truth trodden under foot, and yet we not only let the bishops alone in holding our peace, but most slavishly subject ourselves unto them, fearing the face of a piece of dirt more than the almighty great God of heaven and earth, who is able to cast both body and soul into everlasting damnation." He was still addressing the people in the same strain, when the warden of the Fleet came and placed a gag on his mouth.

Such were the means taken by the archbishop to crush the spirit of the Puritans, and by him not considered sufficiently "thorough." As if for the sole purpose of irritating his opponents, the king, by his advice, ordered a proclamation, called the Book of Sports, to be read by ministers after service, declaring that certain games, such as leaping, vaulting, and wrestling were lawful on Sundays. It had been originally published by James, but its reading not enforced. Now no minister might escape. Thirty who refused to obey in the diocese of Norwich—a stronghold of Puritanism—were suspended. Some temporized. A London minister read the proclamation, and after it the ten commandments. "Dearly beloved," he said, "you have heard the commandment of God and of man, obey which you please."

'Lecturers' put down. The Puritans raised subscriptions for purchasing from laymen their right of presentation to livings and for hiring lecturers to preach on afternoons in market towns. But Laud, not content with ordering that lecturers should wear the surplice and read the service, determined to break up the whole association. The trustees were declared by the Court of Exchequer to have misused the funds with which they were entrusted, and the whole were forfeited to the king, to be used for the good of the Church and the maintenance of conformable ministers. The Church, however, lost its hold on the people, when it lost the most earnest and most popular of its preachers. Into the livings of the ejected Puritans were put ignorant men or court clergy, who bade their people be passively obedient, while they lost their cherished liberties. Of such pastors Milton wrote, as—

> " Blind mouths that scarce themselves know how to hold
> A sheephook, or have learned aught else the least
> That to the faithful herdsman's art belongs !
> What recks it them ? What need they ? They are sped ;
> And when they list, their lean and flashy songs
> Grate on their scrannel pipes of wretched straw ;
> The hungry sheep look up, and are not fed,
> But swoln with wind and the rank mist they draw,
> Rot inwardly, and foul contagion spread ;
> Beside what the grim wolf with privy paw*
> Daily devours apace, and nothing said."

While Laud thus awoke the hate of Puritans by intolerance, he aroused that of the laity generally by endeavouring to raise the political importance of the Church. As a politician, he was both ambitious and unscrupulous, as might be expected of one who had risen to power at the heels of Buckingham. Courts held by bishops now sent out writs in their own names, instead of in that of the king. Clergymen were made justices of the peace in place of country gentlemen. Bishops sat in the king's council and in the Court of Star Chamber. Juxon, Bishop of London, was appointed by the king to the influential and coveted office of lord treasurer. "Now," wrote Laud in his diary, "if the Church will not hold themselves up under God, I can do no more."

In order to escape persecution and tyranny, new homes were sought in America. In Virginia a Church of England colony had been founded by adventurers in 1607. The earliest settlers in New England were the Pilgrim Fathers, a body of persecuted sectarians, who had sailed across the Atlantic in the "Mayflower," in 1620. Rhode Island was colonized in 1634, and liberty of conscience established. Lord Baltimore, a Roman Catholic, granted the same boon to all settlers in Maryland (1638). In the ten years preceding 1640, the number of emigrants to New England was estimated at 21,200. *Emigration to America.*

The Presbyterian Church had been long since established in Scotland by an act of the Scotch Parliament (1592). James I., however, had succeeded by not very creditable means in restoring Scotch bishops to the possession of their former titles, though to little of their former influence and position.

* For the conversions to Popery, see p. 60.

Charles and Laud now determined on setting up a church government in Scotland, to answer in all respects to that established in England. Canons, to regulate the Church of Scotland, were drawn up by the Scotch bishops, and afterwards revised by Laud, in which no place was left for the action of any Presbyterian assemblies. The following year, in place of "Knox's Liturgy," as the Service-book ordinarily used by the Scots was called, a new Prayer-book, nearly the same as the English, was ordered to be read in all churches, from the 23rd July, 1637. In St. Giles', the cathedral church of Edinburgh, no sooner had the dean opened the new liturgy, than all the lower order of people in the church began to scream, clap their hands, hiss and groan, making such a hideous outcry that no one could either hear or be heard.

Episcopacy in Scotland. The cry was, "Sorrow, sorrow, for this dreadful day; they are bringing Popery amongst us." Sticks, stones, Bibles, stools, were hurled at the dean's head. In other places the Prayer-book received a like reception. By most it was looked on as little better than the mass itself. Its very exterior gave offence to the Presbyterian; the red and black type, the Gothic letters, pictorial capitals, and other illustrations, seemed to imply a revival of Catholic times. The nobles were afraid of being required to restore church property acquired at the Reformation; when not moved by religious fervour themselves, their interests made them at heart on the side of the rioters.

The whole nation was enraged. When James I. had introduced changes into the Presbyterian form of church government, he had at least obtained the sanction of a corrupt church-assembly and parliament. But Charles was endeavouring to establish the Episcopalian Church in the place of the Presbyterian, upon his own sole authority, as though he were indeed an absolute monarch, able to make laws without the consent of his subjects.

The king, to whom a tumult raised by the rabble seemed no cause for alarm, sent orders that the new Service-book was still to be read. The lords of the Scotch council, however, dared not put his commands into execution. They were themselves assaulted in the streets of Edinburgh by an infuriated mob, and only rescued from death by the nobles and gentry, who now, following the example of the people, came flocking into the capital to sign an accusation against the bishops (18th Oct., 1637).

The tumults rapidly took the form of rebellion: a council was chosen, composed of members from the four classes, nobles, gentry, clergy, burgesses, which soon became a new power in the State, more formidable than the king's council (15th Nov., 1637); at last, a national league was formed under the name of the Covenant (a forerunner of the 'Solemn League and Covenant' with the English in 1643), binding the signers to reject the new canons and liturgy, and to defend their sovereign, their religion, their laws, and liberties (1st March, 1638). An assembly of the Church, which met at Glasgow, refused to dissolve at the instance of the Duke of Hamilton, the king's deputy (28th Nov., 1638), and proceeded to abolish liturgy, canons, and episcopacy itself. After thus defying the royal authority, the Covenanters prepared for war. The question of war had also to be debated in the king's council at home. The critical moment was now come, when the strength of the government was put to the test. "I am not for war," wrote one of the privy council; "in the exchequer there is but £200; the magazines are totally unfurnished; commanders are there none for execution or advice; the people are so discontented, there is reason to fear a greater part of them will be readier to join the Scots than to draw swords in the king's service." Wentworth, who did not despair so quickly as these panic-stricken councillors, began to increase the size of the army in Ireland, and to call for sterner measures against defaulters. Yet to advise Charles to do nothing by halves, to introduce episcopacy into Scotland, and to govern that country as he himself governed Ireland, was much like telling a man with a palsied hand to drive the nail home. The deputy, so proud of his Irish government, could not, or would not, read aright the signs of the times. Some of the council advised the calling of a Parliament, but Charles could not hear the proposal with patience. Money was therefore raised by loans and other illegal means. By the spring of 1639 an army of some 12,000 men was fitted out, and the king proceeded to York, followed, not only by his court, but by all the nobility and most influential gentry of the kingdom, whom he summoned to attend his person at their own charge, as had been customary in feudal times. He hoped by this display to overawe his needy Scottish subjects.

*Scots enter into a covenant in defence of religious laws and liberties*

*War with Scotland.*

*Charles and court proceed to York.*

But the Scots were too much in earnest, and too well understood the state of feeling in England, to be easily overawed. By the time Charles reached Berwick, it was evident that they could not be reduced that summer. The first English force that saw the face of an enemy, made a precipitate retreat. The courtiers who longed for a return to their pleasures, the nobles and gentlemen who desired a redress of their wrongs, all urged the necessity of coming to an agreement with the Covenanters. Charles found himself obliged to sign a Pacification at Berwick, in which it was agreed that both a Parliament and a Church Assembly should be summoned in Scotland, for the settlement of all grievances, religious and civil (18th June, 1639).

*Pacification of Berwick.*

The king, however, signed the agreement merely as a temporary measure, and with the full intention of raising a larger force and renewing the war next summer. The Scots had plenty of friends in England to warn them of the policy pursued; how Wentworth had been summoned from Ireland, and created Earl of Strafford; how the Irish army was being increased in size; how a new army was being raised in England, and every nerve strained to get money.

In foreign policy meantime Charles had been inconsistent and wavering. At one time he had entered into negotiations with France, at another with Spain, for the restoration of the palatinate to his nephew. Now, therefore, that he was involved in difficulties with his subjects, governments which had received cause of offence assumed an unfriendly attitude. The pope forbade the Catholics to be so ready in lending money and offering to serve in the army, for after all, Laud's religion, which did not acknowledge the pope as head of the Church, was no more the Catholic religion than that of the Puritans. The Dutch grew so insolent that they destroyed a Spanish fleet which was riding in the Downs under Charles' own protection, while the English ambassador wrote from Spain that the Spaniards were instigating the Irish to rebel. Richelieu, bearing in mind the expeditions in aid of Rochelle, now took the opportunity to repay his injuries by sending supplies of money and arms to the Covenanters. A copy of a letter written by the Scots to Louis XIII. was intercepted by Charles, who thought that with this proof of treason in his hand, he might venture on meeting a Parliament. But indeed, the neces-

*Foreign governments unfriendly to Charles.*

sity of calling a Parliament if the war were to be continued, was daily becoming more and more manifest. 'Men's consciences awoke,' and forbade them to pay ship money. Even in Yorkshire, where Strafford possessed so much influence, gentlemen refused to equip soldiers without receiving some security for repayment of the money. Strafford advised the lords of the council to send for them to London, and "lay them up by the heels."\* "What," he asked, "should become of the levy of 30,000 men in case the other counties should return the like answer?" A pregnant question, for everywhere the same spirit was manifested; London refused loans, country gentlemen made excuses, and the king was at last driven to that resource, which last year he would not hear mentioned. He summoned his fourth Parliament on the 13th April, 1640.

*Illegal demands opposed.*

Charles asked for an immediate grant of money. Pym rose, and in a speech of two hours, while speaking respectfully of the king, laid bare the offences of the government against religion, justice, and the power and privilege of Parliament. The House, with deep attention, heard him out, and then voted that they would find a remedy for their grievances before granting the king a supply. The letter of the Scots to Louis XIII. did not trouble the Commons at all, and was no fair proof of treason, as it was dated before the Pacification of Berwick. "The people," it was said, "would sooner pay subsidies to prevent the unhappy war than to carry it on." Grievances formed such an ample subject of debate, that Charles, growing impatient, sent a message saying, if the Parliament would grant him twelve subsidies, to be paid in three years, he would never levy ship money without consent of Parliament (4th May, 1640). Though the Commons felt indignant that they should be asked to purchase immunity from an illegal tax, they were about, after a long debate, to put the question to the vote, whether a supply should be given to the king, without, for the present, specifying any particular sum, when Sir Henry Vane, Charles' secretary, rose and said it was of no use to put that question, for the king would not accept less than he had asked. In disgust the House broke up; and the next morning, Charles having lost patience, dissolved the Parliament (5th May, 1640).

*Charles' fourth Parliament.*

---

\* *I.e.*, to fetter, or put in gyves. See Shaks. Henry VIII. v. 3.

Arbitrary measures were now again employed to raise money for the war; and refusers of loans were imprisoned. But no severity was able to suppress the spirit of opposition. The gentry of Yorkshire sent a petition to the king, complaining of the billeting of unruly soldiers, "to whose violence and insolence we are so daily subject, as we cannot say we possess our wives and children in security. Wherefore," continues the petition, "we are emboldened to present these our complaints, beseeching your Majesty that, as the billeting of soldiers in any of your subjects' houses is contrary to the ancient laws of this kingdom confirmed by your Majesty in the Petition of Right, this insupportable charge may be taken off."* Riots broke out in London; the militia refused to serve; officers and soldiers said they would not fight 'to support the power and pride of bishops.' Soldiers had to be pressed, and artisans were daily dragged from the shops and forced on board the fleet. A disorderly army was at length formed; when formed it would not fight. Some regiments dispersed of themselves; others killed officers who were Catholics; others broke open the prisons, and made havoc of the country through which they passed. Before Strafford, the general of the army, reached the camp, his soldiers fled before the enemy; this was at Newburn Ford, on the borders of the two kingdoms (28th Aug., 1640). The Scots, having by this easy success gained possession of the passage of the Tyne, entered Newcastle without opposition, and continued to advance in the direction of York.

Charles' weakness was now proved. Doubtful and despondent, he knew not what to do or whither to turn for counsel. The Irish army, though in good training, was only about 5000 strong, and was required in Ireland to overawe the people. The Scots were in the kingdom, masters of the four northern counties, while his own army refused to fight. Yet a Parliament seemed a terribly caustic remedy to apply to his difficulties, and he bethought himself of calling an assembly, composed solely of peers, as had occasionally been the custom of English kings four centuries before, when the House of Commons was hardly recognized as an integral part of the government. Perhaps, thought some credulous courtier, this assembly of peers might even vote

* Petition of Yorkshire gentry, 28th July, 1640, MSS. Clar. Pap. and Rushworth.

the king money. But the nation thought otherwise. "If," said two lords consulted by the king's council, "it be intended to raise money by any other way than a Parliament, it will give no satisfaction."* Charles was left in no doubt of his subjects' wishes; counties sent petitions for a Parliament; twelve of the chief peers of the realm signed a petition for a Parliament; the City of London petitioned for a Parliament; the Scots sent a petition: 'they were loyal subjects, their grievances were the cause of their being in arms; they begged their king to settle a firm and durable peace by advice of a Parliament.' So at last, forced by necessity, Charles yielded. When the peers met at York (24th Sept., 1640), he informed them that he had already sent out writs for a Parliament, and asked their advice for treating with the Scots. "They were so taken," writes the king's secretary, "with his Majesty's speech and with his Majesty's offer of a Parliament that whatever was afterwards proposed they yielded to. . . . There is no doubt but this black storm will be dispersed."†

Charles summons his fifth Parliament.

Sixteen peers, none of them favourable to arbitrary government, negotiated with eight Scottish commissioners at Ripon. It was agreed that a cessation of arms should be made for two months; that both armies should remain where they were; that the northern counties should support the Scottish army by paying it £5600 a week, until a peace should be concluded in London (23rd Oct., 1640). Then king, lords, and Scottish commissioners hastened to the capital, where Charles met his fifth and last Parliament (3rd Nov., 1640).

* Clar. State Papers, 1—112.
† Windebank to Sir A. Hopton, 1st Oct., 1640, MSS. Clar. Papers in Bodleian.

## CHAPTER IV.
### MEETING OF LONG PARLIAMENT AND TRIAL OF STRAFFORD.
### 1640—1641.

Had I but served my God with half the zeal
I served my king, he would not in mine age
Have left me naked to mine enemies.—HENRY VIII., iii. 2.

WESTMINSTER HALL, in the year 1640, was just the same building that we see to-day: but the house in which the Commons sat was utterly different. At right angles to the hall, between it and the river, stood a building which was once a chapel of the old palace of Westminster, but was now fitted with tiers of horseshoe benches for the members of the Commons. The building itself was small, somewhat dingy and gloomy; though sittings were generally by day, on winter afternoons candles were placed on a table in the centre. The appearance of the members, however, belied the meanness of their meeting-house; for these were peers' sons, country gentlemen, merchants, lawyers, distinguished in their towns or counties for birth or wealth, or both; their dress displayed their quality—the sword by the side, the velvet coat, the large frilled linen collar to protect the lace and gold or silver trimming from the long hair falling in curls upon the shoulders, were sure signs that the House did not count among its members any of the fanatics from the lower orders, who cut their hair close and prided themselves upon the especial plainness of their attire. Chief amongst the many notables of that assembly were John Pym, John Hampden, Lord Falkland,* Edward Hyde, Oliver Cromwell. Pym, the old opposer of tyranny in the previous reign; Hampden, the ship-money hero, gentle and affable to all, and now the most popular man in the House; Lord Falkland, whose truthful, generous nature made him the declared enemy of injustice in high places; Hyde, afterwards Earl of Clarendon, and

*House of Commons.*

*Leading members.*

---

* He had succeeded his father (Sir H. Cary, Deputy of Ireland), as second Viscount of Falkland, in the county of Fife, in Scotland. He sat as burgess for Newport, Scotch peers being eligible before the Act of Union (1707).

the Royalist historian of the Rebellion, now carried along with the stream, and as eager as his friend Falkland to restore the old government of England by Parliaments; Cromwell, member for the town of Huntingdon, a country gentleman, dressed in a plain cloth suit, and as yet little remarked, save for his activity in defending the poor of his own neighbourhood from oppression.

The members of both Houses of Parliament, urged by a hundred different motives, were almost unanimous in their determination to make the agents of the government answer for their conduct, and above all, the chief offender, Strafford. The noble ruinously fined in the Star Chamber; the courtier of whom Strafford had used sharp words, as 'that the king would do well to cut off his head;' the merchant, forced to pay illegal customs; the patriot, indignant at the judges' verdict that ship-money was a just and legal tax; the Presbyterian fined and insulted by the Court of High Commission, were all alike eager to gratify, as the case might be, their desires for reform, or justice, or revenge. *Grievances, delinquents.*

The House proceeded to business at once. Votes were passed that all monopolists should be deprived of their seats (9th Nov.), that ship-money was against the laws of the realm (7th Dec.),* that all agents of the crown who had taken part in the collection of ship-money, or had shared in any other acts condemned by the

---

* Lord Falkland felt and spoke strongly on the extra-judicial opinion the judges had given at Charles' request, on the king's right to ship-money. "No meal undigested," he said, "can lie heavier upon the stomach than that unsaid would have lain upon my conscience." He complained that the judges, "the persons who should have been as dogs to defend the flock, have become the wolves to devour it;" that they had exceeded their functions, "being judges of law and not of necessity, that is, being judges and not philosophers or politicians;" that to justify the plea of necessity, they have "supposed mighty and eminent dangers in the most quiet and halcyon days, but a few contemptible pirates being our most formidable enemies;" they also "supposing the supposed doings to be so sudden that it could not stay for a Parliament which required but a forty days' stay, allowed to the king the sole power in necessity, the sole judgment of necessity, and by that enabled him to take from us what he would, when he would, and how he would." He especially declaimed against the Chief Justice (at this time Lord Keeper) Finch, who importuned the other judges "as a most admirable solicitor, but a most abominable judge." ... "He it was who gave away with his breath what our ancestors have purchased with so long expense of their time, their care, their treasures, and their bloods, and strove to make our grievances mortal and our slavery irreparable," ... "he who hath already undone us by wholesale [and now as chancellor] hath the power of undoing us by retail."—MSS. Clarendon Papers, No. 1464, and Rushworth.

House, were 'delinquents,' and might be proceeded against at any moment. This made offenders of all ranks tremble, lords of the Council and Star Chamber, lords-lieutenant of counties, sheriffs, judges, besides a host of inferior officers. It was not so much the intention of the Commons to proceed against all these delinquents, as to terrify them into submission. The chief criminals alone had real cause to fear.

Strafford* had seen the storm gathering and was anxious to return to Ireland, but Charles wrote him a positive command to come to London, assuring him, 'as he was King of England, he was able to secure him from any danger, and the Parliament should not touch one hair of his head.' The king was in fact afraid of meeting his enraged Parliament unsupported. Accordingly Strafford came prepared with charges of treason against some of the leading members, for having encouraged the Scots in rebellion. They were aware of his intention and determined to strike first. No time was lost. Pym's feelings at this crisis are analyzed in Browning's lines:

*Strafford trusts in Charles.*

"Now, by Heaven,
They may be cool who can, silent who will—
Some have a gift that way! Wentworth is here;
Here, and the king's safe closeted with him
Ere this. And when I think on all that's past—
. . . . . . . . . how all this while
That man has set himself to one dear task,
The bringing Charles to relish more and more
Power—power without law, power and blood too—
Can I be still?"

Strafford had only been one day in London when, on the 11th of November, Pym proposed in the House of Commons to impeach of high treason the man who, "according to the nature of apostates, had become the greatest enemy to the liberties of his country, and the greatest promoter of tyranny that any age had produced."

*Impeachment of Strafford.*

The process by impeachment has been described in Buckingham's case,† it is still more familiar to us from the trial of Warren Hastings in the following century (1788). The king having no part in an impeachment, and the House of Lords being judge, the only preliminary required is a resolution of the Commons to pro-

* Wentworth created Earl of Strafford, 12 Jan. 1640.    † See page 34.

secute. The Commons now agreed to the proposal without a dissenting voice, and Pym, followed by a train of three hundred members, went up straight to the Lords' house, and there accused the earl of high treason, desiring that he might be lodged a prisoner in the Tower, until the time of his trial came on.

Thus, at one blow, was the king deprived of his ablest adviser, and Strafford himself of the awe with which power had previously invested him. Strafford was in consultation with the king when the news came. Hastening to the Lords' house with a "proud, glooming countenance, he makes towards his place at the boardhead. But at once many bid him void the house. After consultation, being called in, he stands, but is commanded to kneel, and on his knees, is delivered to the keeper of the black rod, to be prisoner until he was cleared of those crimes the House of Commons had charged him with. As he passed through the gazing crowd outside to find his coach, no man capped to him, before whom that morning the greatest of England would have stood discovered, all crying, 'What is the matter?' He said, 'A small matter, I warrant you.' They replied, 'Yes, indeed, high treason is a small matter.'" *Strafford sent to Tower.*

The next month Laud was impeached too (18th Dec.), and followed his friend to the Tower, amid the curses and howlings of the populace. Windebank, the king's secretary, wise in time, jumped into an open boat, and, steering through the mist, succeeded in putting the Channel between him and his foes. Finch, though known as the first adviser of imposing ship-money on the inland counties, hoped much from the graceful defence he made before the Commons. But the temper of his hearers was too stern; "There be birds," said one, "that in the summer of Parliament will sing sweetly, that in winter turn into birds of prey!" The most he could effect was to be allowed, like others, to escape into exile. *Other 'delinquents.'*

Judge Berkeley, the principal supporter of ship-money, was also a marked man. The messenger of the Lords entered Westminster Hall, while the courts of justice were sitting, and then and there carried him off to the Tower, impeached by the Commons of high treason. The gazing crowd felt awe-struck, while the consciences of some of Berkeley's brethren gave them uneasy qualms.

Reparation to sufferers.  Hand in hand with justice went reparation. The prison doors were opened to men shut up for five or eight or ten years, as the case might be. Chambers, the merchant, came out ruined; Leighton, a minister, unable to walk or stand or see; Lilburne, with a tale to tell of starvation, irons, and the scourge. Prynne, Burton, and Bastwick came from their distant prisons in Jersey, Guernsey, and Scilly, to forget the shame of the pillory and the loss of their ears, in the triumph of the day when they were welcomed back to London by thousands of men and women decked with white rosemary and bay and filling the air with their acclamations.* Large numbers of sufferers brought their cases before committees of Parliament, and had the satisfaction of hearing their sentences declared illegal, while many received compensation in money for their losses.

But the event which above all others excited men's minds, was the trial of Strafford. Until March, a committee of Parliament was engaged in examining witnesses and preparing the case. The Scots joined in the prosecution, accusing Strafford of having been the cause of the war, and even the Irish, lately so submissive, now sent over charges against the deputy. On the 22nd of March the trial began. In the cold spring morning, Scene of trial.  as early as five o'clock, crowds might be seen gathering about Westminster. A stage was erected, reaching right across the end of the hall. Here sat the judges, the members of the House of Lords, about eighty in number, 'wearing their red robes lined with white ermine.' The lawn of the bishops was not seen at trials for life. At one end of the stage sat the committee of the Commons who conducted the impeachment, at the other Strafford's secretaries and counsel. Behind the lords' seats was the empty throne; the king and queen, though present, sat in a gallery concealed by curtains. On both sides of the hall, east and west, the forms rising one above another to the roof were occupied by the members of the Commons, with the Scottish commissioners, and some favoured friends. Ladies paid high prices for seats in galleries, and diligently took notes of the proceedings.

About eight Strafford was brought from the Tower by water. All were struck with his appearance. Clad in black, his coun-

* May, Long Parl., 54; Baillie, i. 222.

tenance pale through suffering, his body bent by illness, he bore himself with a proud humility, implying excess of courtesy, and not defect of confidence. Having first bowed to the court, he took his place in a small desk in front of his judges, where he stood or sat at pleasure.

Precedents of harsh procedure too often return to plague the inventors. The difficulties put in the way of state criminals whom kings attacked, were now all cast in the way of Strafford, whose life the people were seeking. He had himself to examine witnesses brought against him, and to speak as to the truth of the facts of which he was accused. His counsel were only allowed at the close of the trial to argue that the facts did not fall within the legal definition of high treason. *Course of state trials in seventeenth century.* Though most of his witnesses were in Ireland, he had not been allowed to summon them to attend, until three days before the trial. He did not know from day to day what charges would be brought against him, but after his accusers had spoken, was allowed half an hour to sit down with his secretaries and prepare his answer. The time given was not favourable for quiet thought. During these intervals the whole hall rose to its feet, judges, prosecutors, spectators, talking and laughing ; bread and meat were handed about, bottles of beer and wine 'went thick from mouth to mouth,' and all this in the king's eyes, who, in the excitement of the trial, with his own hands tore down the curtains in front of his gallery, and there sat visible to all, but as unregarded as if he had not been present.*

Thus unaided for seventeen days, from eight in the morning until three or four in the afternoon, Strafford had to hear and answer his accusers and their witnesses.

The crime of high treason was defined by a statute of Edward III. (1351), to consist of seven offences. *Law of high treason.* Five of these did not touch Strafford. The two under which he was prosecuted were those of 'levying war upon the king,' and 'compassing the king's death.' Of all legal procedure, prosecutions for high treason are the most unintelligible to the ordinary mind. The interpretations of the judges had extended the meaning of 'levying war,' to mean any overt act which was considered objectionable ; that 'of *Forced interpretation of judges.*

* Baillie, i. 259, 265.

compassing or imagining the king's death,' to mean any objectionable purpose which was not carried into act. To understand this process it is necessary to recall the origin of the act, and the fact of the dependence of the judges upon the crown. The act was brought forward by the nobles as a safeguard to themselves, by defining more clearly in what treason consisted. They had found before that if the crown wished to confiscate their lands, it could make out anything to be treason; but though they hoped much from a clearer definition, they gained little; first, because the judges extended the meaning of the words of the law; secondly, because untrustworthy evidence was admitted as to the facts. As an instance of the first, a rioter who had joined in an attack upon Laud's palace at Lambeth, was convicted of high treason for 'having levied war upon the king.' Of the second, Sir Walter Raleigh's case may serve as an epitome.* The evidence on which he was convicted of having intrigued with Spanish emissaries to set Arabella Stuart on the throne, was the written accusation of one witness, who retracted, and then retracted his retractation, and was never confronted with the prisoner. A correspondent of the time wrote of Raleigh's trial thus: "The evidence was no more to be weighed than the barking of a dog. I would not for much have been of the jury to have found him guilty."†

*Laxity of evidence.*

These forced interpretations of the judges and their laxity about evidence, were unjustifiable enough, but there was another process at work, of a perfectly legitimate character, which had enlarged the meaning of laws containing the king's name. In England the constitution has continually changed in fact, without changing in form, and the fictions of the constitutional lawyers have been the regular means by which, as liberty has advanced, new facts have been brought under old forms. It is on this principle, that from the doctrine of the irresponsibility of the king, the constitutional lawyers have justly treated the name of king as meaning not the mere fallible being who wears the crown for the moment, but the true king who acts in accordance with the constitution he represents. The obvious plea, that Strafford had acted according to Charles' wishes and therefore could not have levied war upon the king, no lawyer would have thought of urging in the earl's defence. The king, the ideal king of English

*Ideal king of English law.*

\* See page 23.      † Jardine: Criminal Trials.

## TWO MAIN CHARGES.

law, 'can do no wrong,' and under all circumstances is the maintainer of the rights and liberties of his subjects. Though illegal acts are done by a king's command, a court of justice is bound to set this fact aside, and regard them as committed contrary to his wishes. The minister, therefore, who attacks the liberties of the subject, is also in the eye of the law attacking the authority of the king.

Yet the managers of the prosecution had a difficult task in trying to bring Strafford's acts within the definition of treason. As to the question of law, there were two main charges, which must be kept clearly distinct. The first and finally successful charge was the billeting of soldiers upon the people of Ireland, *in order to make them submit to illegal commands*, which was said to amount to 'levying war upon the king,' as it was really reducing the country by conquest. It must be allowed that technically Strafford had broken the law, and that what he had done amounted to treason within the meaning of the statute. But his counsel could argue that like arbitrary acts of power had been committed by previous deputies, and that he had not committed the offence in a manner systematic enough to be found guilty upon a liberal interpretation of the law.

*'Levying war upon the king.*

The second and unsuccessful point was the 'compassing the death of the king,' which they interpreted as meaning an endeavour to subvert the laws of the realm represented by the king. This accusation rested on Strafford's having advised Charles in council to bring over the Irish army to reduce 'this kingdom,' meaning England, to subjection. They had to prove both the question of fact and the question of law.

*'Compassing the king's death.*

As to the facts, Strafford could point to a straining of evidence, and could show up some charges as absurd in themselves, others as breaking down in proof. The prosecutors could retort, they were sufficiently proved, the sufficiency being in the custom of the time, and the usage of the courts which Strafford had administered. The fact that was most stoutly contested was 'the advising Charles to use the Irish army to reduce this kingdom.' The witness to this was no less than Sir Henry Vane, the king's secretary. Strafford's answer was that 'this kingdom' meant not England, but Scotland, which was then in rebellion, and he brought other members of the council to swear that they had no recollection of his advising Charles to use an army against English liberty. The importance which the Commons attached to the proof of this fact will be shown in the sequel.

Cumulative treason. As to the question of law, the Commons argued that it did not depend on this single article, but that the whole of the charges, twenty-eight in all, mounted up to a sort of accumulative treason, proving that Strafford had formed a scheme to subvert the laws of the realm, and govern by means of a standing army. This design of enforcing submission by means of an armed force was what moved the Commons most deeply. If that was not high treason, the constitution was a mockery indeed. If the law of high treason was to protect the sovereign power of the State, and if this sovereign power was not the king only, but the king acting through his Parliament, then to destroy Parliament was to destroy the vitality of the king. Was it 'compassing the king's death?' Well, would it not have been the death of the constitution? It would, no doubt, and should certainly have been included in a good law defining high treason against the State. But it was not. Pym felt this himself when he made the following grand rhetorical appeal to the earl's judges. "Shall it be treason to embase the king's coin, though but a piece of twelvepence or sixpence? and must it not needs be the effect of a greater treason to embase the spirit of his subjects, and to set up a stamp and character of servitude upon them, whereby they shall be disabled to do anything for the service of the king and the commonwealth?" The king can indeed have no interest but the good of his subjects, and Pym's view was here as ever that of the true constitutional statesman, but it lacked the support of precedents to commend it to judges. Strafford's plea of moderation on the other hand was easily met. "His moderation! when you find so many imprisoned of the nobility! so many men, some adjudged to death, some executed without law! when you find so many public rapines on the state, soldiers sent to make good his decrees, so many whippings in defence of monopolies, so many gentlemen that were jurors, because they would not apply themselves to give verdicts on his side, to be fined in the Star Chamber, men of quality to be disgraced, set in the pillory, and wearing papers and such things—can you, my lords, think there was any moderation?"

On the 10th of April, additional evidence, hitherto kept back, was read in the House of Commons, in support of the charge of advising the king to use the Irish army against English liberty. Before the meeting of the present Parliament, young Sir Henry Vane had found in his father's despatch box some notes made in council of the very debate in which Strafford advised the king to use the Irish army to reduce 'this kingdom.' He had shown them to Pym, who had made a copy, now produced. The double evidence upon the same article was considered conclusive of Strafford's guilt, and Sir Arthur Haslerig proposed to proceed against him by Bill of Attainder,* in other words to vote him guilty by act of Parliament. The motive for this change in procedure was "to avoid delay, which was now of extreme dangerous consequence." The known faithlessness of the king, and the peril impending from it, justified much informality. When a prisoner's friends threaten violence, they can hardly complain if his foes quicken the slow processes of law.

Bill of Attainder.

It has generally been supposed that this measure was brought in by the extreme patriots; but a member's notes, made in Parliament at the time, have revealed the fact that whereas it was warmly supported by the moderates, such as Hyde,† Falkland, Culpepper, and others, who took the Royalist side in the war; it was opposed by both Pym and Hampden, who preferred to ask the Lords to give judgment on the trial by impeachment. They had a quiet confidence in the goodness of their case, and were anxious to avoid even the appearance of differing from the Lords. However, on finding those who supported them were bent on the measure, they acquiesced, sharing, as they did, the universal conviction that, if Strafford escaped with his life, the king would restore him to power. But others gave utterance to the criticism to which such measures are undoubtedly open.

"I do not say," said the Royalist, Lord Digby, "but the charges may represent him as a man worthy to die, and perhaps worthier than many a traitor.

---

* Bills of Attainder were first introduced by Henry VIII. The last instance of the legislature's passing a Bill of Attainder, was in the case of Sir John Fenwick, in the reign of William III. See a remarkably clear statement of the character of such bills in Macaulay's Hist., c. 22 and 23.

† It is a significant fact that, among the Clarendon State Papers at Oxford, none are to be found relating to Strafford's trial. As there must have been such, it is presumed that Hyde destroyed them, wishing to conceal that he had acted on the popular side. His name is not in the list of 'Straffordians.'

I do not say but they may justly direct us to enact that they shall be treason for the future. But God keep me from giving judgment of death on any man upon a law made *à posteriori*. Let the mark be set on the door where the plague is, and then let him that will enter, die. I believe his practices in themselves as high, as tyrannical, as any subject ever ventured on; and the malignity of them largely aggravated by those rare abilities of his, whereof God has given him the use, but the devil the application. In one word, I believe him to be still that grand apostate to the commonwealth, who must not expect to be pardoned in this world till he be despatched to the other. And yet let me tell you, Mr. Speaker, my hand must not be to that despatch."

The bill, however, easily passed the Commons (21st April); only fifty-nine members voted against it, whose names were posted up in the streets of London, as 'Straffordians, enemies to their country.' The trial by impeachment in Westminster Hall still continued. Strafford made a brilliant defence, in which he carefully turned the attention of his hearers away from the billeting or 'levying war upon the king,' the weak point of his case, to the weak point of the prosecution, the charge of 'compassing the king's death.' The highway, which brought him to the Tower, furnished a simple illustration which seemed to demolish their laboured construction.

Strafford's defence.

"My lords," he said, "I do not conceive that there is either statute law, or common law, that hath declared this—endeavouring to subvert the fundamental laws—to be high treason. Jesu! my lords, where hath this fire lain all this while, so many hundred years together that no smoke should appear till it burst out now, to consume me and my children? Hard it is, and extreme hard, in my opinion, that I should be punished by a law subsequent to the act done. . . . If I pass down the Thames in a boat, and run and split myself upon an anchor, if there be not a buoy to give me warning, the party shall give me damages; but if it be marked out, then it is at my own peril. Now, my lords, where is the mark set upon this crime? where is the token by which I should discover? if it be not marked, if it lie under water and not above, there is no human providence can prevent the destruction of a man instantly and presently. My lords, I have troubled your lordships a great deal longer than I would have done; were it not for the interest of those pledges, that a saint in heaven left me, I should be loath, my lords [here his weeping stopped him]—what I forfeit for myself is nothing ; but I confess that my indiscretion should forfeit for them, it wounds me very deeply; you will be pleased to pardon my importunity, something I should have said, but I see I shall not be able, and therefore I will leave it. . . .'"*

---

* Nalson, ii. 123.

And then lifting up his hands and eyes, he said, 'In te, Domine, confido ne confundar in æternum.' Strafford's defence had laid bare the real principle at issue, as far as the court was concerned. A law has a relation to the innocent as well as to the guilty. If the law of high treason meant that those guilty of such and such crimes should die, it meant just as much that those not guilty of them should have their lives safe, as far as the crime of treason was concerned. Such stretching of a law might be as dangerous to the liberty of the subject as the offences with which Strafford was charged. For if the words, 'compassing the king's death' should at one time be made to include a scheme of subverting the laws, they might, he argued, at another be made to include some other offence equally far from their literal meaning, and thus men's lives, finding no protection in the law, would lie at the mercy of any party in power. Strafford carried his judges with him in thus repelling the charge of compassing the king's death. Peers indeed had no wish to extend the responsibility of ministers too far. The prosecutors, however, felt that the extension of this principle was the only security for their lives; they considered that the simple meaning of the words could not be trusted as a complete exponent of the cases included, without implying a perfection of form in English law which did not exist, and that the gist of his argument was, that a malefactor who found a new way to break the principle of a law should get the benefit of his ability at the expense of their liberties, while, as to the possibility of future consequences from such straining of law, they felt that their chief fear in that respect was from Strafford himself. It had fallen to Pym to reply to the earl's defence. As he ended his speech, he caught the eye of his old friend earnestly fixed upon him: he faltered, turned over his papers, and, with difficulty recovering himself, asked their lordships to close the proceedings for the day. Strafford's friends, meanwhile, were not idle. The queen, fond of exercising power, and anxious to avert this blow to royalty, now exerted herself in his behalf. Torch in hand, she was nightly to be found holding conferences with popular lords, offering them, as she thought, all they could desire, if only they would save Strafford's life.* A compromise was proposed: Charles offered to form a ministry out of the opposition leaders both in

Opposition refuse office.

* De Motteville, i.

Lords and Commons; the Earl of Bedford was to be treasurer; St. John, a member of the Commons, had already been made solicitor-general; places were to be found for the Earl of Essex, for Hampden, Pym, Hollis, and others. The new ministry, on their side, were to allow Strafford to escape with his life, and to ward off any attack made against the bishops by the Presbyterians. The compromise, however, was never effected. Bedford died, Essex was not to be persuaded: "Stone dead," said the blunt, plain-spoken earl, "hath no fellow;* if he be fined or imprisoned, the king will grant him his pardon as soon as the Parliament is ended." Pym and Hampden were not less far-sighted than Essex, and had even better reasons for distrusting any advances from the king.

Army plot. The Scottish and English armies were still in the northern counties, awaiting the ratification of the treaty, after which the one was to be disbanded and the other to return to Scotland. The Parliament, looking upon the Scots as friends, who would, in case of need, render assistance against the king, had voted them £300,000 as a free gift. But the English army had no love for the Parliament, which had no wish to do anything for them. The soldiers had become discontented because their pay was in arrear, while of the officers, many were Catholics, almost all devoted partizans of the king. Ill-feeling towards the Parliament was so general, that some of the leading officers in London ventured on talking over with the queen an ill-matured plan of bringing up the army to coerce the Parliament. Charles gave his assent, though at the very time he was negotiating with the leaders of the Parliament. Naturally he would sooner have seen Hampden, Pym, and Essex changing places with Strafford and Laud in the Tower, than have had them sitting by his side in the council chamber. Still, such a double-dealing game was a hazardous one to play, and Pym was not an easy man to overreach: he had his spies abroad to tell him the tavern discourse of too sanguine officers; he had his friends even in the court circle; in fact, the whole plan had been betrayed by Lord Goring, one of the conspirators, and Pym was only holding back his knowledge from the Parliament until he should find the fittest moment for revealing it. While these

* Clar. Hist., i. 395.

negotiations and army plots were going on behind the scenes, the nation still had its attention fixed on the Bill of Attainder, which did not easily make its way through the Lords. Charles tried to intimidate by threatening to refuse his assent. He summoned the two Houses, and told them that he did not consider the earl fit to serve him even in the position of a constable, but that no fear, no respect whatsoever should make him act against his conscience in consenting to his death (1st May). But if the king threatened on the one side, the people threatened on the other. The next day was Sunday; the London pulpits preached the duty of justice upon a great delinquent. By the Monday London was roused; some thousands of apprentices and others, armed with swords and cudgels, gathered around Westminster Hall, crying, 'Justice on Strafford, justice on traitors,' and demanding from every lord as he went into the house, 'that they might have speedy execution on the earl, or they were all undone, their wives and children.' The Lords, dismayed at their violence, spoke them fair, and sent word to the Commons to demand aid in suppressing the tumult. But the messenger could gain no admittance; the doors of the Commons' house had been locked since seven o'clock in the morning, and remained locked until eight o'clock that evening. Within, fear, horror, and amazement sat on the faces of the members, for Pym was revealing to them, not only that grand idea of bringing up the army to crush the Parliament, but various other desperate designs formed by the friends of Strafford; how there was a plan of sending a hundred picked men into the Tower, where Strafford was confined, under the name of a guard; how bribery had been attempted on the governor to let his prisoner escape; how, lastly, there was some dark design of bringing over a French force into Portsmouth.

A protestation was drawn up on Pym's motion, to defend the privileges of Parliament and the lawful rights of the people, and signed by every member present. Hyde, who had written his name second on the list, took it up to the Lords himself to receive their signatures.* Great was the panic in London when the doors of the Commons were unbarred. To think of an army led by Royalist and Papist officers, marching into their city, the strong-

* Forster: Lives of British Statesmen, iii. 185. Grand Remonstrance.

hold of Presbyterian faith! Rumours of plots, true and false, were in every man's mouth, and easily found credence. The Lords began to think their own lives in danger from the populace, if they delayed the trial any longer. Having already voted the facts of some of the articles of impeachment proved, they now appealed to the judges on the question of law. The judges unanimously declared 'that upon all their lordships had voted to be proved, the earl was guilty of high treason.' On this the Lords passed the Bill of Attainder, voting the earl guilty, not upon all the articles, but only upon the fifteenth, the quartering of troops upon the people of Ireland, and the nineteenth, the imposing an unlawful oath upon the Scots in Ireland. In voting on the bill, it is important to observe, that they acted as nearly as possible as if they had been giving judgment on the impeachment, for they used the forms in which they were accustomed to vote as judges, not as legislators.* Thirty-four lords stayed away; twenty-six voted for the bill, nineteen against it (7th May).

*Lords pass Bill of Attainder.*

Strafford's warning that the precedent of the case might be used against others no doubt had weight with many who had supported the king in unconstitutional acts, but these only succeeded in protecting themselves so far as to insert a clause in the bill, to the effect that the judges should count nothing as treason in consequence of this bill which was not treason before. As the judges had pronounced the acts were treason, the clause was unmeaning. But now Charles' turn was come. If he had in him the courage to resist, if not to resent, intimidation, in these desperate circumstances he had still the opportunity of securing one of two triumphs, either of saving the life of the earl, or of throwing on Parliament the reproach of executing him against law, for that he possessed the legal right to refuse his consent to any bill was at that time undisputed. It might have been thought, therefore, that the king would have been glad of the substitution

---

* The difference between voting on a Bill of Attainder and an impeachment is, that in giving judgment on the latter a peer professed to be bound by the letter of the law and of the rules of evidence; in voting for the former, though bound by the spirit, he professedly held himself emancipated from the letter. Further, there was a great difference in form. In voting for a bill a peer says 'aye' in his seat, and if a division is called, walks in silence past the teller of his side; in voting on an impeachment each peer stands up in his place, puts his hand on his breast, and says, 'Guilty (or not) on my honour.'

of the bill for the impeachment, since the change gave him an opportunity of making good his promises to Strafford. But these were not Charles' feelings. His chief misery lay not in the fact that Strafford must die, but that his own hand must consent to his death. The angry rabble followed him to Whitehall, with their shouts of "justice, justice, we will have justice." The queen wept bitterly, in fear, it seems, for her own safety, as she began to make preparations to leave the country. In anguish of soul Charles asked his councillors how the rioters were to be suppressed; they bade him please his Parliament and pass the Bill of Attainder: he asked five bishops how he was to remove his scruples of conscience; all but one told him he had both a public and a private conscience, and that the duty of saving the life of a friend or servant was as nothing compared with that of preserving his kingdom. The same day a letter was handed him from the earl bidding him pass the bill—"Sire, my consent shall more acquit you herein to God than all the world can do besides; to a willing man there is no injury done." {Charles passes Bill of Attainder.}

"My Lord of Strafford's condition," said Charles, "is more happy than mine."* He shed tears, but sent a commission for others to sign the bill, a mode of relieving his conscience suggested to him by his council. 'Put not your trust in princes, nor in the sons of men, for in them there is no salvation,' Strafford exclaimed when told that the king had consented to his death. After passing the bill, Charles sent a letter to the House of Lords by the hands of the Prince of Wales, requesting the Parliament to commute the punishment of death into that of perpetual imprisonment; the letter, however, had a postscript: 'If he must die, it were charity to reprieve him till Saturday.' But the discovery of the plot for Strafford's release had made longer imprisonment impossible, and the House ordered the execution for the next day (12th May).

In forming a judgment on the justice of the conviction upon which Strafford suffered, it must be repeated on the one side that the lawyers and judges in serving the interests of the crown, had really enlarged the statute; that undoubtedly the earl had technically offended against the {Question of justice of Strafford's conviction.}

* Radcliffe's Life in Straff. Despatches.

law, by quartering troops to coerce the people ; that the Commons heard the points of law argued at length in their house, and decided that his acts fell within the provision of the statute, before they passed the third reading of the bill ; that after this the judges declared that the facts voted to be proved amounted to high treason by law ; that the Lords, by voting judicially upon the bill, were acting as supreme judges when they also declared that in their view the offences came within the statute ; and lastly, that proceeding by bill only gave the king a chance of exercising his prerogative of mercy, which he would not otherwise have had. Briefly put, the case would amount to this, that the judicial competence of the House of Lords was unquestioned, but in this case Strafford's peers, acting simply as a jury, declared certain facts proved, the judges of the land declared the law on these facts against him, and the peers then pronounced the verdict ; and though the fact that the conviction itself was on small and technical grounds might well be pleaded as an extenuating circumstance to reprieve him from the full punishment of death, yet his own conduct towards others deprived him of any such claim to exceptional mercy. It has hardly been sufficiently observed that, whatever the contemplated object of the bill, its actual effect was not to enlarge the statute retrospectively, but only to alter the procedure. If we apply the standard of the nineteenth century to judge of the procedure of the seventeenth, we shall say that this conviction of treason was not just, though it was far more just than any other of that day.

So far as to the technical issue. At the bar of history, Strafford is arraigned as a traitor to the constitution. He is proved guilty by the undoubted evidence of his own correspondence. The two restraints on the executive are, the freedom of Parliament and the independence of the judges. According to Strafford's scheme, judges were to receive percentages on verdicts for the crown, and dismissal for verdicts against it. Parliament was only to vote subsidies, and not inquire into grievances. Discontent at grievances unredressed was to be quelled by a standing army. This standing army was to be supported by taxes levied, like shipmoney, on the sole authority of the crown. If we turn now to Pym's ideal, since realized, and look upon this picture and on that, we shall with Hallam 'distrust any one's attachment to the English constitution, who reveres the name of the Earl of Strafford.'

## CHAPTER V.
### GRAND REMONSTRANCE.—IMPEACHMENT OF FIVE MEMBERS.
### 1641—1642.

\* \* It is not so, thou hast misspoke, misheard ;
Be well advised, tell o'er thy tale again :
It cannot be ; thou dost but say 'tis so :
I trust I may not trust thee ; for thy word
Is but the vain breath of a common man:
Believe me, I do not believe thee, man ;
I have a king's oath to the contrary.—KING JOHN, iii. 1.

DURING Strafford's trial, the Commons had not been unmindful of reform. Early in the year Charles had given his consent to a bill which required that a Parliament should be elected once every three years, and that no future Parliament should be dissolved or adjourned, without its own consent, in less than fifty days from the opening of the session (16th Feb.). In order that the act might not remain a dead letter, it provided that if the king failed in his duty, various officers employed in the Government should send out writs for elections in his stead ; and that if these failed in their duty, the electors should meet of themselves and choose their representatives.

The too long continuance of the same Parliament changes the character of the House of Commons from that of a popular assembly to that of an oligarchical senate, by making the members heedless of the wishes of their constituents, and apt to sacrifice their duties to their interests. The too frequent election of new Parliaments renders members subservient to their electors, so that instead of following some settled course of action according to their own convictions, they act merely as delegates apt to reflect every prejudice that obtains amongst the multitude. There is no universal rule of right in this matter. In the seventeenth century, new Parliaments might, without injury to their character, have been elected every year, so slight was the control constituents possessed over their representatives. The House of Commons was subject to the influence of the court; the county members were gentlemen by birth, often connected by blood or marriage with peers and ministers; while the members for small boroughs were returned according to the directions of neighbouring peers and gentlemen. No public meetings were held for the debate of political questions. No petitions of a political character had been presented to any previous Parliament. No newspaper press existed before the commencement of the civil war. The votes of members were unrecorded. Parliamentary debates were never published. The privilege of excluding strangers from the House was constantly exerted by the Commons. London, however, in stirring times, knew much and judged freely; but at duller periods there was a want of the coffee-houses of a later date to bring public opinion to a focus. The knowledge of events in London took months in circulating through the country. The action, therefore, of a Triennial Bill would have been beneficial in itself, and the experience of the last eleven years had shown the absolute necessity of a guarantee for the meeting of Parliaments. The measure which followed was of a different character.

At the same time that he gave his consent to the Bill of Attainder, Charles, sick at heart, without heeding its contents, passed a second bill, depriving him of the right to dissolve the Parliament without its own consent (10th May). This bill had been introduced into the Commons upon the disclosure of the Army Plot, which gave Pym and Hampden good cause to doubt, whether their own lives or the liberties of the people would be safe, were the Parliament once dissolved.

*Parliament cannot be dissolved without its own consent.*

If too long Parliaments become oligarchical, much more will a Parliament which is indissoluble. It may now, in fact, be taken as an axiom that a Parliament which can only dissolve of its own consent, will never dissolve unless forced to do so by some power external to itself. Either it is in accordance with the popular feeling, in which case there is no reason it should dissolve as it is still representative; or, again, if the pulse of popular opinion beats feebly, it feels it can go on governing as it likes; or, lastly, public opinion is strongly against it, and under these circumstances it feels that dissolution is suicide, so it is then most determined to ride over the storm and wait for a time when sympathy is restored. But in a moment of terror like this such far-sighted calculations would have seemed

*Danger of assembly which cannot be dissolved.*

but mistrust of the patriotism of fellow-members.* It is not the only occasion on which the disregard of future dangers, induced by the terrors of the present, has brought countries into a constitutional dead-lock.

Statutes were passed to abolish those great engines of tyranny, the courts of Star Chamber, of High Commission, and of the North, and deprive the king's council of all jurisdiction, criminal or civil, and of the power of imprisoning without showing legal cause† (July); as also to prevent the recurrence of what was practically confiscation, by fixing the extent of the royal forests; and, lastly, to declare the illegality of all customs levied without consent of Parliament. Illegal courts abolished.

In the Church, reform was also carried on. The times were likened to 'a little Doomsday;' ministers who frequented taverns instead of teaching and preaching, those who burned three hundred wax candles in honour of our Lady, who called the communion table, altar, who taught the people that all they had belonged to the king, or in other ways had the character of being popishly or slavishly inclined, were now all alike turned out of their livings, fined, and imprisoned. Reform in Church.

All over the country the Presbyterians and sectarians rose again to the surface. The Presbyterians looked forward to overthrowing the Episcopal Church; the aspirations of the sectarians, or Independents, as they were often called, from the name of their most influential sect, looked rather to securing liberty to worship as they pleased. Men who had lain hid in corners, or migrated to New England, re-appeared to spread their special doctrines. Conventicles were filled, preachings held, by the poorest of the people. No wonder, it was said, "that chandlers, salters, and such like preached, when the Archbishop of Canterbury, instead of preaching, had busied himself in projects about leather, salt, soap, and the like. They had but reciprocally invaded each other's calling."‡ Nevertheless there Presbyterians and Independents.

---

* According to an act passed in the first year of George I. (1717), Parliaments now sit for seven years, unless previously dissolved by the crown.

† The statute abolishing the arbitrary courts contained a clause, that any person imprisoned by the command or warrant of the king, or any of his council, should be entitled to a writ of *Habeas Corpus* from the Courts of King's Bench or Common Pleas, without delay on any pretence whatsoever. —See p. 16.)

‡ May, L. P., 75.

were numbers both in the Parliament and the country unwilling to see strange forms of Church government, free preaching, and the growth of schism uncontrolled by the authority of the bishops. Hence when religious matters were debated, the House was far from being at unity. 'Let us keep the Church as it is,' said Hyde and his Church party. 'Let us allow bishops to keep their office, but shut them out of all share in State government, and lessen their power over the clergy,' said Pym and Hampden and the political reformers. 'Let us bring them down, root and branch,' said a third, the Presbyterians. The Independents joined their votes to the Presbyterians, for although they did not wish the Presbyterian Church to be established by law, they knew there was little hope of escaping persecution, until the old rule of Episcopacy was overthrown. "I can tell you, sir, what I would not have, though I cannot tell you what I would," said Cromwell, their leader, one day when pressed to declare his views.*

The country was as divided in its wishes as the House. The abolition of Episcopal government was demanded by a petition of 15,000 Londoners (11th Dec., 1640), its maintenance by nineteen petitions from different counties.

After the discovery of the Army Plot, the force of the Presbyterians in the Commons was much increased, for Pym and Hampden, with the political reformers, though not ill disposed to the Church, found it necessary to form an alliance with the Presbyterians. Hence for the present, in religious or political questions alike, these two sections voted as one. The results of this powerful coalition were soon shown in the introduction into the Lower House of a bill called the 'Root and Branch Bill,' which required, not simply that the clergy should be deprived of all civil power, and the bishops consequently of their seats in the House of Lords, as one did that had already passed the Commons (1st May), but that the very order of bishops should be abolished, their titles, their power over the clergy, their revenues, all taken from them (27th May). On this parties plainly declared themselves, and the previous unanimity gave way to a fierce division, which crushed the bill. Men such as Hyde and Falkland drew back from further change whether in Church or State. The work of reform and justice, they argued, had now been completed;

* Warwick, Memoirs, 177.

Strafford had paid the full penalty of his tyranny; Laud was in the Tower, a prisoner for life; other culprits had been punished by fine, imprisonment, or banishment; to ensure liberty, new statutes had been made, and the illegal courts abolished. If more was demanded of the king, the Commons would be trespassing on his just rights, and altering the ancient form of government as it had existed before Charles first encroached on the liberties of the people. On the other hand to Pym, Hampden, and their followers, the Army Plot, and other intrigues in Strafford's behalf, were convincing proofs that Charles was not to be trusted. Granted he had consented to many bills, how had he given this consent? His deep reluctance was not subdued, it was only biding its time till he could use force to recover what he had lost? Even now the queen was talking of going to Spa, nominally to recover her health, really to try and gain some foreign aid to help her husband in crushing the Parliament; Charles, of a journey to Scotland, no doubt to strengthen his party there, and maybe to foster the discontent of the English army he would pass through. And what then? So old friends parted company. The party of Hyde and Falkland, now become royalist, went one way; that of Pym and Hampden, followed by all the Presbyterians and Independents, another.

*Royalist party formed.*

*Political reformers.*

Charles, on his way to Scotland, visited the English army, at the time disbanding (Aug.), and readily obtained promises of assistance from Papist officers and soldiers of fortune. But his opponents were generals enough to have organized their intelligence department well: they numbered friends among the king's friends, and one wrote to the Earl of Essex, that strange attempts had been made to pervert and corrupt the army.

*Tampering with army.*

Arrived in Scotland, Charles granted the Scottish Parliament the establishment of the Presbyterian Church and triennial Parliaments, and bestowed honours and pensions upon the leading Covenanters, hoping by such means to win the favour of nobles and people, and prevent them from befriending his enemies in England. At the same time he sought to obtain proofs against the leaders of the Parliament of having been in communication with the Covenanters in 1640, and on these he intended impeaching them of high treason on his return.

*King in Scotland.*

"I believe after all be done," he wrote to his secretary, who reported Pym's apparent cheerfulness, "that they will not have such great cause of joy." While his conduct, narrowly scanned as it was, was making Parliament more and more doubtful of his good faith, an act fell out that cast upon him the suspicion of all his Protestant subjects. On the 1st November, the Commons, holding their breaths through horror, heard that on the 23rd of October, the Irish of Ulster had risen in arms, and nearly surprised Dublin, and all over their own province were driving the Scotch and English from their homes with robbery, plunder, murder, while they displayed a commission, stamped, as they said, with the king's great seal, authorizing them to take up arms. Every week with fresh despatches the tale increased in horror. Ulster was the province where the settlers were most thickly planted, but the rebellion and its attendant massacre spread fast from county to county, from province to province. The scattered remains of Strafford's army, still some 3000 in number, joined the insurgents, the 'degenerate English,' also Papists, uniting with the Irish. It was a fearful time, a whole people in rebellion to avenge years of oppression and wrong, a people, moreover, brutal through ignorance, burning with fanaticism. Heartrending were the accounts that came to England, how men, women, and children were mercilessly butchered; how people of all conditions, spoiled and stripped, with only rags for coverings, some wounded to death, others frozen with cold, came crowding into Dublin, now almost their only asylum, until barns, stables, and outhouses were over-filled with dying wretches; how the Irish boldly declared their purpose to extirpate English Protestants, and not to lay down arms until the Romish religion was established, the government settled in the hands of natives, and the Irish restored to the lands of their ancestors.\*

<small>Irish Rebellion.</small>

<small>King and queen suspected of complicity in rebellion.</small> Though Charles declared that the commission published in his name was a forgery, and offered to commit the care of the war entirely to the Parliament, he did not succeed in counteracting the prevailing and persistent opinion that both he and the queen had been concerned in the rebellion.

\* Lingard, vii. 283, from Nalson.

History has revealed that there was grave cause of suspicion. Charles, when the 'Parliament had insisted on his disbanding Strafford's army, had sent private instructions to the Earl of Antrim, in Ireland, to get the same forces together again, and to engage the lords of the Pale to seize possession of Dublin castle, and declare for himself against the English Parliament. But it is ill playing with edged tools. The native Irish, who had planned an insurrection on their own account, possibly with the knowledge and consent of the queen,* seized the occasion to wreak vengeance for the seizure of their lands, and rising before the English Catholics were ready to join them, began the rebellion with the inhuman massacre of the Protestant settlers.† The king seems now to have cherished the strangely mistaken idea that the horrors of the rebellion might make his English subjects more inclined to support his own authority. "I hope," he wrote to his secretary, "this ill news in Ireland will hinder some of these follies in England."

It had, of course, quite the opposite effect. Before Charles returned from Scotland, Pym and Hampden caused a Remonstrance to be drawn up, which it was intended afterwards to print and disperse throughout the country. This Remonstrance began by indicting the king's government for all its past errors, the voyage to Cadiz, the loss of Rochelle, the long imprisonments and cruel sentences of the Star Chamber, and the death of one whose "blood still cries for vengeance, or repentance of those ministers of State who at once obstructed the course both of his Majesty's justice and mercy."‡ Next followed a statement of the reforms effected by the Parliament, the abolition of the illegal courts, the beneficial laws passed, the justice meted to evil councillors. After this came a complaint against the enemies of the Parliament, who had tampered with the army, and whose "designs defeated in England and Scotland, had succeeded in Ireland," and this led up to the final demand that for the future the king should select councillors in whom Parliament could confide. To understand the motives which led a body of country gentle-

<small>Grand Remonstrance.</small>

---

* The suspicion against the queen was revived at the Restoration by the extraordinary exertions she then made to procure for Antrim the restoration of the estates forfeited by his treasonable help to Cromwell. It was supposed he knew some dark secret; and the only other motive her apologist suggests was certainly inadequate. See Carte's Ormond, 277—293.
† Godwin, ii.   ‡ See p. 58.

men to propose what was in fact the first step to a revolution, we must imagine ourselves environed with the dangers that they saw around them on every side.

In England, Pym's life had been attempted, not only by a loathsome attempt to inoculate him with the plague, but in Westminster Hall another man had been stabbed by mistake for him. From Scotland accounts came of a plot to assassinate both Hamilton and Argyle; there were suspicions, which history has confirmed, that the would-be murderer was Montrose. The popular leaders had strong reasons for believing that there was a second Army Plot brewing in Scotland, by which Parliament was to be crushed. Meantime, within the House the union which had been strength was gone; the Lords were inclined to retrace their steps; in the Commons, the longer Parliament lasted the more court influence increased. The secession of Hyde had carried with it even Falkland, though noted as a lover of justice, and of Parliament as the fountain of justice. Outside there was one of the reactions which ensue on revolutionary legislation, however salutary. The weak are alarmed; the violent remain dissatisfied; while the masses, on finding their wild and unreasonable hopes have met with an inevitable disappointment, are apt to echo the cries of the privileged classes who resent or dread interference. The people in such a mood will sacrifice their friends, and let slip all they have gained, unless some leader appears to restore confidence by showing clearly what is yet to be done, and how. The Remonstrance was Pym's manifesto. In its pages the good of government by Parliament was contrasted with the well-known evils of government by Prerogative; the remedy was shown; the old method of electing the king's council must give way to a new and more constitutional one; and the country must be governed by ministers in whom the Parliament had confidence, whether the king had confidence in them or not. After a debate which lasted for more than fifteen hours, the House divided on the question whether the Remonstrance should be presented to the king. The yeas numbered 159, the noes 148. Whereupon a member moved that it should be printed at once. To print it was to appeal from the king to the people. Hyde and Colepepper said, if the motion were persisted in, they should ask leave to enter their protest in the journals of the House, a custom occasionally adopted in the Upper House, but unknown in the Lower. Pym and Hollis referred to the usage of the House. An opponent then, putting aside the question of leave, called out that he did then and there protest for himself and for all the rest of his party. 'All! all!' shouted the enemies of the Remonstrance, waving their hats over their heads and snatching their swords from their belts. In the passion of the moment, blood might have been shed within the walls of the Commons' House itself, had not Hampden, ever ready, calmed the turbulent spirits by a few well-timed words. Debates were then by day and not by night, but though no further vote was taken, it was not until two o'clock in the morning that the wearied members, depressed or elated by that majority of eleven, left their gloomy chamber for their homes* (Nov. 22).

So far the political reformers had gained a victory, but they were still far from carrying the whole sense of the House or the nation with them. Even in London, among the wealthier citizens a royalist party appeared, and celebrated the king's return from Scotland by a great manifestation. A royalist Lord Mayor was elected, who, attended by the city aldermen in their scarlet robes, by troops of horsemen, by gentlemen richly clad in velvet coats and chains of gold, went out to meet the king and queen, and entertained them royally in the city. Royalist party.

Charles, elated by the rise of a royalist party, and with the lightly-given promises of Scotch nobles and army officers fresh in his mind, felt confident that he should yet be able to get the better of his enemies in the Parliament. But his acts gave warning of danger. A proclamation for the enforcement of laws against Puritans was published; the trainband that formed the guard of the two Houses, was dismissed by his orders; Balfour, a friend of the Parliament, was removed from the command of the Tower; and Lunsford, a cavalier of bad reputation, appointed in his place (22nd Dec.). On the news of this appointment, tumults arose in the city, where there was already excitement enough to warn Charles that his friends were not so many as he thought. But though he consented to cancel it within twenty-four hours at the representation of his friend the Lord Mayor, he could not allay the suspicion to which such peculiar measures had given rise.

The Remonstrance, printed by order of the House (15th Dec.), was

* Forster's Grand Remonstrance; Warwick's Mem.

already in the hands of the citizens. Reports were abroad that a charge of treason was intended against some members of Parliament. At this critical time, a bill to deprive the bishops of their seats in the House of Lords, was rejected for the second time, owing, as was said, to the opposition of papist peers. It was the Christmas holidays ; and apprentices, watermen, workmen, crowds of all sorts, came flooding out of the city to Westminster, threatening the lords opposed to the bill, and insulting the bishops.

*Bill for depriving bishops of seats.*

Meanwhile, there had gathered round Charles at Whitehall, officers from the late disbanded army, young students from the inns of court, gentlemen from the country, eager for a fight with the Parliament. "What !" said one, in actual hearing of some members, "shall we suffer these base fellows at Westminster to domineer thus ? Let us go into the country and bring up our tenants to pull them out ?"* These reckless men, spreading themselves between Whitehall and Westminster, soon drew their swords upon the citizens, who were often armed only with clubs. In Westminster Hall, in Westminster Abbey, frays took place ; citizens were wounded, and a knight, who supported the Parliament, was slain. The names of Roundheads and Cavaliers were now first heard, bandied as epithets of reproach. The spiritual peers, as the cause of the quarrel, suffered most from the insolence of the mob ; one day the Archbishop of York nearly had his robes torn off his back; on another, in real or pretended fear, the bishops slipped out of the House by back ways, or went home in the coaches of the popular lords.

*Frays between 'Cavaliers' and 'Roundheads.'*

After this last adventure, eleven bishops, following the lead of Williams, Archbishop of York, who, as some think, had arranged the whole matter with Charles, drew up a protestation declaring that all that should be done during their compelled absence from the Parliament was null and void. The protestation was presented to the king, who ordered it without delay to be read to the Lords (30th Dec.) fancying that now any bill passed by them during the bishops' absence would be recognized as void in law. The Lords, deeply offended at the conduct of the absentees, sent the protestation down to the Commons, who

*Protest of bishops.*

* Ludlow, i. 19.

immediately impeached the bishops of high treason, for endeavouring to subvert the fundamental laws of the realm (30th Dec.). The violence offered in no case seems to have been great, in fact three prelates still continued to frequent the House; and, if a bishop had met with injuries while attending his post in the House of Lords, the question might have entered the minds of those not unfriendly to the Parliament, whether, after all, the tyranny of a king was not more tolerable than the tyranny of a mob. But, at the very time when his friends might have won golden opinions as the victims of violence, he laid himself open to the suspicion of double dealing. Straws show which way the wind blows; and his message only made the House think that he intended hereafter to declare acts of Parliament null and void, because the bishops had been too timid to face the menaces of a crowd. The suspicion in Pym's mind was not removed by a secret offer now made him of the chancellorship of the exchequer. At a previous crisis, such an offer had tempted one of the ablest leaders of the opposition to forsake the principles he professed. But Pym was not Strafford. The Remonstrance was not a bid for office, but a demand for a constitutional ministry. This demand could be satisfied not by a secret concession to one of its subscribers, but by the public resignation of a point of prerogative. The secrecy was itself a proof that there was no concession of the principle. Failing Pym, Charles sought new ministers out of the party of his friends.

*Bishops impeached.*

*Pym refuses office.*

Lord Falkland, with reluctance, became secretary of state. "I choose to serve the king," he said to his friend Hyde, "because honesty obliges me to it, but I foresee my own ruin." Charles, who had made him his minister only because of his influence in the Parliament, felt no gratitude; a man who objected to the opening of letters, or the employment of spies, was of little use for the measures he contemplated. Sir John Colepepper, another member belonging to the same party, was made chancellor of the exchequer (1st Jan., 1642). Hyde refused office, only to serve the king's interests in the House with less suspicion of his honesty. Charles, however, had framed his policy before he appointed his ministers; for he now determined on carrying into execution a deep-laid plot, which he had been discussing with the queen and his confidants ever since he went to Scotland. Among patriots, vague rumours of impending danger

*Falkland and Colepepper take office.*

thickened. The Commons, growing more and more suspicious, petitioned the king to allow the restoration of their proper guard (31st Dec.). Charles took three days in replying, and then sent a refusal, concluding thus: "WE DO ENGAGE UNTO YOU SOLEMNLY, ON THE WORD OF A KING, THAT THE SECURITY OF ALL AND EVERY ONE OF YOU FROM VIOLENCE IS, AND SHALL EVER BE, AS MUCH OUR CARE AS THE PRESERVATION OF US AND OUR CHILDREN" (3rd Jan.). Upon the same day that this message was received, the king's attorney impeached of high treason, in the king's name, at the bar of the House of Lords, Lord Kimbolton, and five members of the Commons, Pym, Hampden, Hollis, Haslerig, and Strode; and desired immediate possession of the persons of the accused. He read seven articles of accusation, but the real charge, which Charles hoped hereafter to substantiate by proof, was the fourth, that of having invited a foreign foe to invade England. This referred to secret encouragement that had been given by some of the popular leaders to the invading Covenanters of 1640, the very men on whom the king had just been conferring honours in Scotland; and though such a charge could not stand good at law, by reason of an Act of Oblivion, passed in 1641, it was quite possible that, the members once in his power, he could find means to ensure their suffering the penalty of high treason. Shortly after the articles of impeachment had been read in the Upper House, a sergeant-at-arms entered the Lower and said, "In the name of the king, my master, I am come to require Mr. Speaker to place in my custody five gentlemen, members of this House, whom his Majesty hath commanded me to arrest for high treason." The Lords had refused to deliver up Lord Kimbolton; the Commons replied by sending a committee to the king, in which were both Falkland and Colepepper, to inform him that their members should be forthcoming as soon as a legal charge was preferred against them (3rd Jan.). The answer of the Commons meant more than it said, for the king's whole method of proceeding was illegal: 1st, a commoner cannot be called to answer at the suit of the crown to a criminal charge, unless the articles contained in the bill of accusation are first declared by a grand jury not to be groundless; 2nd, a commoner, unless impeached by the Commons before the House of Lords, can only be tried for treason before the common law judges by a petty jury, after the bill of accusation has been 'found' by a grand jury ; 3rd, the king cannot arrest in person or by a messenger, but only by a warrant drawn up and signed by a magistrate or councillor ; and for this reason, that, if the arrest is illegal, an action may be brought against a fellow-subject, but not against the king, who, in the eye of the law, is himself the fountain of justice.

Though the members, who should have been prisoners, were the heroes of the hour, Charles was far as yet from doubting his triumph. The next morning the queen at Whitehall was urging him not to hesitate in playing out the second act of his plan. "*Allez, poltron,*" said she, as he seemed to hesitate, " go, pull those rogues out by the ears, *ou ne me revoyez jamais.*"* " In an hour," said the king, as he kissed her, " I will return master of my kingdom ;" and, followed by a train of some three hundred armed men, proceeded to Westminster to arrest his enemies in person.

The Commons had received intimations from various quarters that some violence was intended, and were sitting, foreboding evil, when a friendly officer, who had climbed over the roofs of some neighbouring houses to be in time, entered the House with the information that, from this vantage point, he had seen the king set out from Whitehall, attended by his guards and a long train of cavaliers. The five members slipped out through the Speaker's garden, and thence took boat for the city, not a moment too soon, as they were hardly out of the House before Charles was entering Palace Yard, outside Westminster Hall. He came to the door of the Commons' House, and taking his nephew, the elector palatine, in with him, commanded all others upon their lives to stay without. " So the doors were kept open, and the Earl of Roxburgh stood within the door leaning upon it. Then the king came upwards towards the chair with his hat off, and the Speaker stepped out to meet him ; then the king stepped up to his place, and stood upon the steps, but sat not down in the chair. And after he had looked a great while, he told us he would not break our privileges, but treason had no privilege ; he came for those five gentlemen, for he expected obedience yesterday, and not an answer. Then

* De Motteville.

he called Mr. Pym and Mr. Hollis by name, but no answer was made. Then he asked the Speaker if they were here, or where they were. Upon this, the Speaker fell on his knees, and said, 'May it please your Majesty, I have neither eyes to see nor tongue to speak in this place, but as the House is pleased to direct me, whose servant I am here, and humbly beg your Majesty's pardon, that I cannot give any other answer than this, to what your Majesty is pleased to demand of me.' 'Well,' replied the king, 'since I see all the birds are flown, I do expect from you that you shall send them unto me as soon as they return hither, otherwise, I must take my own course to find them. But I assure you, on the word of a king, I never did intend any force, but shall proceed against them in a fair and legal way.' He then left the House, amid cries of 'Privilege! privilege!'" (4th Jan.).

Notwithstanding his protest, the House felt that bloodshed had only been averted by the narrow escape of the five members. The next morning, still adhering to his resolution of obtaining the persons of the accused, Charles, unattended by any guards, drove from Whitehall into the city. As he passed through the streets, cries were raised of 'Privilege of Parliament,' and some daring hand flung into his coach a paper inscribed, 'To your tents, O Israel!' a menace of revolt like that of the ten tribes to Rehoboam. Arrived at Guildhall, he addressed the lord mayor, aldermen, and common councilmen, demanding them not to shelter in the city those whom he had accused of high treason, and saying repeatedly he must have those traitors. But he had come on a bootless errand. Even among the city dignitaries his friends were few, while his foes were many, and cries of 'God bless the King,' were drowned by those of 'Privilege of Parliament.'\* "I have," said Charles, "and will observe all privileges of Parliament, but no privileges can protect a traitor from a trial" (5th Jan.). Westminster being regarded as no longer safe, the Commons were installed in the Guildhall, where the city set a guard to defend them. There was no chance of Charles getting the members into his power, unless by force. The citizens were completely alienated. Even those who had doubted the reports of previous plots against the Parliament, now believed in them all,

*King drives to Guildhall, and demands persons of five members.*

\* Forster, Five Members.

and recognized the foresight of Pym and Hampden, whom they had thought alarmists. All that had been whispered of Ireland was now talked aloud and printed, while the shops of the city were shut, as if an enemy were at the gates. "Our late troubles have been attended with one benefit," said Hampden to Hyde, "that we know who are our friends. I know well you have a mind we should be all in prison." Whether Hyde and the two new ministers did know or not, is still a moot point. Every one disclaims complicity in a plot that has failed. In Hyde's case even a knowledge of the intended impeachment involved treachery to friends he had long worked with. According to Hyde's own account, Charles had promised nothing should be done without their knowledge, and then concealed this from them. The best solution is to suppose that Hyde knew he was not to know.

*City alienated.*

There was now no hope of reconciliation between the two parties, short of Charles submitting to rule through a ministry responsible to Parliament. The march of those 300 on Westminster was in fact looked on as the declaration of war, or rather as war without a declaration. Men who remembered Eliot's fate, could not renounce self-defence after such a hair-breadth escape. Charles' hope had been, Periander like, to cut off the ears that overtopped. History has shown that a country can be unmanned by such a policy for a time. But by failure he had rather given the party heads than taken them away.

*War inevitable.*

The 11th of January was a gala day, a day of triumph for Presbyterians and reformers. While the London train-bands marched along the banks of the Thames, to the sound of drum and trumpet, as a guard, the five heroes of the day went by water from London Bridge to Westminster, followed by hundreds of boats and barges thronged with people and adorned with flags and streamers. Whitehall was silent as they passed. Charles had retired the day before to Hampton Court with his family to avoid the spectacle. "Where now are the king and his cavaliers? What has become of them?" cried the people, as with shouts of triumph they rowed on to reseat the members at Westminster. On landing the members were met by 4000 gentlemen and freeholders, who had come on horseback from Buckinghamshire, Hampden's native county, as a guard of honour for their insulted representative, bringing with them a petition to the Parliament against the king's evil councillors.

The king had made a great mistake. A momentary triumph, if won, is not a final victory; and no successes won by violence or chicanery can make up for the lost vantage ground of clean hands and frank conduct. Charles was especially unfortunate; his secret plots were always revealed, always failed, and always precipitated the discussion of vital questions. It was now necessary to raise forces to send against the Irish rebels. To whom was the right of commanding and calling out the county militia to belong? By the statute of Winchester, passed in the thirteenth year of Edward I., every man was required to possess arms in quantity and value according to the value of his lands and goods, so that each county was provided with a sort of feudal militia, which was called out in lieu of police by the lord-lieutenant of the county, in case of any tumult or riot. Two rights with regard to this militia the king of England had always exercised; first, that of nominating the lords-lieutenant and other officers in command;* secondly, when invasion was threatened, that of sending so-called commissions of array to the lords-lieutenant, bidding them call out the militia and train them for service. But whether in time of peace the king could summon his subjects to service outside their respective counties, was a question that had never yet been determined, or if at all in the negative, as Charles had just passed a bill which deprived him of the power of pressing troops into his service.

Both sides were equally keen on the question. The failure that rankled in Charles' breast was due, he thought, to the fact that his volunteers were enough to overawe the Commons, but not enough to overawe the capital. The Parliament had seen to what use Charles intended to put the sword, if he got it. Accordingly the Commons sent a petition to the king, asking that Parliament should nominate the commanders of fortified places, and the lords-lieutenant and other officers of the militia forces. The people beset the Upper House, demanding that the lords should both join in petitioning for the militia, which they had refused to do, and pass the bill removing ecclesiastics from all civil offices.

Between the 20th of January, and 5th of February, numbers of

* Hallam, Const. Hist. i. p. 552.

petitions to this effect flowed in from town and country, from young men, apprentices, seamen, tradesmen, porters, women. Many lords left the House in disgust at the noise and violence of their petitioners. Those that remained yielded in both the points required, and an ordinance was at once prepared to transfer the command of the militia from the king to the Parliament (Feb.). Since his departure from London, Charles had been preparing for war. The queen was to cross to Holland to procure arms and ammunition by the sale of the crown jewels. He intended himself to fix his residence at York, where it was expected his friends would gather round him, and the people be found more devoted to their king than in the immediate neighbourhood of London. When the bill to deprive the bishops of their seats in the House of Lords was presented to Charles, Colepepper urged him to yield, hoping that he might save the command of the militia. 'It is better,' he said, 'to satisfy them in one or other of these bills; this one can easily be repealed, and while the sword remains in your hands, there will be no attempts to make further alterations.'\* 'Is Ned Hyde of this mind?' asked the king. 'No, he does not wish that either of the bills should be passed; a very unreasonable judgment, as times go.' 'It is mine too, though,' replied Charles, 'and I will run the hazard.' Finding the king obstinate, Colepepper went to the queen, and assured her that in consequence of this refusal, the Parliament would stop her journey abroad. Henrietta, eager to get out of a country in which she felt herself always hated and now defenceless, never ceased importuning her husband with tears till he gave his consent to this bill.

*Lords pass Bishops' Exclusion Bill.*

*Charles consents to Bishops' Exclusion Bill,*

At Newmarket, on his way to York, Charles gave his final answer to the commissioners sent by the Parliament to ask his consent to the Militia Ordinance. 'Talk of your fears and jealousies,' he said indignantly, after hearing a bitterly worded declaration read, 'what would you have? Have I violated your laws? Have I declined to pass one bill for the ease and security of my subjects? I do not ask you what you have done for me. God so deal with me and mine as all my thoughts and intentions are upright for the observance of the laws of the land.' 'I wish,' said one of the commissioners, 'your

*but refuses Militia Bill.*

\* Clar. Mem. 114.

Majesty would reside nearer your Parliament.' 'I would you had given me cause; but I am sure this declaration is not the way to it.' 'Might not the militia be granted for a time?' 'By God, not for an hour. You have asked that of me in this, was never asked of a king, and with which I will not trust my wife and children' (9th March).

At York, Charles found himself again in possession of power. The Cavaliers followed in eager crowds; friends, who had been forced into exile, returned to his side, and many gentlemen from the neighbouring counties came to offer their support to his cause. His first step was to demand admittance to Hull, at that time the arsenal of the north. On his approach he found the gates shut, the bridges drawn, the walls manned, as though an enemy were expected: and Sir John Hotham, who had been lately sent down as governor by the Commons, came upon the walls and, kneeling down, said he durst not open the gates, being placed in trust by the Parliament (April). When the Commons were attacked as endangering the foundations of private property by thus denying the king access to his own arsenal, Pym replied by attacking as unconstitutional the principle, "that his Majesty hath the same right and title to his towns and magazines that every particular man hath to his house, lands, and goods. . . . This erroneous maxim, being infused into princes, that their kingdoms are their own, and that they may do with them what they will (as if their kingdoms were for them, and not they for their kingdoms) is the root of all the subjects' misery, and of all the invading of their just rights and liberties. Whereas, they are only iptrusted with their kingdoms. . . . By the known law of this kingdom, the very jewels of the crown are not the king's proper goods, but are only intrusted to him for the use and ornament thereof; as the towns, forts, treasures, magazines, offices, and people of the kingdom, and the whole kingdom itself, are intrusted unto him for the good, and safety, and best advantage thereof; and as this trust is for the use of the kingdom, so it ought to be managed by the advice of the Houses of Parliament, whom the kingdom hath trusted for that purpose; it being their duty to see it be discharged according to the condition and true intent thereof."

*Charles refused admittance into Hull*

Even the pretence of peace could hardly be maintained much

longer; and events were hurried on by the gentlemen of Yorkshire, who held a meeting in which it was proposed to raise a guard for the king's person (14th May). On the other side, after a century and a half of civil peace, the great body of the nation, whatever the injuries they suffered, were not willing to see the flames of civil war re-lighted; and now, while the gentlemen were assembling, the freeholders of the county came crowding into York, declaring that they also ought to have been summoned, for the knights and gentlemen had no right to act in their names. To satisfy them, a second meeting was held on the 3rd of June, at Heyworth Moor, where some 40,000 men assembled to meet the king. The freeholders had prepared a petition, begging him to dismiss the Cavaliers and be at accord with his Parliament. The Cavaliers, indignant at its contents, tore the petition out of the hands of those who were reading it to approving groups. Yet the freeholders had their wish, for young Thomas Fairfax, a Yorkshire gentleman, who sympathized with them, forced his way right up to the king, and falling upon one knee, fixed a copy of the petition upon the pommel of the royal saddle. *[Meeting at Heyworth Moor.]*

The Parliament, on its side, was making active preparations. First it formed itself into a war-council, eliminating obstructives. The House had made up its mind on the end to be pursued, and freedom of discussion was confined henceforward to the means. Open supporters of the royal enemy were put in confinement for a time or expelled the House.* One by one, as occasion or excuse offered, the king's friends fled to York; the House of Peers, in which, when the Parliament first met, had sat above eighty, now dwindled down to twenty members;† of the House of Commons sixty-five departed, amongst them Hyde and Falkland. An order was passed for raising troops and money (10th June); the money lent was to receive eight per cent. interest, the Parliament promising repayment on the nation's credit. Within a few days, such an amount of money and plate was brought to the treasurer at Guildhall, that there was hardly room to stow it; the wealthy bringing their large bags and goblets, the poor women their very wedding-rings, and their gold and silver hair-pins, thimble and bodkin money,‡ as the royalists contemptuously called it. The city was treated as a *[Parliament becomes a war-council.]*

\* Clar. Mem. 134.     † Hallam, i. 537.     ‡ May, 139.

camp; one who called the leaders traitors as a spy. In the artillery grounds in Finsbury fields, the muster ground of the volunteer troops, citizens were nearly all day at drill. The Presbyterians, who had formerly looked on the grounds with disfavour, as the resort of courtiers and gentlemen, now hastened thither to practise themselves in arms, and enlist in the London trained bands. Major-General Skippon soon commanded eight regiments, above 8000 soldiers. The militia ordinance was put in force without further care for the king's consent. In the same counties, in the same towns, sometimes on the very same day, appeared the officer appointed by the Parliament, and the officer appointed by the crown, the one summoning the people to arms in the name of the ordinance, the other in that of the king's commission of array.

Without slackening their preparations, the Parliament sent to the king at York nineteen propositions, for the first time formally tabulating their demands. Their hope was not so much that the king would grant them, as that the blame of the war would fall upon him for his refusal. They asked, that he should resign to Parliament (1) the nomination of his privy councillors and other officers of state, (2) the command of the militia and all fortified places; (3) that he should suffer the Church to be reformed by the advice of Parliament, and (4) not marry his children without asking its consent. Though securities practically equivalent to these are now incorporated in the constitution, the king of the seventeenth century was indignant at their bare proposal. "These being passed," he said, "we may be waited on bare-headed, have swords and maces carried before us, and please ourselves with the sight of a crown and sceptre, but as to true and real power, we should remain but the picture, but the sign of a king." The Commons fixed on the Earl of Essex as the general for their army. He had fought in his youth for the Protestant cause in the Low Countries. Charles had appointed him lieutenant-general in the first Scotch campaign, and after it had dismissed him with studied discourtesy. In earlier times he had suffered a deeper wrong from the Stuart court, for James the First had caused him to be divorced from his wife, in order to marry her to his own profligate favourite, Robert Carr, afterwards Earl of Somerset. Thus experience and personal antecedents seemed alike to fit him for the post. His nomination was acceptable to the Pres-

*Charles refuses propositions of York.*

byterians, who sympathized with his creed ; to gentlemen, who would have scorned to serve under a general of inferior rank ; to the people at large, who loved his honest, straightforward nature. On being voted general (4th July), he proved at once his honesty and courage, by accepting the dangerous honour, defeat meaning death to the leader of a rebel army. Several members of the Parliament received commands ; St. John, Hampden, Hollis, were named colonels of regiments of foot ; Cromwell, Haslerig, Fiennes, of regiments of horse. Great excitement prevailed in London ; everybody went about decorated with orange ribands, the colour of Essex' house, the shops were closed, and civil business was almost at a standstill. *[sidenote: Essex appointed general.]*

The king was not idle ; the queen sent arms and money from Holland, and, as soon as a small force was collected, he raised his standard on a hill near Nottingham (23rd August). Thence he marched into the west, making many friendly speeches to the people on his way, declaring his good intentions towards the laws and liberties of the kingdom.\* His nephews, Rupert and Maurice, sons of the Elector Palatine, came over from Germany to fight for him ; the Catholics lent him money, and by the middle of October he mustered at Shrewsbury an army of about 12,000 men. *[sidenote: King raises his standard.]*

And now the people had to choose between King and Commons. Declarations and pamphlets were eagerly devoured. Though half a year had passed, the Grand Remonstrance still served as the chief manifesto of the Parliament. In that document the king had been depicted as the tyrant, imprisoning without law, and taxing without right ; as the friend of Rome and the persecutor, cruelly maiming his subjects' bodies, and more cruelly maiming their souls' health ; while the Parliament stood forth as the upholder of true and tempered liberty, who kept the property of the rich safe from the grasping hand of confiscation, the hard-won earnings of the poor from being wasted by monopolies and illegal customs ; who enabled peer and peasant to walk again on English soil, free of all constraint but the well-known laws ; and above all as the protector of tender consciences, godly itself, and *[sidenote: Charles depicted by Parliament as tyrant and persecutor.]*

---

\* May, 134.

a shield to the godly against the courts which formed the new English Inquisition.

*Commons depicted by Royalists as rebels and fanatics.* In the royalist pamphlets the king was God's anointed, ruling by divine right, a pillar of the Church, the preserver of order, the upholder of the ancient constitution, yet giving up his right at his subjects' desire, and passing every law that conduced to his people's good; while the Commons were rebels, bent on encroaching alike on the king's prerogative and the rightful authority of the peers, friends of anarchy and misrule, ready to plunge the country in civil war to gratify their inordinate ambition, with a sullen and fanatical religion, which could neither take enjoyment itself, nor tolerate it in others; in fact, with that in them which might make a tyranny of many, far worse than any tyranny of one.

*Charles the deceiver.* But since the Remonstrance the king had unfortunately added to the reckoning his enemies kept against him. Not only had the tyranny received a new illustration in their eyes from the attempted arrest of the five members; the friendship with Rome by the muster of Catholics, and the persecution from a proclamation against Puritans; but a new count of crime was added. The solemn assurance to the Commons, that their preservation was as much his care as that of his wife and children, had been used to lull them into a false security; the oath that, on the honour of a king, he had never intended force, stood blankly contradicted by his armed retinue at the door. The untruthfulness of character suspected from his answer to the Petition of Right, and more than suspected from the army plots, now seemed a certainty. To the Parliament the king was not only the tyrant and the persecutor, but the deceiver. This count was really the cause of the war. Charles was not incapable of the position of a constitutional governor. He had ability above the average, dignity of manners, and a higher dignity, raising him above all low tastes; and he had not that unbending obstinacy, which would amount to incapacity, as a governor. But he was believed to have admitted an unfortunate distinction between a public and private conscience, which dispensed him from the necessity of keeping faith with political opponents. Measures past, concessions obtained, promises to observe the law, all these the cherished victories of peaceful patriots, seemed as unavailing as bands to bind a Proteus. The very awe of majesty requires a king's truthfulness to be above suspicion. But the leaders of the Commons had to work with a vision of the Tower ever before their eyes: the fairer the offers made to them the more the dread of foul play. This prevented the due action of that safety-valve of the State, a constitutional opposition. Even in foreign diplomacy, where bad faith is not uncommon, the discoverer of fraud is held justified in laying arbitration aside and drawing the sword at once: at home the interests of king and subjects being really identical, deceit has still less occasion for practice.

Devoted partisans on either side were not very many in number. Those of the king were mostly to be found in the soldiers of fortune from Germany, and the more reckless of the country gentlemen, who looked forward to the excitement of war. On the Parliament's side the Presbyterians and sectarians, seeing in their own cause the cause of God, strove for the overthrow of the Established Church with all the ardour of religious enthusiasts. But between the views of these two extreme parties opinion generally fluctuated, and men took sides doubtingly as their natures or circumstances prompted.

The greater part of the nobility and gentry either openly joined the king, or tried to remain neutral, and generally had sufficient influence over their tenantry to cause them to embrace the same side as themselves. To many it seemed absurd to hazard wealth and a secured position to avoid paying a few shillings arbitrarily raised; an upheaval from below was more dangerous to them than pressure from above; others, again, who recognized the importance of the principle at stake, were still inclined to their king by the instincts of chivalry, or the abhorrence of fanaticism. On the other hand, the inhabitants of manufacturing towns, independent county freeholders, merchants, and others, who had made fortunes in trade, and afterwards bought land in the country, showed themselves, as a rule, friendly to Parliament. Besides being influenced by religion and a sense of independence, these classes had especially suffered from the monopolies and extortions which had raised the price of necessaries and shackled the enterprise of trade. There were exceptions, however, on both sides. Many gentlemen felt that the cause of the Parliament was so good, they were bound to take up arms in its defence; many yeomen and burghers adhered to their

county magnates and their king. As a general rule, where the contagion of neighbourhood or the necessities of religion did not decide the question, the king was preferred to the Parliament. It was only the men of strong convictions, of unusual foresight, who would coolly and deliberately embark on an unknown sea, without chart or compass of guidance, and risk all for the sake of liberty, and the doubtful gratitude of posterity. So with unwilling hearts did men array themselves. One Royalist wrote to his wife, that though he loved not his side, 'grinning honour' compelled him to stay by it, for he could not bring himself to fight for the Parliament, and if he remained neutral he should be called a coward.*
"You," said Sir Edward Verney, the king's standard-bearer, to Hyde, who reproved him for looking melancholy, "are satisfied in conscience that the king ought not to grant what they desire. I have eaten my master's bread, and served him near these thirty years, and will not do so base a thing as to forsake him, but for my part I do not like the quarrel, and wish he would yield."†

Sir William Waller, one of the Parliament's commanders, wrote to Sir Ralph Hopton, a Royalist officer : "The great God, who is the searcher of my heart, knows with what reluctance I go upon this service, and with what perfect hatred I look upon a war without an enemy. The God of peace in His good time send us peace, and in the meantime fit us to receive it ! We are both on the stage, and we must act the parts that are assigned us in this tragedy ; let us do it in a way of honour, and without personal animosities."

At any rate, thought these unwilling enemies, one battle will decide everything, so that, whatever the consequences to the vanquished, our country will soon rest again on 'the gentle bosom of civil peace.'

\* Forster, B. S. iii. 50. † Clar. Mem. 160.

## CHAPTER VI.

### FIRST YEARS OF THE WAR.—BATTLES OF EDGEHILL AND NEWBURY.—1642—1643.

> They stood aloof, the scars remaining,
> Like cliffs which had been rent asunder,
> A dreary sea now flows between,—
> But neither heat, nor frost, nor thunder,
> Shall wholly do away, I ween,
> The marks of that which once hath been.
> COLERIDGE.

*Constitutional attitude of Commons.*

It must not be supposed that the Commons declared war against the king. The popular leaders were most careful to maintain a quasi-legal ground for their resistance. Novel and subtle as their principles seemed at the time, they have since been largely accepted. Pym's speeches in fact may be said to have laid down the lines of the theory on which modern constitutional government is based. Thus the Remonstrance was framed as an attack, not on the king, but on his councillors; and when the king objected that actions which he avowed as his own were 'censured under that common style,' Pym's answer was, "How often and undutifully soever these wicked counsellors fix their dishonour upon the king, by making his Majesty the author of those evil actions which are the effects of their own evil counsels, we, his Majesty's loyal and dutiful subjects, can use no other style, according to that maxim in the law, 'the king can do no wrong,' but if any ill be committed in matter of State, the council must answer for it: if in matters of justice, the judges."* So now the Commons went to war with the actual king to protect the ideal king of the constitution from evil counsellors. This appears in their declaration "that, whereas the king was seduced by wicked counsel to make war against the Parliament, who proposed no other end unto themselves than the

* Forster, British Statesmen. Pym, p. 269.

care of his kingdom and the performance of all loyalty to his person, it was a breach of the trust reposed in him by his people, and tending to the dissolution of his government." The legal maxims of the royal lawyers of the past had received a new reading from the popular lawyers of the present. The new wine seemed bursting the old bottles, but the bottles have since expanded to the strain. That these ideas were genuine beliefs of the time, is shown as well by the cherished clause of the covenant, "to preserve the king's person and authority," as by the real horror felt when Republicans first broke through this reserve, or when Cromwell averred that his pistol would be no respecter of persons. The patriots were not, however, wanting in readiness to chastise their 'poor, semi-divine, misguided father, fallen insane.'*

Essex marched from London into the west (9th Sept., 1642), and took up his head-quarters at Worcester, where he remained without venturing to offer the Royalists battle. Charles, wishing to fight before the rebel army could be reinforced, broke up his camp at Shrewsbury (12th Oct.), and marched across the country in the direction of London, feeling certain that Essex would follow him to protect the city. He went by way of Wolverhampton, Birmingham, Kenilworth, and passing Southam, on the road to Banbury and Buckingham, arrived at Edgecote, without having any knowledge of his enemies' movements (22nd Oct.).† Here, however, Rupert, who was encamped with the rear at Wormleighton, learnt from his scouts that fires were to be seen from the Dassett hills, and that Essex had his head-quarters that night at the village of Kineton, half way between Warwick and Banbury, and only ten miles to the north-west of Edgecote. The king, aroused from sleep at three in the morning, on hearing this news, at once summoned a council of war, in which it was agreed to hold without delay a general rendezvous of the army on the top of Edgehill.

To appreciate the tactics of the time it is necessary to remember the nature of the weapons. The soldiers on either side were armed after the same fashion. The introduction of fire-arms had caused the defensive armour of the ordinary horse and foot soldiers to be reduced to a back and breast piece and a broad iron hat, commonly called a pot; calves'-leather boots reaching up to the knees, and a long buff coat worn under the armour,

Armour of
footsoldiers.

* Carl. i. 160. † See Map, p. 127.

completed their equipment. Officers often wore open helmets, arm and shoulder pieces, and tassets or skirts to protect the thighs.

The cavalry was divided into three classes—the cuirassiers, the carabineers, and the dragoons.* The cuirassiers being almost without exception gentlemen, arming themselves at their own expense, came to battle magnificently appointed, with silver-hilted swords, plumes of feathers waving above open helmets, and buff coats gay with gold and silver trimmings. Their usual weapons were the sword and pistol. The carabineers were so called from the name of their carbine or musket. The dragoons were light armed, having only the buff coat and iron hat, and were like mounted riflemen, fighting as much on foot as on horse, but with swords for cavalry work. *Cavalry,— three classes.*

The infantry was divided into bodies of pikemen and musketeers, the use of musket and bayonet not yet being combined in the same weapons. The pike, made of ash, was fifteen or sixteen feet long, and headed with steel. *Musket and pike.*

The musket or matchlock was not advanced beyond the first stage of invention. The spark to fire the gunpowder was applied from the outside, instead of being produced by the concussion of flint and steel. The match consisted of little ropes of tow, boiled in spirit; these, when lighted at one end, smouldered on until the whole was consumed. The musket was still such a heavy and cumbersome weapon that it had to be fixed on a rest. This rest was made of ash-wood, headed at one end with iron to fix in the ground, and having at the other a half hoop of iron. Before the end of the war the musketeer was relieved of this additional burden. Rests were disused owing to the introduction of lighter and more portable muskets. To a belt, fastened round the musketeer's left shoulder, hung a bullet bag, some twists of spare match, a flask of touch powder, and a bandeleer, with twelve little cases, made of leather or tin, each of which contained a separate charge of powder. As loading and firing were both long operations, only one rank fired at a time, and the

* The dragoons are said to have received their name from the locks of the first muskets in use amongst them, on which was represented a *dragon's* head with a lighted match in its jaws, a natural image of a death-dealing engine. Both weapon and name came from France. The cuirassiers were so called from the original name of the back and breast piece, a cuirasse. Like other pieces of defensive arms the cuirasse was made of leather (cuir) before it was made of iron. Buff was leather like buffalo-hide; it would often turn a sword-cut.

musket was by no means so great an advance in the art of destruction as we might suppose from our experience of the modern rifle. Field guns were also cumbersome, and seem to have done little execution. It was when the ranks had come to push of pike, or when the victors mercilessly cut down the flying foe with the sword, that the dead fell thickest. There were no regular uniforms. Different regiments of infantry on either side often wore buff coats dyed the colour belonging to the house of their colonel. Thus Hampden's men wore green coats; Lord Grey's blue; others, red, purple, and gray. All the officers of the Parliament wore orange scarfs, the colour of the house of Essex. But in the confusion of the battle, a twig of green, a sprig of broom, or a bit of coloured riband, fastened to the hat, with the help of the word for the day, was the chief guide by which to distinguish friend from foe.

Edgehill, which forms 'the face or edge of the tableland of the north of Oxfordshire,' looks abruptly down on the Warwickshire level below, and as it is approached from Kineton, stands out a long bold line of hill against the horizon. The eastern slopes rise more gently, and hither on Sunday morning, the 23rd of October, came the Royalist regiments from their scattered quarters on the Southam and Banbury road, many of them having to march eight miles or more before they reached the summit. The side of the hill, which faces Kineton, is now covered with large trees, wearing on an October day all the varied tints of autumn, but then only a few bushes were scattered over it. The undulating plain below, lying between Kineton and Radway, now all brought under cultivation and crossed by innumerable hedgerows, was then an open desolate-looking pasture ground; one long hedge alone, which survives to the present day and probably marked the enclosure of an old homestead there, struck across it about midway between the two villages.

Essex saw the Royalist horse moving on the top of Edgehill before eight o'clock, and at once formed his army in front of Kineton, facing south-east, ready to fight if the king should come down and offer battle on equal terms. Several causes induced Charles to gratify the wishes of his enemies, and abandon his unassailable position on the summit of Edgehill. Extreme confidence prevailed amongst the Cavaliers. Rupert made no doubt of victory, and urged immediate battle. It was known

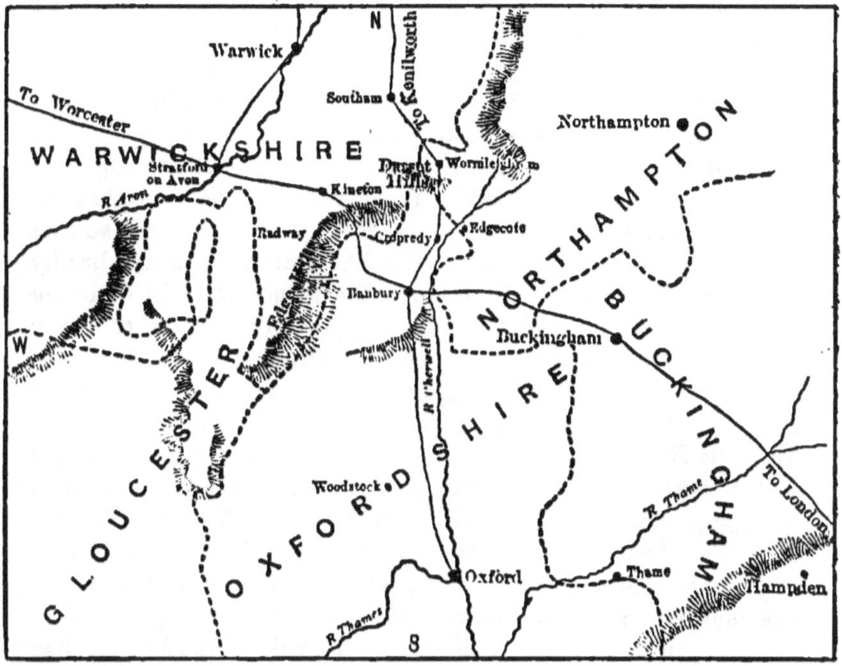
N
Warwick
To Worcester
Southam
To Kenilworth
Northampton
WARWICKSHIRE
Stratford on Avon
Kineton
R Avon
Radway
Edgecote
Cropredy
Banbury
Edge Hill
NORTHAMPTON
BUCKINGHAM
Buckingham
W
GLOUCESTER
OXFORDSHIRE
R Cherwell
Woodstock
To London
R Thame
Thame
Oxford
Hampden
R Thames
S

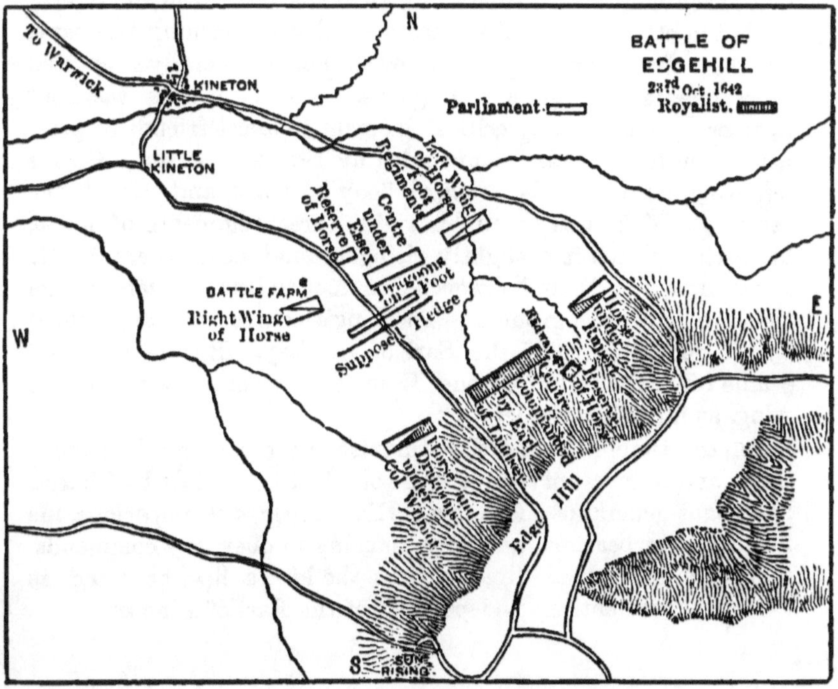
To Warwick
N
KINETON
BATTLE OF EDGEHILL
23rd Oct. 1642
Parliament
Royalist.
LITTLE KINETON
Left Wing of Horse
Foot Regiments
Centre under Essex
Reserve of Horse
Dragoons of Foot
BATTLE FARM
Right Wing of Horse
Supposed Hedge
W
E
Radway
Horse under Rupert
Reserve of Horse
Centre commanded by Earl of Lindsey
Horse and Dragoons under Col. Wilmot
Edge Hill
S
SUN RISING

that two regiments of horse and one of foot under Colonel Hampden were a day's march behind the rest of Essex' army, engaged in bringing up some artillery, which it was hard to drag through the heavy clayey soil. Lastly, ever since the army had reached Kenilworth, there was no food to be got. The country people, in these Midland counties more inclined to the Parliament than to the king, and frightened by reports of the cruel and plundering habits of the Cavaliers, had hidden their provisions, so that some of the common soldiers were half starved, and had hardly eaten bread for forty-eight hours. The prince thought no better remedy could be found to bring the people to their reason than a victory gained over the rebels. Accordingly the Royalists formed on the top of Edgehill, fronting the north-west, ready to march down the hill and give the enemy battle on the level between Radway and Kineton. The king's army was about 12,000 strong; that of Essex about 10,000. Both were disposed according to the tactics of the time. The main body of foot held the centre. Every corps of infantry consisted of pikemen and musketeers, the pikemen drawn up in the centre, the musketeers in the flanks. The lines were rarely less than ten deep, in order that when the front rank of musketeers had fired, they might have time to retire to the rear, form and reload, while the other nine ranks were severally performing the same motions. In either wing was placed the horse, generally supported by regiments of infantry or dragoons. A body of horse was kept in reserve, ready at any critical moment to assist friends or press hard upon foes. Essex commanded his centre in person. On his left wing, he placed his principal body of horse, and part of five regiments of infantry; on his right, three regiments of horse, his artillery on some slightly rising ground near where Battle Farm now stands, and dragoons on foot to line the long hedge that ran across the ground. The king's centre was commanded by his general-in-chief, the Earl of Lindsey. Rupert was half a mile off to the right; Colonel Wilmot, who commanded the left wing, as far off on the left.

*Disposition of armies.*

Rupert, though far more distinguished for courage than judgment, and only twenty-three years old, had been made by Charles lieutenant-general of the horse. His temper was imperious, his manners overbearing, and now, refusing to obey any commands, except those received directly from the king's lips, he acted as though he was entirely independent of the Earl of Lindsey.

About one o'clock, the Royalists, having a front of two miles, streamed down the hill in three lines, their two wings gradually converging towards their centre as they approached the enemy. It was already three o'clock, and the October day on its decline, before the battle commenced. "Come life or death," said Charles to his principal officers, as he left his tent, "your king will bear you company," and with his own hand fired the first piece of artillery.

As Rupert was advancing upon the enemy's left wing, Sir Faithful Fortescue, a major in Essex' army, and his whole troop of horse, rode forward and joined the ranks of the prince. Thus encouraged, the Cavaliers charged impetuously, while the Parliament's horse, inexperienced, and panic-stricken by the base desertion of their comrades, having once fired their pistols into the air, turned their horses' heads and fled, throwing into confusion several regiments of infantry behind them, which also took to flight, in spite of all the efforts of their officers. Essex' left wing routed. "The Lord Mandeville's* men would not stand the field, though his lordship beseeched, nay cudgelled, them ; no nor yet the Lord Wharton's men ; Sir William Fairfax his regiment, except some eighty of them, used their heels." Horse and foot fled in one confusion together towards Kineton, whither they were closely pursued by Rupert, who was intent on plundering the baggage carts, which could be seen standing unguarded in the village streets.

Meanwhile, on the king's left wing, the Royalists had been equally successful in clearing the field of the larger part of the Parliamentary horse. But whatever advantage Essex' right wing routed. these mounted gentlemen gained over the raw recruits of the Parliament, who had but just learnt to sit a horse or fire a pistol, was all lost through want of subordination to their general. For what folly in Rupert to be plundering at Kineton, instead of seeing how the battle went under Edgehill ! What rashness in the king's reserve of horse, whose special function it was to decide the day by a charge at the critical moment on the critical point, and as a reserve never to follow up an advantage till the whole field was theirs, to clap spurs into their horses, and without orders join in this idiotic pursuit of one wing of the enemy, while his centre was still unbroken ! These heedless acts lost the king his victory. In the absence of all the Royalist horse from the field,

* Lord Kimbolton (p. 111), afterwards Earl of Manchester (p. 155).

the Parliament's reserve, after charging through the enemy's lines, and spiking several pieces of cannon, fell upon the rear of his centre. At the same time Essex, supported by the officers from his broken wings, who, scorning to fly with their men, had rallied around their own main battle, put himself at the head of his infantry, and fiercely charged the Royalist ranks in front. And now came the real struggle of the day. Charles, conspicuous in his steel armour and black velvet mantle, on which glittered his Star and George, rode into the leading ranks, encouraging his troops to hold their ground. But no valour could resist the odds against which his men were fighting, attacked at once in front and rear, and outflanked through the absence of their own wings and the superior numbers of the enemy. What slope of the ground there was favoured the troops of the Parliament; the slain and wounded fell by scores in the space of a few yards; the Earl of Lindsey, badly shot, was carried off the field by the enemy; the king's standard-bearer was slain, and his standard placed in the hands of Essex. But a gallant Royalist captain, by the simple artifice of fastening an orange scarf to his person, and riding boldly up to the earl's secretary, to whose keeping the prize had been entrusted, succeeded in quietly taking it from him, saying it was not fit for a penman to have the honour of carrying that standard; then bearing it back in triumph to the king, he was knighted beneath its shadow.

<small>Meeting of centres.</small>

Charles, though he had only a hundred horse about him, and was within half a musket-shot of the enemy, refused to retire. He ordered Charles and James, his two boys of twelve and nine years old, who were by his side, to be taken out of danger. His physician, the great Harvey, the discoverer of the circulation of the blood, having retired with the princes to the shelter of some bushes, took a book out of his pocket, and read, quite regardless of the turmoil round him, until a bullet grazed the ground close by, and warned him to remove his charges out of range.

Meanwhile Rupert and the Cavaliers, after plundering the baggage, were following up the pursuit of the Parliament's horse, when they were stopped at a hill a little beyond Kineton, which is still known as Rupert's headland, by the approach of Hampden's three regiments with the artillery. Rupert retreated hastily, but only to find the Royal infantry forced up under the foot of the hill, and the ground he had occupied in the morning now held by the troops of the Parlia-

<small>Rupert retires before Hampden.</small>

ment. "I can give a good account of the enemy's horse," he said, when he saw the confusion of his party. "Ay!" exclaimed a Cavalier, with an oath, "and of their carts too." As it was now half-past five, it was quite impossible to distinguish friends from foes, and the two armies drew apart. The Royalists passed the night at the foot and on the side of the hill, where, pinched with cold and hunger, they made what fires they might out of the few bushes growing about. Essex' troops also spent that Sunday night on the field, in little better plight than their enemies. "I had tasted no meat," says one, "since the Saturday before, and having nothing to keep me warm but a suit of iron, I was obliged to walk about all night, which proved very cold by reason of a sharp frost." Large numbers on both sides deserted during the night, and the next morning there was, in either army, a general unwillingness to renew the battle. The king retired, over Edgehill into Oxfordshire; Essex to Warwick, whence he had come.*

Though the Parliamentarians laid claim to a victory, the results of the battle seemed to favour the king. Banbury, Abingdon, Henley, opened their gates without a show of resistance; and soon Rupert and the Cavaliers were plundering the country in the very neighbourhood of London. Results of battle.

The disposition of London was most important. Not only did the opinions and acts of the Londoners exercise weight all over the kingdom, but on the readiness of the city merchants to lend money was likely for some time to depend the pay and maintenance of the Parliament's army. Though often terrified, the city never failed in its support to the Parliament, nor was it unfairly called by Charles "the nursery of the rebellion." It opened wide its coffers; sent out apprentices by thousands to enlist in the army; organized a formidable force of its own under the name of the city trained bands; and, in fact, was always ready to give the nation some striking, if not turbulent, proof of its zeal. Disposition of Londoners.

The principal motive that urged the citizens to support the war was their eager longing to be allowed to worship according to the forms of the Presbyterian Church. Had Charles at this time granted toleration to Presbyterians, he would have deprived the Parliament of some half of its most zealous supporters. The day

* Clar. Hist., iii.; Ludlow, i.; Ellis, Orig. Letters, 2nd series, iii. 303; May, 23; Warwick Mem., 231; Beesley, Hist. of Banbury, 308, 320; Grose, Hist. of Ancient Armour.

after Essex' arrival in London, Lord Brook,* who had fought at Edgehill, addressed a crowded audience at the Guildhall (8th Nov.). "Gentlemen, citizens of London," he said, "you must not think to fight in the sighs and tears of your wives and children. Therefore, when you hear the drums beat, say not, I beseech you, I am not of the trained band, nor this, nor that, nor the other, but doubt not to go out to the work, and this shall be the day of your deliverance. What is it we fight for? It is for our religion, and for our God, and for our liberty and all. And what is it they fight for? For their lust, for their wills, and for their tyranny; to make us slaves, and to overthrow all. Gentlemen, methinks I see your courage in your faces. I spy you ready to do anything, and the general's resolution is to go out to-morrow, and do as a man of courage and resolution, and never man did like him."†

In spite, however, of the exhortations of the leaders of the Parliament, and the presence of Essex and his army, fear was so prevalent in the city that the Commons sent a petition to the king, proposing a treaty. Charles, after returning a gracious answer, in which he called God to witness his great desire for peace and offered to treat at Windsor or wherever else he might be (12th Nov.), took advantage of a thick mist to advance unperceived from Colnbrook, and fall upon a few regiments of foot and a small party of horse, that garrisoned Brentford and protected the road to London (13th Nov.).‡ For this action he was accused by his enemies of treachery. Since no ces-

*Proposed Treaty. Attack on Brentford.*

---

\* Heir to Sir Fulke Greville, to whom James I. granted the barony, with Warwick Castle. † Parl. Hist., ii.
‡ On this occasion Milton fixed this sonnet on his door, claiming the reverence Lysander showed to the city of Euripides, and Alexander to the poet of Thebes:

> Captain or colonel, or knight in arms,
> Whose chance on these defenceless doors may seize,
> If deed of honour did thee ever please,
> Guard them, and him within protect from harms.
> He can requite thee, for he knows the charms
> That call fame on such gentle acts as these,
> And he can spread thy name o'er lands and seas,
> Whatever clime the sun's bright circle warms.
> Lift not thy spear against the muses' bower:
> The great Emathian conqueror bid spare
> The house of Pindarus, when temple and tower
> Went to the ground: and the repeated air
> Of sad Electra's poet had the power
> To save the Athenian walls from ruin bare.

sation of arms had been made, he was justified, by the rules of war, in seizing any advantage that offered him an opportunity of treating from a more favourable position. Still he had been trusted as a king rather than as an enemy, and the citizens were exasperated on finding that his gracious answer to their petition had been intended as a mere blind, and that his hope, when he gave it, had been to enter London at the sword's point. Not a word was any longer heard of a treaty. All the night after the action at Brentford, the indignant city was pouring out men, encouraging its apprentices to en- list, and reinforcing the army of Essex out of its own train- bands. "Come, my boys, my brave boys," said their com- mander, Skippon, to these new troops, "I will run the same fortunes and hazards with you. Remember, the cause is for God, and for the defence of yourselves, your wives and children. Come, my honest and brave boys, pray heartily, and fight heartily, and God will bless us." Two days after the fight, 24,000 men were reviewed on Turnham Green, midway between London and Brentford ; yet Essex, habitually cautious, refused to risk a battle, so that the king was allowed to withdraw his troops, without opposition, to the neighbourhood of Oxford, a town devoted to his cause, which he intended making his head- quarters for the winter.  *Indignation in London.*

The whole country now began to take part in the war. Leaders on either side appeared in nearly every county, and maintained a desultory warfare. Towns, castles, houses, were fortified, garrisoned, and besieged. The number of the troops on each side depended on the inclinations of the people. Those counties alone enjoyed peace within their borders, in which one party far outnumbered the other. *Whole country engaged in struggle.*

In the east, where there were many towns engaged in the staple manufacture of England—woollen cloth—as Norwich, Sud- bury, Colchester, Yarmouth, and Lynn, the king's enemies so far outnumbered his friends, that all opposition to the Parliament was quickly crushed by the energy of Colonel Cromwell, who associated the seven counties of Norfolk, Essex, Suffolk, Cambridge, Hunt- ingdon, Lincoln, and Hertford together into a confederacy against the king. In Kent and the other south-eastern counties, though many of the gentry were Royalists, the Parliament's friends were so far the stronger, that little opposition could be offered them.

Berkshire went with Oxford for the king, while Hampshire and Wiltshire were battle-grounds between the two. In the west, where there were fewer freeholders than in the east, the king's friends predominated, though even here many important trading, manufacturing, or fishing towns were held for the Parliament, as Bristol, the second town in the kingdom for size and wealth, Gloucester, Weymouth, Plymouth, and Lyme. The backward district of Wales, and the Cornish, like their Breton brethren in later time, went wholly with their king and feudal lords: but elsewhere in the west, the king's enemies were generally to be found in numbers sufficient to keep the country in a state of constant warfare. In the midland counties, the partisans of the Parliament again predominated, though here the Royalists made head against their enemies, and held a strong garrison at Newark, in Nottinghamshire, by which communication was kept up between Oxford and York. North of the Humber, the two parties were about equally matched. The Earl of Newcastle and his numerous tenantry declared for the king; but many of the county freeholders joined the inhabitants of Bradford, Leeds, Wakefield, Halifax, Manchester, and the other seats of the woollen manufacture, in adhering to the Parliament. Thus, as generally happens in times of movement, the towns favoured progress, the country reaction.

The queen, who had been successful in Holland, through the interest of the Prince of Orange, her son-in-law, returned to England in the spring, accompanied by four ships, laden with arms and ammunition, soldiers and officers (22nd February.) She escaped the fleet of the Parliament in her passage, but about two days after her landing at Bridlington, in Yorkshire, the town was bombarded by Admiral Batten with such effect, that she was forced to fly from her lodging, and seek shelter in a ditch in the open fields, where balls scoured over her head. She escaped however without injury, and by the union of her resources with those of the Earl of Newcastle, a formidable army was soon raised, which was called by the friends of the Parliament 'the Northern Papist Army,' being regarded with special aversion.

Newcastle's army of 'Papists.' Papists there were in plenty amongst its ranks, for Charles, though in his printed delarations he constantly denied the fact, had ordered Newcastle to let any serve who would. "You see," said the joking earl, one day as he pointed out the weakness of some fortifications, "though they call us the army of Papists, we cannot trust in our good works."

The increasing power and success of the Royalist forces now caused discouragement to many friends of the Parliament, who had thought to bring the king to terms within a few months. In the Parliament and in the city, a peace party appeared, composed in large part of men who observed with annoyance the influence into which the war was raising both sectarians and people of inferior rank. It was not pleasant to the lord to hear himself spoken of as on an equality with a plain country gentleman; the Presbyterian did not like to hear the sectarian demanding toleration for all creeds; indignation burnt in more breasts than those of Royalists, when the tale was told how Admiral Batten had done such an ungracious, unchivalrous act as to fire on the very house the queen was in. Some began to think it time to change sides. The governor of Scarborough betrayed his trust, and surrendered the town to the queen. Sir John Hotham, governor of Hull, would now have followed this example, had not the Parliament discovered his intention in time to prevent its execution. Many Presbyterians would gladly have made peace, if only they could have obtained the king's consent to the establishment of their own Church: while the evils of the hour made those who were no friends to arbitrary power overlook the many proofs they had experienced of Charles' ill faith, and forget the importance of the cause for which they were engaged. But the leaders of the Commons, Pym, Hampden, and their close followers, never wavered for an instant; they had taken the resolution of continuing the war until the king was really conquered and forced to submit to terms that would deprive him of power to injure his subjects' liberties, and from this resolution they never swerved. These firmer spirits found their warmest supporters in the sectarians, to whom peace and a consequent triumph of Presbyterians or Episcopalians offered nothing but a prospect of bitter persecution. At Oxford councils were as divided as at Westminster. There also two parties appeared; the one desired to restore Charles to the exercise of absolute power at the sword's point; the other to obtain by negotiations a peace restoring him to the exercise of power bounded by law. The war party was led by the king's nephews, Rupert and Maurice, two imperious young foreigners. "Tush," Rupert would say, when any objection was made to his commands, as contrary to law, "we will have no more law in England but the sword." This party was supported by the professional soldiers from the continent, the Papists, many of the country gentlemen, and by courtiers and self-seekers generally, who thought that if a peace were effected by negotiation, the rebels at Westminster would get too good terms for themselves, and the king be unable to reward his friends sufficiently for their services. The peace party, on the other hand, was composed of men of less selfish and less violent dispositions, who, though fighting under Charles' banner, loved their country's liberties, and grieved over its sufferings. The people, indeed, endured much, and the war was raising up a bitter spirit even between members of the same families. The nearest relations constantly fought in opposite ranks, and it was no uncommon tale to hear of the dying soldier who took his death the more heavily because he had seen the fatal shot fired by a brother's hand. The courteous and affable Lord Falkland was so altered by grief, that to his friends he seemed hardly the same man. He became pale, morose, short in his answers, untidy in his dress; and sitting among his friends would after a long silence cry out passionately, "Peace, peace," and say, "that the very agony of the war, and the view of the calamities and desolation the kingdom did and must endure, took his sleep from him, and would shortly break his heart." So loud was the cry for peace raised, both in London and at Oxford, that the extreme party on either side was obliged to yield and

Peace propositions offered at Oxford.

allow negotiations to be held (March). The propositions now drawn up for the king's acceptance, like those before offered at York, required him to abolish Episcopacy, and to resign the command of the militia and other executive powers to Parliament.

Charles, having been proved a match for his opponents in arms, of course refused these terms. Though he pretended to be exceedingly desirous for peace, he belonged at heart to the war party, and looked forward to being restored to an arbitrary throne by the force of his friends' swords. Angrily interrupting the Earl of Northumberland, when reading as one of the Parliament's propositions, 'A bill to vindicate the five members,' he proposed as his final answer that the Parliament should deliver into his hands forts, towns, magazines, ships, and revenue, and adjourn to some place twenty miles from the capital, in which case he would consent to the disbanding of the armies, and speedily return to London. By this, negotiations were at once broken off (15th April). Soon after a plot was discovered, which had been formed by some of the disappointed peace party. Their design was to seize the leaders of the Parliament, occupy the military posts, and then admit the royal forces into the city (May). {Waller's plot.}

The intercepted letters by which the plot was discovered implicated Waller, the poet, a cousin of Cromwell, and a member of Parliament; and by his confessions, several others were involved. But though it was startling to discover the presence of traitors within the very walls of the Commons' House, Pym, acting with his accustomed moderation, did not increase the irritation of the friends of peace by pressing uncertain evidence. Out of five persons condemned by court-martial, only two were executed. Waller, who had made a most abject submission, was allowed to escape with no greater punishment than a fine and a short imprisonment.

Meanwhile, both parties made ready for a second summer's campaign. The Parliament's officers were divided in counsel. Hampden advised an immediate advance upon Oxford, but Essex persisted in first laying siege to Reading. The war party began to be doubtful of the zeal of their general, and took {Distrust of Essex.} little trouble to see that his troops were well supplied with pay and clothing. His conduct led men to think that he wished, not to reduce the king to the Parliament's mercy, but only to keep up a balance of parties and so bring about a peace by negotiation. After Edgehill, he had retreated to Warwick, leaving the road to London open to the enemy—a movement several of his officers failed to understand. After the action at Brentford, he had refused to risk a battle, saying he dared not trust his young and raw recruits. Men who wished to conquer would gladly have seen Colonel Hampden command in Essex' place. Hampden's regiment of green-coats, raised and trained by himself, was known as one of the best in the army; his military genius he had proved unmistakably in many minor actions; his daring was more likely to lead to victory than Essex' caution. But no one ventured to propose to displace the earl. All the peace party, all the Presbyterians, were warmly attached to him, while many noblemen and gentlemen would have been averse to serving under any one his inferior in rank.

But the first and last duty of a general is to win, and he must be chosen for no other object. A half-hearted policy ruins an army, and either ruins a cause or prolongs the miseries of war. Through the hesitation of their aristocratic leader, a series of disasters now befell the Parliament's forces. Essex' head-quarters were at Thame, a few miles east of Oxford. His army, through disease and desertion, had gradually dwindled down to a force of about 5000 men. Though long urged by Hampden to act boldly on the offensive, or at least to concentrate his troops, now too scattered to be safe, he persisted in maintaining a defensive attitude on a weak and extended line. His troops, thus dotted about in detachments, were hardly able to defend their own outposts, much

*Essex at Thame.* less the neighbouring counties, against the Cavaliers, who weekly, almost nightly, crept out of Oxford to burn and plunder villages and manor houses. It was on one of these occasions that the Parliament experienced the loss of a leader who was not to be replaced. A body of Royalists, commanded by Rupert himself, had surprised a troop at Chinnor on the Chilterns, and were bearing off booty and prisoners in triumph to Oxford. Colonel Hampden started in pursuit from Watlington, and overtook them at Chalgrove Common on their way to the bridge over the Thame at Chiselhampton. A sharp

*Death of Hampden (24th June).* skirmish followed. At the first charge two balls entered Hampden's shoulder and broke the bone. A prisoner brought the news to Oxford. "I saw him," he said, "ride off the field before the action was done, which he never used to do, and with his head hanging down, and resting his hands upon the neck of his horse" (18th June). Hampden only lived for a week more. After receiving the sacrament, he prayed with his last breath that the God of hosts would 'have 'these realms in His special keeping: that He would level in the 'dust those who would rob the people of their liberty, and would 'let the king see his error and turn the hearts of his wicked 'counsellors from the malice of their designs.' "O Lord, save my bleeding country," were almost the last words he spoke. His body, carried from Thame to be buried at his native village of Hampden, was followed as a hero's to the grave by soldiers with heads uncovered, drums and ensigns muffled, arms reversed. The grief of soldier and citizen was real enough. As general and as statesman Hampden had the true leader's spirit, whose presence inspires followers with confidence and commands their sympathy by mere contact. "The memory of the deceased colonel," says a newspaper of the day, "is such that in no age to come but it will more and more be had in honour and esteem; a man so religious, and of that prudence, judgment, temper, valour, and integrity, that he hath left few his like behind." After three hundred and thirty years we can but endorse the verdict.

It seemed as though all the forces of the Parliament were dispirited by Hampden's death. In the north Fairfax, defeated by Newcastle at Atherton Moor near Bradford (30th June), was shut up in Hull, so that the eastern counties lay open to the approach of the northern 'Papist' army. In the west their successful general, Sir William Waller, suffered two severe defeats; in fact, the king's commanders there, Prince Maurice and Sir Ralph Hopton, 'the soldier's darling,' gained one success on another, until the Parliament lost all its hold over the three counties of Devon, Somerset, and Wilts. The Cornish peasants and the Cavaliers united overcame all enemies. The former would ask their commander's leave to fetch off cannon from hills surmounted with breastworks, and dauntlessly perform what they proposed—a feat repeated by their Breton brethren at La Vendée—the latter would think it play-work to storm defences, on which the soldiers of the Parliament would have looked askance. Stories went about amongst the terrified garrisons "that the king's soldiers made nothing of running up walls twenty feet high, and that no works could keep them out." One town after another surrendered during the summer and autumn months; Taunton, Bridgewater, Bath (July), Dorchester, Weymouth, Portland, Barnstaple, Bideford (August), Exeter (September 4). Prince Rupert took Bristol by storm. The governor, Nathaniel Fiennes, capitulated without disputing his entrance by a hand to hand fight in the streets, though Rupert's losses had been heavy enough to warrant the attempt (25th July). It was agreed that the garrison should march off with arms and baggage, and the townspeople be preserved from plunder and violence. But the Cavaliers, without regard to the terms they had made, plundered the waggons belonging to the garrison and sacked the city; and so mercenary was the spirit of some of the Parliament's troops, that they took service in Rupert's army, and pointed out to their new friends the houses

*Royalist successes in north and west.*

*Bristol stormed by Cavaliers.*

where the most valuable plunder might be found. By the middle of the summer, Gloucester was the only important city still held for the Parliament in the west.

*Peace propositions of Lords.* The news of the surrender of Bristol, the second town in the kingdom, caused extreme depression in London. The House of Lords drew up propositions for peace, the most moderate yet brought forward. Both armies were to be disbanded; the militia question was to be settled by a future Parliament, the Church by a future synod. After a long and fierce debate, the propositions were carried in the Commons by a majority of twenty-nine votes (5th Aug.). The vote was an act of political suicide, and the war party appealed from Parliament to the people, knowing that if Charles returned to London on these terms, his word would be no guarantee for the performance of his promises. The result was that *Tumults in London.* two days after the propositions were passed, the Lord Mayor and Common Council came to the door of the Commons to present a petition against peace, followed by a tumultuous rabble of several thousands. The demonstration succeeded, and the House agreed by a majority of seven to lay aside the peace propositions (7th Aug.).

Two days after this scene had occurred, some hundreds of women, wearing white silk ribands in their hats, as an emblem of their mission, came to the Commons' House, bearing a counter-petition for peace. Four or five members went to the door, and telling them that the House was no enemy to peace, ordered them to return to their homes. But dissatisfied with this answer, they stayed on, and by noon there were some 5000 women, with men amongst them dressed in women's clothes, pressing round about the house, allowing none to pass in or out, and crying, " Peace, peace," " Give us those traitors that are against peace," " Give us that dog, Pym."

The Parliament's guards, after firing powder without dispersing the mob, loaded with ball and shot a ballad-singer dead at the moment she was urging her companions on with her songs. A troop of cavalry at the same time coming up, charged in upon the crowd, slashing with their swords at hands and faces, until the women fled on all sides, leaving some seven or eight of their number lying wounded or dead upon the ground (9th Aug.). The friends of peace, disgusted with such scenes and with their own defeat, tried to persuade Essex to make use of his army in forcing the Parliament to offer propositions to the king. But Essex, though he had himself advised the Parliament to treat, was too honourable to think of betraying his trust, and felt indignant that such a proposal should have been made to him. In consequence of his refusal, seven lords and several members of the Commons changed sides and went to Oxford.*

Extreme danger now threatened the Parliament. There was no force between Oxford and London to oppose the king's approach, except Essex' wretched army, whose thinned ranks had not yet been refilled. The Parliament, says May, its own historian, "was then in a low ebb; and before the end of that July, they had no forces at all to keep the field, their main armies being quite ruined. Thus seemed the Parliament to be quite sunk beyond any hope of recovery, and was so believed by many men. The king was possessed of all the western counties from the farthest part of Cornwall, and from thence northward as far as the borders of Scotland. His armies were full and flourishing, free to march wherever they pleased, and numerous enough to be divided for several exploits." Charles judged rightly that the time had come, when one bold stroke might finish the war. His plan was conceived with unusual force and spirit. His own and Newcastle's army were to converge on the capital and form a junction within sight of it. But his generals were jealous of one another, and slow to obey even royal commands. Newcastle was not inclined to give up the independent authority he had in the north, merely to be domineered over by Prince Rupert; so he sent word to Charles, that he could not carry out his orders and march through the associated counties upon London, because he was sure the gentlemen in his army would refuse to leave Yorkshire unless Hull were first reduced. Meanwhile, the desertion of many of the peace party had united the friends of the Parliament, while the extremity of the danger itself inspired them. The Londoners were hard at work raising fortifications for the protection of their threatened city. Thousands were to be seen, men and women of every "profession, trade, and occupation," marching out daily in a body to dig at their appointed place of labour, with colours flying and drums beating before

* Clar., iv. 175 ; May, 214.

them. The tailors went out 8000 strong, the watchmen 7000, the shoemakers numbered 5000 ; the very oyster women from Billingsgate 1000. It was one of those stirring moments when all feel proud to labour, and knights, ladies, and gentlemen might be seen marching out with the crowd, spade and mattock in hand, so that within a few weeks a breastwork was raised all round the city for a circuit of twelve miles, strengthened by twenty-four forts and carrying 212 pieces of cannon.* Before, however, these fortifications were fully completed, the citizens breathed more freely. Newcastle's aversion to leave Yorkshire brought them a respite when their doom seemed fixed. His dislike of the plan, falling in, as it did, with the feeling of many of the officers, induced Charles to try and make the conquest of the west complete by besieging Gloucester, before marching east. The town was known to be badly provided with stores ; everybody said it could not hold out long ; and Massey, the governor, was suspected of an inclination to desert the side of the Parliament. The king summoned the town, fully expecting it would surrender at once, but a stern defiance was brought from 'the godly city of Gloucester' by two citizens, whose plain garb, close cut hair, Scripture phrases, and quiet yet assured demeanour marked them out as undoubted Puritans. "Waller is extinct, and Essex cannot come," replied Charles, quietly, more surprised than disconcerted at the confidence they displayed, so sure was he that the town would be compelled to surrender before the Parliament could find an army for its relief (10th Aug.).†

*March on London deferred.*

Much hung on the resolution of this garrison of 1500 men, who possessed but forty barrels of gunpowder and a slender artillery. If they yielded, Charles would turn immediately upon the disheartened and defenceless capital ; if they resisted, the Parliament would obtain a breathing time in which to recruit its forces. Neither soldiers nor citizens showed any lack of resolution. They set on fire the suburbs of the town, in order to deprive the Royalists of shelter while forming their entrenchments. They made constant sallies, and met the besiegers' mines by counter mines. The women and children daily laboured at repairing the breaches, and sallied out under the eyes of the king's horse to fetch in the turf. There was little

*Siege of Gloucester, 10th Aug.— 5th Sept.*

* Somers, Tracts, iv.; May, 314.
† May, 218; Somers, Tracts, v.; Clar. Hist., iv. 167.

complaining heard in the streets, and no disaffection took place amongst the garrison. Though constant opportunities were offered by the sallies, only three soldiers deserted. Though the country people, whose cattle the Royalists were killing by thousands through mere wantonness, implored the town to surrender, soldiers and citizens endured on, trusting that relief would come to them in time.

"Waller is extinct, and Essex cannot come," Charles, in his confidence, had said. But he was wrong. With wonderful speed the thinned ranks of the Parliament's army were filled up; four regiments of the London train-bands volunteered for the service, and Essex left London on the 24th of August at the head of 14,000 men. He conducted his march with speed and dexterity, driving before him a body of horse sent by the king to oppose him; but the besieged had no knowledge of the succour which was coming, still less of its whereabouts, until, on the 4th of September, they heard the sound of guns fired from the Presbury hills. The next morning they saw the royal forces withdraw from their trenches, fire their huts, and depart. Relief had come but just in time, for the garrison had only three barrels of gunpowder left.* {Essex relieves Gloucester.}

Essex, after re-supplying Gloucester with provisions and ammunition, returned eastwards for the protection of London. The Royalists at first did not know what road he had taken, and he succeeded in surprising their garrison at Cirencester and securing their supplies for himself before pursuit commenced. He had nearly crossed the Wiltshire Downs between Swindon and Hungerford, when Rupert and the Cavaliers attacked his rear while embarrassed in some deep lanes, near Aldbourn Chase, and a sharp skirmish took place, in which the Parliamentarians suffered considerable loss. Charles, while Rupert delayed the enemy, had pressed on with the infantry by forced marches on a more direct road to Newbury, which he entered the following day, so that Essex, on approaching it from the Hungerford side, found the road to London barred (19th Sept.). {March to Newbury.}

South of Newbury, which lies low on the banks of the Kennet, the ground gradually rises, until, at the distance of about a mile from the town, it reaches the level of a long line of hill, running east and west, and dividing the beds of the two rivers, the Kennet and the Emborne. This high ground was then open common;

* Somers, Tracts, v.; May, 222.

## MAP OF NEWBURY.

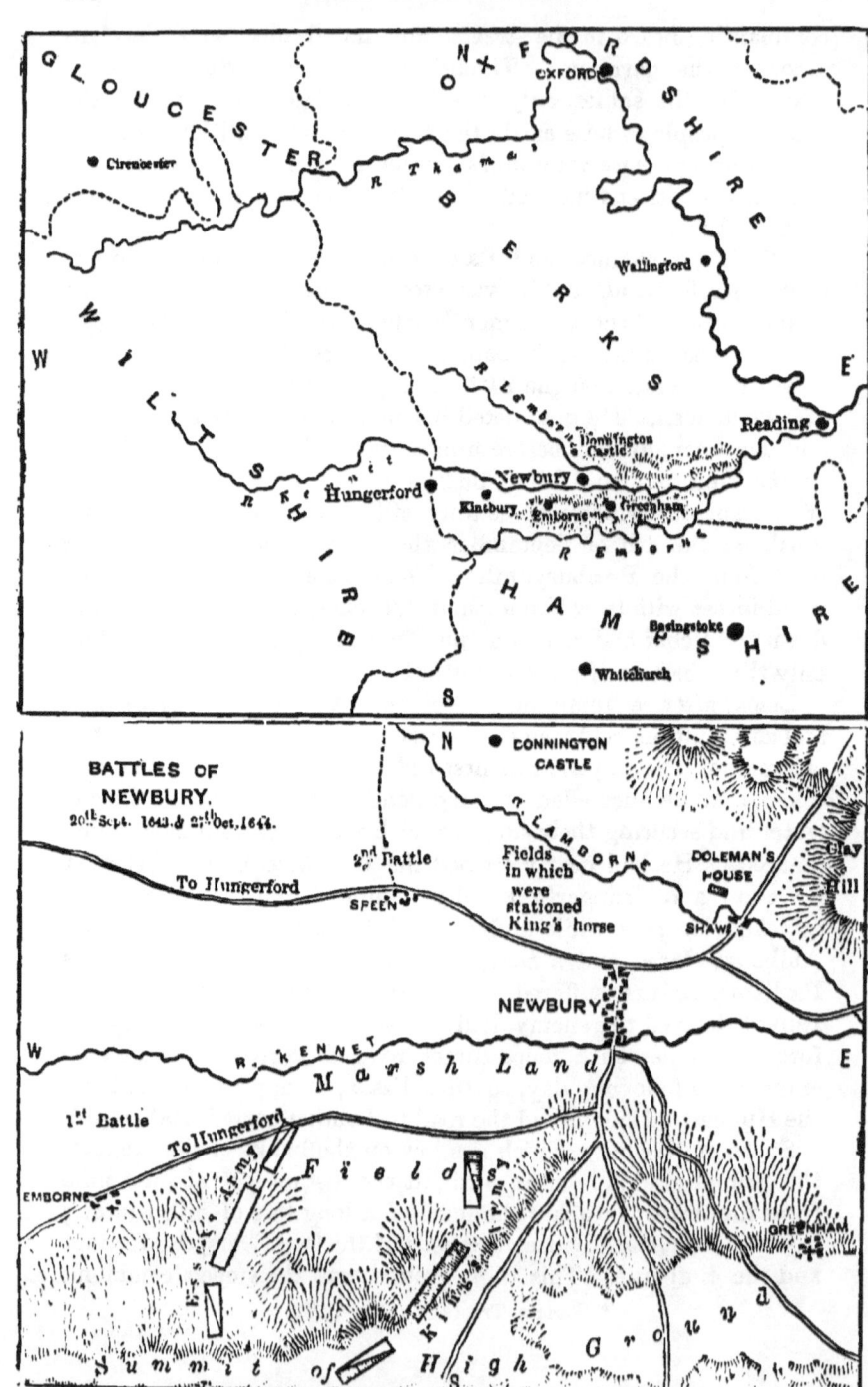

but the side of the spur sloping down to Newbury, as well as much of the low ground lying nearer the Kennet, was under cultivation and crossed by hedgerows. Charles stationed his left wing, centre, and artillery upon the brow of the hill, facing west towards Emborne and Hungerford, his right wing only on the lower ground in front of Newbury, protected by hedges and resting on the Kennet. Aware of the strength of this position, he determined, with the advice of his chief officers, to maintain a defensive attitude there, and not advance to meet the enemy as the more hot-headed subordinates would have liked. The Parliamentarians, on the other hand, could have no choice but to attack, as the enemy lay between them and their supplies, and to attack meant forcing their way up a hillside in the face of an artillery fire before they could come to close quarters.

On seeing the king's tactics, Essex drew up his army upon some open ground in front of Emborne. Two causes compelled him to fight at all hazards. The first, that, for the protection of London, it was necessary he should make his way through the enemy; the second, that, while delay mattered nothing to the king, who could refresh his troops in Newbury, and draw provisions, if necessary, from his garrisons at Wallingford and Oxford, it was fatal to himself, lying in the open fields and in an unfriendly country. The king, on the other hand, failed to reap the advantages of his position; for he could not secure the obedience of his own followers any more than of his Parliament. His own wise resolution was broken by the rashness and insubordination of his officers, some of whom, despising the London militia, and making sure of victory, became so excited at the sight of an enemy drawn up for action that they charged impetuously and, the battle soon becoming general, obliged their friends to advance for their support, leaving much of the artillery behind them on the hill. Many of the officers flung off their doublets in bravado, and led on their men in their shirts, as if armour was a useless encumbrance in dealing with the base-born apprentices, whom they came rather to triumph over than to fight.

Essex' left and the king's right were so impeded by the hedges that they could only engage in small parties. The horse, however, on the king's left found a free passage down a lane by which Essex had intended to advance his right. Essex' horse, though at first thrown into

*Hedges prevent horse from deciding the day.*

some disorder, soon rallied, and returned the charge of the impetuous Cavaliers. But in an enclosed country as this was the cavalry could not have much effect in deciding the day. It was the daring and skill of Essex, and the valour of the troops he led —the very train-bands the Royalists despised—that were destined to win the laurels of the field. The general, "being foremost in person, did lead up the city regiments, and when a vast body of the enemy's horse had given so violent a charge, that they had broken quite through, he quickly rallied his men together, and with undaunted courage did lead them up the hill. In this way he did beat the infantry of the king from hedge to hedge, and after six hours' long fight planted his ordnance upon the brow of the hill. The train-bands of the City of London endured the chiefest heat of the day, for being now upon the brow of the hill, they lay not only open to the horse but to the cannon of the enemy; yet they stood undaunted and conquerors against all, and like a grove of pines, in a day of wind and tempest, they only moved their heads, but kept their footing sure." It was on this hard-fought day that Lord Falkland met his death. In the morning he seemed to have recovered a little of his old cheerfulness, and dressed himself with unusual care, saying, "he was weary of his country's misery, and believed he should be out of it before night." Though his duties as the king's secretary gave him no position in the field, he fought as a volunteer at the head of Lord Byron's regiment of horse. This was on the right wing, where the ground was cut up by enclosures. Byron found his approach to a body of the enemy's infantry impeded by a high quick hedge. A single gap offered a passage through, which was so narrow that only one horse could pass at a time. The enemy stationed on the other side of the hedge were keeping up a hot fire, and as Byron viewed the place his horse was shot under him. While he retired to remount, Lord Falkland, "more gallantly than advisedly," clapped spurs into his horse, and charged through the gap. In an instant horse and rider fell dead together.* His end gives us a painful insight into the misery the more delicate minds endured during such a time. There was no doubt his life had been a burden to him for months.

*Death of Lord Falkland.*

* Lord Byron's account of battle of Newbury, in a letter to Hyde, in MSS. Clar. State Papers in Bodleian, No. 1738.

A patriot at heart, he had chosen his side from chivalry rather than from insight; and, though he followed his king, had no sympathy for that policy of 'thorough' which lay at the root of the civil war.

Darkness at last caused the two armies to separate. Both spent the night on the hill, the Royalists retiring to the further side of it, towards Greenham, and leaving the ground they had held in the morning in the hands of the Parliament's infantry. Essex fully expected the battle to be renewed the next day, and determined to force his way through the enemy or die. But the Royalists were dispirited. Though the loss of life was not so great as might have been expected, it had fallen heavily upon men of rank. More than twenty officers, distinguished for birth or merit, were among the dead. Such a catastrophe seemed to the king's friends in no way compensated by the loss of an equal number of obscure Parliamentary colonels. With these feelings the Royalists withdrew during the night into Newbury. Essex, finding the way by Greenham open before him, continued his march to Reading and London.* Charles, after leaving Newbury, retired to Oxford for the winter.† *Royalists withdraw into Newbury. Essex marches to London.*

* Byron's letter to Hyde leaves no doubt that Essex, instead of marching through Newbury (as is often stated), kept south of the Kennet. "The next morning early, Essex, finding the ground quitted by us, drew his army upon it, and there made a bravado in sight of ours, which was then drawn into the town of Newbury. Prince Rupert marched with such horse as were nearest to him, and fell on the enemy's rear as they marched off. But the country being full of enclosures secured them so that no great execution could be done upon them before they recovered Reading, and thus concluded the battle."

† May, Long Parl.; Clar. Hist.; Rush, Abr., v.; Account in Harl. Miscellany; Lord Byron's letter to Hyde in Clar. Papers in Bodleian, 1738.

# CHAPTER VII.

### RISE OF INDEPENDENTS.—BATTLE OF MARSTON MOOR.—
### SELF-DENYING ORDINANCE.—1643—1645.

Ἐπίπεσι πολλὰ καὶ χαλεπὰ κατὰ στάσιν ταῖς πόλεσι, γιγνόμενα μὲν καὶ ἀεὶ ἐσόμενα ἕως ἂν ἡ αὐτὴ φύσις ἀνθρώπων ᾖ, μᾶλλον δὲ καὶ ἡσυχαίτερα καὶ τοῖς εἴδεσι διηλλαγμένα ὡς ἂν ἕκασται αἱ μεταβολαὶ τῶν ξυντυχιῶν ἐφιστῶνται. ἐν μὲν γὰρ εἰρήνῃ καὶ ἀγαθοῖς πράγμασιν αἵ τε πόλεις καὶ οἱ ἰδιῶται ἀμείνους τὰς γνώμας ἔχουσι, διὰ τὸ μὴ ἐς ἀκουσίους ἀνάγκας πίπτειν. ὁ δὲ πόλεμος, ἀφελὼν τὴν εὐπορίαν τοῦ καθ' ἡμέραν βίαιος διδάσκαλος καὶ πρὸς τὰ παρόντα τὰς ὀργὰς τῶν πολλῶν ὁμοιοῖ.—THUC. iii. 82.

The communities of Greece suffered all the embittering results of civil strife that visit men, and always will visit them, so long as human nature remains the same, though with more or less intensity, and varying in form, according to the special circumstances that arise in each case. The fact is, that, in times of peace and prosperity, states alike and individuals form their judgments in a better spirit from the absence of constraining necessities, while war, by besetting daily life with difficulties, teaches violence, and frames men's temper to suit their surroundings.

THOUGH the Parliament was saved, the Royalists might fairly boast that the balance of success was on their side. In the west they had driven their enemies out of every important town but Gloucester. In the north, the reduction of Hull would leave them masters of the whole of Yorkshire. It might well seem that the current of their success would remain unchecked, or that if there was a check, they could at any moment win a favourable peace by negotiation; but there were causes at work which made either of these results impossible.

Success did not improve the character of the king's troops. *Character of king's troops.* The cavaliers and officers were becoming cruel and rapacious in their habits of warfare; while the common soldiers, often in want of pay, and retained in little discipline, followed the example of their leaders, and plundered the country people without distinction of friend or foe. Though feelings of honour still caused generals and officers to treat prisoners, their own equals in rank, with courtesy if not with generosity, the common soldier was too often ruthlessly handed over to the care of some inhuman gaoler. Rupert, on one occasion, marched prisoners from Cirencester to Oxford, half-clad, bareheaded, barefooted, bound together by cords, with gaping wounds still undressed, though there was a cutting wind and snow on the ground: the king, the two princes, and several lords, rode about a mile out of Oxford on purpose to see Rupert's prisoners come in; Charles was observed to smile: no words of pity, no order for their relief, passed his lips. If a tender-hearted Lord Falkland were by, what wonder he grew weary of his life, when such were the acts of his party? For the captives such marches were but the beginning of misery. Prisoners were kept crowded together for months in noisome dungeons, and sometimes left two days together without food. "I was so hungry," said one prisoner, after making a vain attempt to cut his throat, "the devil tempted me to cut it and be out of my misery."* This cruel usage of prisoners was not confined to the Royalists. The governor of Windsor Castle so starved the common soldiers committed to his keeping, that three men, it was said, fell down dead in the street on their release. Some hypocrites went so far as to parade their brutality as a proof of godliness. "My soul abhors to see this favour done to the enemies of God," said a turn-coat captain, addressing the wife of the governor of Nottingham Castle, as she bound up the wounds of her Royalist prisoners. Tales such as these, sayings ascribed to Puritans or Cavaliers, not to mention the harrowing details of battles and sieges—all these were published weekly, almost daily, in papers and pamphlets, and spread broadcast over the kingdom. No story was too foul or false to be refused a place in these publications. For instance, the *Mercurius Aulicus*, the chief Oxford paper, selecting domestic grief as an instance of God's judgments, after relating in a tone of exultation that death had deprived Hampden of his two eldest children, added gratuitously the lie that of his two remaining sons, the one was a cripple, the other a lunatic.† Slander thus did its part with violence and cruelty in embittering the feelings of men who, in

\* Somers, Tracts, iv. 510, 532.  † Forster, ii. 358.

the outset of the war, had felt almost as friends. Religious animosity helped to broaden the gulf. Ministers especially suffered. If they refused to read out the king's declarations, where the king had power, or the Parliament's declarations, where it had power, they had to fly their parishes to escape imprisonment. Thus deprived of home and livelihood, Puritans and Episcopalians had no choice but to take refuge with the nearest friendly garrison or come to regiments as chaplains. As they suffered most, they hated most. It was not bad usage only; as wars go on, the questions which touch men's hearts most deeply come more and more to the front. The church question was one of these, and one on which the ministers could not but feel deeply. So it was that the religious influence which should have tempered the bitterness of faction, gave its sanction to acts breathing more of the Old Testament than the New; and those who should have been the mediators taught that any parleying with the foe was treason against God. Thus the demands of the Parliamentarians increased, and there was no basis for negotiation, unless Charles would consent not simply to lessen the power of bishops, but to establish a non-Episcopal church. Through Scottish influence, Parliament had already summoned to London an assembly of divines to settle uniformity of worship for the two countries. This, of course, simply meant to discuss the means for the establishment of the Presbyterian Church in England (1st July). The bishops had completely lost all influence in the country, and as far as that went, Episcopacy was already dead. London was quite changed from the time when a gay court was held at Whitehall, when Laud lived at Lambeth, when cavaliers daily visited the artillery gardens, when crowds frequented the theatres. The grass was already growing in the courts of Whitehall;* Lambeth Palace was deserted, and was soon to be used as a prison. In the artillery gardens, once so gay, grave citizens now learnt the use of pike and musket; the theatres were all closed by order of Parliament (September 2nd, 1642). Services, preachings, and fasts had taken the place of the old bonfires, dances, and feasts. The book of sports had been burnt by the common hangman by another order of Parliament (5th May, 1643).

*Sufferings of clergy.*

*Assembly of divines.*

*London a Puritan city*

---

* Scotsman's letter in Somers Tracts, v.

Services were no more conducted with vestments and postures, lighted candles, and choirs. The wearing of any vestment was become a matter of indifference; the liturgy was read or prayers extemporized as minister and congregation pleased; organs, images, altars, were gone from churches. The beautiful old crosses, remains of Catholic times, and still left standing in the streets, were removed by order of Parliament. Presbyterians rejoiced to see bonfires made of "fine pictures of Christ and the saints, of relics, beads, and the like remains of Catholic superstition."*

The gaming houses were put down, and laws and ordinances for the punishment of vice† so strictly enforced, that no swearing was to be heard, no drunken man to be seen in the streets. Everybody led, or affected to lead, a life of strictness; for he who failed to attend some place of worship, or in public swore or drank, was looked upon as a reprobate, and could not hope to exercise any influence amongst his fellows. Sundays were no longer holidays of pleasure, but were strictly spent in religious services. In the evening men might pass through the town, and hear nothing but the voice of prayer and praise, from private houses as from churches.‡ No fruiterer or herb woman dared stand about and sell in the streets; no milk-woman cry her milk; no one but travellers by necessity might be received in taverns. Even if a child danced round a maypole, its parents were fined twelvepence for the offence. Fast days were observed after each success or failure, and, soon after the breaking out of the Irish rebellion, an order of Parliament was issued, enacting that the last Wednesday in every month should be kept regularly as a solemn fast and day of humiliation (8th January, 1642).

The Presbyterians, who now ruled, regarding as they did their own as the true church coeval with the early ages of Christianity, were unwilling to tolerate any other worship, and had they possessed the power would have been as despotic as the bishops. As it was, they persecuted as far as they dared. They hunted out Catholic priests, and put to death on an average about three a year;§ others they sent into banishment or left to die in prison. To keep under the

*Presbyterian intolerance.*

\* Birch, ii. 355; Baillie, i. 425.     † Neal, ii. 506.
‡ Neal, ii. 503; iii. 37.     § Lingard, viii. 35, 323.

sectarians, they tried to restrain the liberty of the press by passing an ordinance for the suppression of slanderous papers and pamphlets (11th June). But the sectarians were now too numerous to be crushed, and could disobey the ordinance with impunity.

Ideas grow rapidly in times of revolution. The habit of private judgment grows still more rapidly. The very means by which the popular leaders have carried the mass to their point of view, soon carry it beyond them. The pamphlets of the Presbyterians and Episcopalians had made the people controversialists; and in many cases undermined the authority of the teachers who had converted them. The same phenomenon occurred in the region of political strife. The war of words, bandied between patriots and Royalists, discussing the rights of King and Parliament, had familiarized the people with the discussion of constitutional questions. When such questions are left to popular discussion moderation is soon lost; violent opinions grow apace, and the claims of custom and prescription evaporate, like subtler elements, in that rough crucible. Out of the ranks of the sectarians arose a new set of political reformers, who no longer ascribed the divisions existing between King and Parliament to evil counsellors, but spoke of Charles as personally in fault. Some went further. A pamphlet was published, saying that if the king did not yield to what was demanded of him, he and his race ought to be destroyed. Henry Marten, one of the Independent party, defended the writer in the Lower House. "I see no reason," he said, "to condemn him; it is better one family should be destroyed than many." "I move," said another member, "that Mr. Marten be ordered to explain what one family he means." "The king and his children," replied the Republican boldly. The use of such language horrified the Presbyterians, and Marten was for some time expelled the House.

*New political reformers.*

It was evident that there was an advanced party with whom the Presbyterians were as much at issue as they were with the Royalists. But the presence of a common danger checked a schism for the time. The Presbyterians still far outnumbered all other sections on their side, and the misfortunes that befell the arms of the Parliament in this summer of 1643, made the Independents not merely rally to them, but agree to call in the aid of Scotland on terms which would require the establishment of the national church of the north. The interest of the Scots was really identical with that of the English Presbyterians, for if Charles and Episcopacy were restored together, Scotland would not long be allowed to retain her own form of worship. They tried, therefore, to bind their allies down by prescribing a solemn league and covenant (August). Subscribers to this document bound themselves: (1.) To endeavour to reform religion in England and Ireland according to the Word of God, and practice of the best reformed churches, and to bring the three churches in the three kingdoms to uniformity in confession of faith, form of church government, and directory or prayer-book for worship; (2.) To extirpate Popery, prelacy, schism; (3.) To preserve the liberties of the kingdom, the king's person and authority, and to bring malignants to punishment; (4.) To assist and defend all such as should enter into the covenant. All civil and military officers, all ministers holding livings, and all members of Parliament were required to take the covenant. Thus Episcopalian representatives were obliged to leave the Assembly of Divines, and over 1500 ministers resigned their livings.

*Solemn league and covenant.*

Union in a State must of course necessitate many sacrifices of the individual. A subject must often be required to give a passive submission, and sometimes an active co-operation, to acts of which he does not approve. There are two limits to such interference. Firstly, it should be confined, as far as possible, to political as distinguished from religious duties, since it is only when religious questions have taken a political form that they can lead to the disruption of the State; and further, in political matters the duty of bowing to the majority is more clear, and the conscience less tender, than in cases which seem to touch the intercourse of man with his Maker. Secondly, the interference should be limited to overt acts as distinguished from opinions; if a man does what is required by the law, he should not be required to make a declaration of his feelings. Such a requirement is simply inquisitorial, and generally defeats its own ends, by encouraging either open defiance, or a disregard of the sanctity of oaths. The Presbyterian system recognized no such limits to interference. Some of the Independents, indeed, had learnt the lesson of a higher duty, and strove earnestly to make the league with Scotland a political league only, and not a religious covenant; in fact, Sir Henry Vane, had power been in his hands, would have

*Covenant a test.*

been ready to grant toleration even to Catholics. The Scots, however, were impracticable, and all Vane could do was to procure the insertion of the ambiguous words "to endeavour the reformation of religion according to the Word of God and the best reformed churches." These words, though, when taken in connection with their context, they obviously referred to the Presbyterian Church, yet served as a loophole for the Independents in the army, the Parliament, and the Assembly of Divines, who subscribed in numbers to a test which was intended to eliminate them. The 2nd clause left the Episcopalians no such opening, yet many followed the example of the Independents, putting some forced meaning on the words to suit their own consciences. Such laxity of conscience must not be too severely censured. In these cases the real guilt lies rather on those who induce hypocrisy than on those who practise it. The determination of successive governments to exact oaths of fidelity to themselves resulted finally in a general relaxation of the moral fibre of the nation.

<small>Failure of test. Covenant subscribed to by Independents.</small>

For the time, however, the power of the Presbyterians seemed to have overwhelmed the Independents. Four Scotch ministers were admitted into the Assembly of Divines; a Scotch army was engaged to enter England early in the ensuing spring; and Scotch commissioners were joined with a committee of the two Houses, who sat in the capital at Derby House to direct the operations of the war.

<small>Causes of decline of Presbyterian ascendancy.</small>

In spite, however, of Scotch support, the ascendancy of the Presbyterians was already on the decline; for though superior in position and in numbers, their leaders were no match for the Independents in ability. Hampden's death had been a blow to the moderate party. Pym, like Hampden, had possessed the trust of both parties, of Independents, because of the vigour with which he had prosecuted the war, and of Presbyterians because he seemed to acquiesce in their views of church matters, and had agreed with them politically in advocating a limited monarchy. Himself sincere, yet no bigot, he had long kept the peace between the intolerant Presbyterians and Independents. His death now came after a short illness, in which he preserved his usual calmness of temper, telling his chaplain "that it was a most indifferent thing to him to live or die; if he lived, he would do what service

<small>Death of Pym (8th Dec.).</small>

he could; if he died, he would go to God whom he had served, and who would carry on his work by others " (8th Dec.).

In Oxford bonfires were lighted the night the news came that Pym was dead, and the Cavaliers "drank deeper healths than usual to the confusion of the Roundheads." In London there was real sorrow among all parties. The Commons paid off a sum of £10,000, the amount of debts their great leader had incurred in his country's service, and erected a monument in his honour in Westminster Abbey.

The political reformers, who hitherto had implicitly followed Pym, now drifted to the right or the left, and either became absorbed in the ranks of the Presbyterians, or passed over to the new men who were now rising into influence. Thus after Pym's death the breach with the Independents widened rapidly, and the Presbyterians were soon in a false position. Obliged to continue the war, because the king refused to grant them the establishment of their Church, they were, at the same time, afraid of winning a decisive victory, which they saw would only encourage the sectarians and men of new ideas in politics. *False position of Presbyterians.*

On the other hand, the Independents desired nothing more than to crush the king's forces, and so bring the war to a speedy end. They were already in possession of a force fitted, if any, for the accomplishment of the task. Cromwell, lieutenant-general of the horse to the Earl of Manchester, had been very active in forming a new army, raised by order of Parliament in the eastern counties. He had long seen that Essex and Waller's half-hearted soldiers were not the men to gain great victories. "Your troops," he said one day to Hampden, "are most of them old decayed serving men, and tapsters, and such kind of fellows; their troops are gentlemen's sons, younger sons, and persons of quality; do you think that the spirits of such base and mean fellows will ever be able to encounter gentlemen, that have honour and courage and resolution in them; you must get men of a spirit; and take it not ill what I say—I know you will not—of a spirit that is likely to go as far as gentlemen will go— or else you will be beaten still." Hampden thought the notion good, but impracticable. Cromwell undertook to put it into practice. He sought out soldiers amongst the more independent classes, the sons of freeholders and artisans, sectarians, who fought not for pay and plunder, but with the *Eastern counties' army.* *Cromwell's Ironsides.*

higher motive of winning liberty to worship God according to their own fashion. From the very first, when Cromwell only commanded a troop of horse in Essex' army, it was observed that his men were of a different stamp to their fellow-soldiers. They did not plunder or drink; he who swore paid his twelvepence; he who drank was put in the stocks. And now Cromwell was forming a whole army on the same principles, not heeding to what despised sect his recruits belonged, so long as they proved good soldiers. "I raised such men," he boasted long afterwards, "as had the fear of God before them, as made some conscience of what they did, and from that time forward, I must say, they were never beaten, and wherever they were engaged against the enemy, they beat continually." The valour of the troops thus raised was early attested by their popular name of "The Ironsides."

The rise of the Independents created no alarm at Oxford, as Charles expected to reap a new advantage from the divisions of his enemies. He exulted, moreover, in having found a fresh means of increasing the strength of his own armies.

Since the rebellion broke out in 1641, the war in Ireland had been carried on with great success on the part of the Catholics, and a Catholic council of twenty-four persons established at Kilkenny now ruled the larger part of the kingdom. The old English settlers at the head of this party were, however, now eager to make peace with the king, and caused numerous petitions to be sent to Oxford, begging for the free exercise of the Catholic worship, and the calling of a Parliament. Charles, making no absolute promises, agreed to a cessation of arms for a year, and then ordered the Duke of Ormond, his general in Ireland, a devoted and able Royalist, to send over to England ten regiments of the troops that had hitherto been engaged in fighting Irish rebels.

*Cessation of arms with Irish.*

This truce with the Irish Catholics excited indignation not only amongst Charles' enemies, but also amongst his Protestant friends. It was believed that many rebels were to be found among the regiments sent over by Ormond. "The queen's army," it was commonly said, "of French and Walloon Papists, the king's army of English Papists, together with the Irish rebels, are to settle the Protestant religion, and the liberties of England."*

* May, Brev.; Whitelock.

Hyde suggested to the king that, in order to make his cause more popular with the nation, which reverenced the very word 'Parliament,' he should summon to sit at Oxford those members whom fear had driven from Westminster. Charles unwillingly consented; he feared the proposed assembly would force peace on him, and so mar the success he hoped from the new accession to his forces. His fears proved correct. This body, though it was Royalist, showed a strong dislike to certain of the council, as Papists, and as having been the old instruments of tyranny. They even showed some suspicion of the king's own intentions; and, in fact, this half Parliament was evidently inclined to make peace with its other half at Westminster. All overtures, however, proved nugatory, for "the Lords and Commons" of the Long Parliament refused to hold any communication with the king while he spoke of the Oxford assembly as on an equality with themselves. After a three months' session, Charles gladly adjourned the Parliament of his friends (16th April), which he described, in writing to his wife, as "this mongrel assembly, the haunt of cowardly and seditious motions."

*Oxford Parliament.*

When hostilities re-commenced, the Parliament had no less than five armies afoot; the army of Lord Fairfax, now moving freely in Yorkshire, as the siege of Hull had been raised by the advance of the Scots; that of Essex, now being recruited in London after its successes at Gloucester and Newbury; that of Waller, now reinforced after its expulsion from the west; the eastern counties' army, under the command of Cromwell and Manchester; and, lastly, the army of the Scots, 21,000 strong, commanded by a Scotchman, Lesley, Earl of Leven.

*Armies of the Parliament.*

Charles had two large armies—his own, at Oxford, of 10,000 men; that of Newcastle, in Yorkshire, of 14,000 men; besides several considerable forces scattered over the country, and regiments of English and Irish troops landing from time to time in Wales, and at Chester and Bristol.

*Armies of the king.*

The Parliament had laid on the country heavy taxes for the maintenance of its armies. Custom duties were levied on various articles of export and import. An ordinance had been passed for a weekly assessment of £10,000 on London, and of £24,000 on the rest of the kingdom. This tax, like the subsidy, was levied on lands and goods, but not after the same

*Taxes.*

fashion. The subsidies had been levied after an old rate, and by commissioners appointed by the Chancellor from amongst the inhabitants of the county or borough. Through the laxity of these commissioners the receipts had steadily decreased. Now a specific sum was laid upon each county, and raised by commissioners named by Parliament. By further ordinances, the excise duty, a tax hitherto unknown in England, was introduced, which consisted of a tax on the manufacture of commodities as distinct from the custom duties on their importation, and as touching home rather than foreign produce. The ignorant always prefer customs to excise, because the incidence of the former is less visible; but the objection to customs is that they take much more out of the pocket of the consumer than they bring to the exchequer. Customs, being mainly levied on raw produce, have to be paid by the merchant; his payment has to be recouped by the manufacturer and the dealers, besides other intermediaries, all of whom require a profit on the money sunk in the payment of the tax. Excise, being levied on the last stage before sale, is, therefore, a more economical tax. The Dutch had employed it before this, but its introduction into England was due to the genius of Pym.

Such excise was now laid upon many articles of every-day use and consumption; upon ale, cider, perry, wine, oil, sugar, pepper, salt, silk, soap, and even meat (May, 1643—July, 1644). Counties under the power of the Royalists were no better off than those under the power of the Parliament. The Oxford Parliament copied that of Westminster, and laid on an excise; irregular contributions were constantly levied by the king's troops, and his whole army, when unpaid, as it now often was, lived at free quarters.

The committee of the two nations, sitting at Derby House, directed the movements of the generals. Fairfax, Manchester, and Lesley received instructions to attack Newcastle's army, and lay siege to York; Essex and Waller to invest Oxford. When it was known within Oxford that a siege was impending, Discontent faction and discontent broke all bonds of control. in Oxford. Money was getting scarce, and everybody was out of humour. The queen took fright, and departed for Exeter, bidding Charles her last farewell. Courtiers grumbled, and considered themselves neglected. The officers wanted to govern everything, and quarrelled with the civilians in the council. The number of Papists in the town annoyed many of the king's Protestant friends. Charles was incapable of silencing discontent and making men work together. He had no faculty for putting the right man into the right place. Promotion went by caprice or importunity. His officers quarrelled with one another for command. In fact it was a reign of jealousy before; and now, to gratify his nephews Rupert and Maurice, he displaced and offended some of the best and most trustworthy of his servants.

Oxford was already nearly invested, when Charles, by a skilful manœuvre, saved both his army and the town. At the dead of night, accompanied by his cavalry and 2500 foot, he passed undiscovered between the two armies of Essex and Waller (3rd June), and proceeded by quick marches to Worcester, and thence across the Severn to Bewdley. Rupert, in command of his Cavaliers and some of the troops which had been sent over from Ireland, was now in Lancashire, engaged in reducing the fortified places which were held for the Parliament. But Charles, hearing that Newcastle—who was closely besieged in York—could not hold out for six weeks longer unless relieved, sent orders to Rupert to march straight to York and relieve it by engaging the Scots.

Meanwhile, the Parliamentary leaders, as soon as they became aware of Charles' escape, agreed that Waller and his army should pursue the royal forces, while Essex and his army reduced the towns in the west. Waller thought the king was making for Lancashire to join Rupert, and so kept ahead of him on the eastern bank of the Severn. But Charles' plan was much bolder; on hearing the Parliament's forces were divided, his aim was to regain his head-quarters immediately and attack before his enemies could re-unite. With this view he crossed the river behind Waller, and on the 20th June was again in Oxford. Without giving any time for Essex to reappear, he marched out at once at the head of his whole army, and soon fell in with Waller, who, on hearing of his movements, had returned in haste to cover the road to London. The two armies were in sight of one another as they marched northwards from Banbury, Charles being on the eastern, Waller on the western, bank of the Cherwell.

About midday, Waller, observing that the rear of the king's army was some distance behind the main body, forced a passage across Cropredy Bridge, and fell upon it in front, while at the same time he sent a body of

Battle of Cropredy Bridge. (Map, p.127.)

horse to make their way over a ford about a mile lower down the river. Charles, seeing his rear about to be attacked on two sides, at once recalled his advanced troops, and a succession of skirmishes followed, in which the Royalists were generally victorious, taking several pieces of cannon, and beating the enemy back both over the ford and the bridge. Fighting lasted until night caused the two armies to separate. The action in itself might have been called indecisive, but the king gained all the advantages of a victory, for death and desertion soon reduced Waller's army to half its numbers.

Three days after the battle of Cropredy Bridge, the eastern counties' army was brought into action in Yorkshire. It was supporting the Scots in besieging York; but the generals of the Parliament, on hearing that Rupert was marching from Lancashire with 20,000 men to raise the siege, withdrew from their entrenchments to Hessay Moor in order to oppose his approach (30th June). The prince, however, disappointed their expectations, for instead of following the high road from Knaresborough, over Skip Bridge, he crossed the Ouse with his army above its junction with the Nidd, and entered York the same evening without opposition (1st July).

As Rupert had already effected his object in relieving the town, Newcastle wished to avoid, or at least delay a battle; urging in the first place that divisions would probably break out in the enemy's army, composed as it was of Scots and English, Presbyterians and Independents, in the second, that he was expecting a reinforcement of 3000 men, and that no battle ought to be fought until after their arrival. But Rupert, confident of victory, put forward the king's letter: "I have his Majesty's commands," he said; "I am bound to fight." "I am ready to obey your Highness," replied Newcastle, "as if the king himself were here." The prince's army was encamped a few miles to the north of York, and it was agreed that Newcastle's foot should be ready by two o'clock at night to march out and unite with it. Their sudden and unlooked-for deliverance seemed, however, for the time to have demoralized the York forces. Some of the soldiers were out seeking for booty in the deserted trenches of the enemy; others were already drawn together, when a report spread that before marching they were to receive their pay; at once the men broke from their ranks and dispersed, and some hours elapsed before they could be gathered together again.* Rupert rode out of the town at daybreak, without waiting for Newcastle, and proceeded to lead his army across the Ouse at Poppelton, where the Scots had left standing a bridge of boats (2nd July).

The counsels of the Parliament's generals were, like those of the Royalists, divided. The English were for seeking out the enemy and fighting, but the Scots proposed to retreat to Cawood, where, by forming a *tête-de-pont* to defend the bridge at the junction of the branches of the Ouse, they might oppose Rupert's further advance south. The Scots' counsel prevailed, and the army drew off from Hessay Moor southwards, in the direction of Tadcaster: those in the van had already advanced some miles, when it was attacked in the rear by Rupert's horse at Marston village and forced hastily to turn and form in order of battle.

Both Hessay and Marston Moors form part of a low plain, watered by the Ouse and the Nidd. Drainage and tillage have now changed the character of a tract that was then in the main really moor, open and unenclosed. Immediately south of the road that joins Tockwith and Marston, the dead level ends, and an easy ascent of ten minutes leads to the summit of a line of higher ground, running from one village to the other. The Parliamentarians on the first attack promptly faced about to the north, and formed upon the brow of this hill, on Marston Field, a large enclosure with crops of rye then dotted over it. Their right wing, consisting of Sir Thomas Fairfax' regiments of horse and foot, together with the larger part of the Scotch horse, and a reserve of Scottish infantry, occupied a position immediately west of Marston village, where the elevation is highest. Their main battle was composed of Scotch and English infantry, commanded by Lords Leven and Manchester and Sir Thomas's father, Lord Fairfax. Still farther west, resting on the village of Tockwith, where the hill is much lower than at Marston, was the left wing, comprised of three regiments of Scottish cavalry and the eastern counties' horse, under the command respectively of David Lesley

* There is a curious account of the 'battle of York' (*i.e.*, Marston Moor) in the Clarendon State Papers at Oxford. The writing is in the same hand as a paper printed in the Clar. State Papers, ii. p. 181, which is endorsed by Hyde, 'Sir Hugh Cholmeley's Memorials.' The writer, whoever he is, tells us he received his account 'from a gentleman of quality of that country who was a colonel and had a command there and present all the time.' The other accounts of the battle given by eye-witnesses are nearly all written by Parliamentarians.

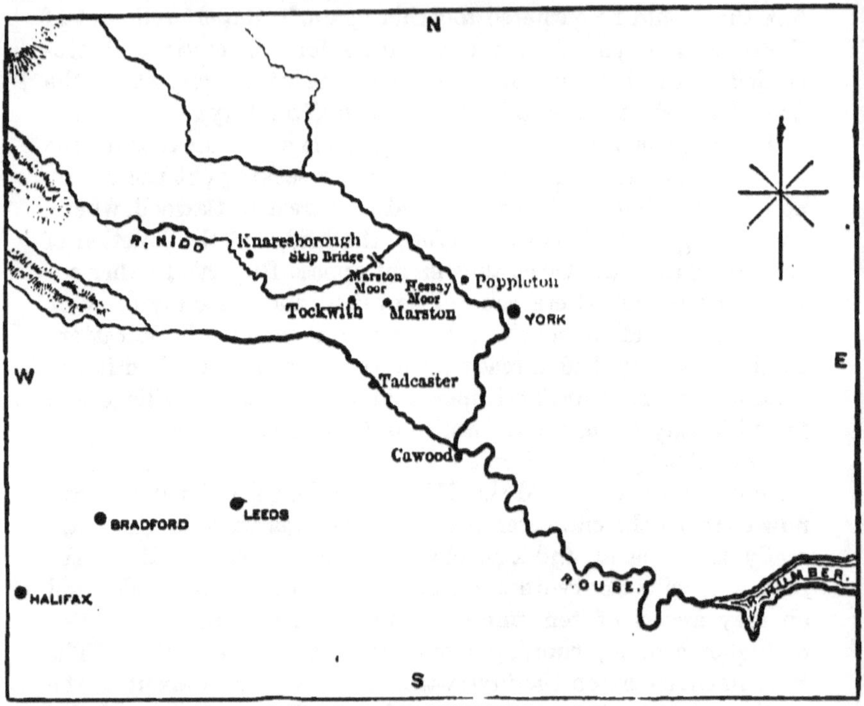
N
R. NIDD
Knaresborough
Skip Bridge
Marston Moor
Hessay Moor
Poppleton
Tockwith
Marston
YORK
W
E
Tadcaster
Cawood
LEEDS
BRADFORD
HALIFAX
R. OUSE.
R. HUMBER.
S

N
RIVER NIDD
BATTLE OF
MARSTON MOOR
2nd July, 1644.
Parliament
Royalist
MARSTON MOOR
HESSAY
End of present Moor Lane
Reserve of Irish Foot
5000 Horse under Rupert
Rupert's foot Regiments
Porter's Division
Newcastle's Whitecoats
4000 Horse under Goring
Supposed Ditch
TOCKWITH
End of old lane
W
5000 Horse under Fairfax
To York
E
LONG MARSTON
6000 Horse under Cromwell
Manchester's Foot
Centre consisting mainly of Scotch Foot
Fairfax' Foot
Two Brigades Scotch Foot Reserve
To Tadcaster
S

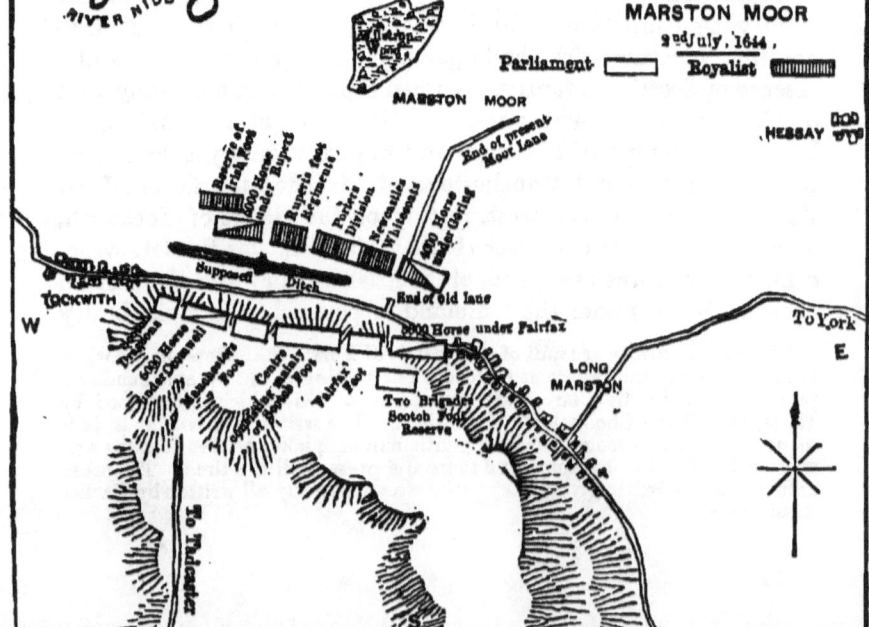

and Lieutenant-General Cromwell. Its outer flank was supported by a body of Scotch dragoons.

Rupert, who was following from the north-east, finding that his enemies were facing about to accept battle, formed his army upon Marston Moor, awaiting meanwhile impatiently the arrival of the York forces. After some delay the marquis, "accompanied with all the gentlemen of quality which were in York, came to the prince, who said, 'My lord, I wish you had come sooner with your forces, but I hope we shall yet have a glorious day.' The marquis informed him how his foot had been a-plundering in the trenches, and that it was impossible to have got together all at the time fixed, but that he had left General King about the work, who would bring them up with all the expedition that might be. The prince, seeing the marquis' foot were not come up, would with his own forces have been falling upon the enemy, but the marquis dissuaded him, telling him that he had 4000 good foot as were in the world coming. About four o'clock in the afternoon General King brought up the marquis' foot, of which yet many were wanting, for there was not above 3000. The prince demanded of King how he liked the marshalling of his army, who replied, he did not approve of it, being drawn too near the enemy and in a place of disadvantage. Then said the prince, 'They may be drawn a further distance.' 'No, sire,' said King, 'it is too late.'"

The two armies were drawn up so close together that "their foot," says a Parliamentarian, "was close to our noses." Rupert had been beforehand in gaining possession of a deep ditch that ran in a straight line between them. In this he placed four bodies of musketeers opposite the eastern counties' army. His right wing he led in person. Newcastle's foot fell into position on the extreme left of the main body, which was placed under the command of General King; the left wing was commanded by Colonel Goring. A few fields cut up the moor on this side, so that the only approach for the horse on the enemy's right lay up a narrow lane with a hedge on one side and a ditch on the other, both lined with dismounted dragoons. All along the line waved banners magnificent with gold and silver fringes. Here a red pennon with a white cross, and motto, 'Pro rege et regno;' there a black coronet and sword reaching from the clouds, 'Terribilis ut acies ordinata;' while far on the right the presence of the prince was marked by a standard nearly five yards long and broad, with a red cross in the centre. Each army was nearly 23,000 strong, so that never before in the course of the war had such large forces met face to face. The Parliamentarians wore as their mark a white paper or handkerchief in their hats; their word for the day was 'God with us.' The Royalist mark was to be without bands or scarfs; their word 'God and the king.'

Since two o'clock the cannon had been booming, but still the two armies delayed to join battle. The Parliament's generals, trusting in Rupert's proverbial daring, waited for him to disorder his lines by being the first to charge across the ditch. Their soldiers meanwhile 'fell to singing psalms,' a sign that they at least were nerved and ready for any odds.

When the forces from York had at last arrived, Rupert's impetuosity was restrained by the representations of Newcastle and King, both of whom were averse to fighting because of the lateness of the hour. He declared accordingly his intention of delaying the battle till the next day, ordered provisions to be brought for his army from York, and with most culpable neglect suffered many of his horsemen to dismount and lie on the ground, with their horses' bridles in their hands.

But that long summer's day was not so to end. It was already seven o'clock when Leven, who acted as commander-in-chief, finding that the enemy would not charge him, determined to charge them, and ordered the whole line of his army to advance. "We came down the hill," says Oliver's scout-master, "in the bravest order, and with the greatest resolution—I mean the left wing of our horse, led by Cromwell, which was to charge their right wing, led by Rupert, in which was all their gallant men." At the sound of the enemy's alarums, the prince in hot haste sprung to horse and galloped up to the front of the field. He found his own regiment taken by surprise, and in some disorder. "'Swounds!" he cried, "do you run—follow me!" and fiercely led the way to meet the enemy's charge. Meanwhile Manchester's foot, in the face of a fierce fire, dashed down the hill at a bit of level, where there was a break in the ditch, and thus taking the Royalist musketeers in flank, drove them out of their shelter. A desperate struggle ensued. The horsemen discharged their pistols, and then, flinging them at one another's heads, fell to with their swords. A company of Cavaliers, led by Rupert in person, charged Cromwell's own division of three hundred horse in front and flank. A shot grazed the lieutenant's-general's neck. "A miss is as good as a mile," he exclaimed, and, scattering his assailants before him "like a little dust," pressed onwards till he broke through the lines of the enemy. "Manchester's foot, on the right hand, went on by our side," says Oliver's scout-master again, "dispersing the enemy's foot almost as fast as they charged them, still going by our side, cutting them down that we carried the whole field before us, thinking the victory wholly ours, and nothing to be done but to kill and take prisoners." Soon Rupert's whole wing, horse and foot, was in full flight, and the Cavaliers were swept off the field, flying northwards " along by Wilstrop woodside as fast and thick as could be."

Meanwhile the Parliament's troops on the right wing found their advance impeded by the hedge and ditch which protected the enemy's left. They could only march up the lane three or four abreast, and were exposed all the while to a hot fire from the musketeers stationed by Rupert on either side. After forcing their way to the open ground at the end of the lane, they were received by large bodies of the enemy, who fell upon each party as it emerged. Fairfax, indeed, in face of all difficulties, charged right through Goring's squadrons, at the head of four hundred horse. But finding himself left unsupported, he was fain to take the white handkerchief out of his hat, and pass for a Royalist commander while he rode hastily back to his own side.

Meantime his van, composed of newly-levied regiments, had wheeled round before the enemy, and disordered his own infantry and the Scots' reserve, so that on his return, he found his whole wing broken and already in flight. Some of the Cavaliers, with their usual impetuosity, pursued the flying enemy over the hill which shut out their view of the field, and miles on to the south in the direction of Cawood and Tadcaster ; others tarried to plunder the carriages and baggage left by the Parliamentarians on the top of the hill ; others under the command of Goring joined Newcastle's regiment of Whitecoats, and wheeled round on the unprotected right flank of the enemy's centre. Thus attacked in front and flank, the Scots' infantry on this side gave way. In vain Leven exhorted his men to stand. "Though you run from your enemies," he cried, "yet leave not your general." Believing the battle to be lost, he joined the stream of fugitives, and never drew rein until he came to Leeds.

**The general confusion — account of an eye-witness.**    The confusion was not confined to the Parliament side. "I knew not for my soul," says one who was there looking for Rupert, "whither to incline: runaways on both sides, so many, so breathless, so speechless, not a man of them able to give me the least hope where the prince was to be found, both armies being mingled, horse and foot. In this terrible distraction did I scour the country, here meeting with a shoal of Scots crying out, 'Wae's us, we're a' undone!' then with a ragged troop, reduced to four and a cornet, by-and-by with a little foot-officer, without hat, band, or anything but feet."

It is a time of confusion such as this that gives an opening for the calm and collected officer who has his men well in hand. Half the Royalist left wing were far away, triumphantly driving the blow home, as they thought, by a hot pursuit. Goring had only Newcastle's Whitecoats and a sprinkling of his own Cavaliers, when the fading light revealed to him a new enemy occupying the very ground he had himself held in the morning.

**Cromwell redeems the day.**    It was the Parliament's left wing, led by Cromwell and Leslie; who, after dispersing the Royalist right, had relinquished pursuit and crossed the battle-field to support their less fortunate friends. Once again Cavaliers and Ironsides fiercely charged, and once again victory remained with the Ironsides. The Cavaliers fled the field, while Newcastle's regiment of Whitecoats, a thousand brave Northumbrians raised out of his own tenantry, scorning to receive quarter or to fly, were all, save some thirty, cut down to a man, in the same order and rank in which they stood. Major-General Porter, who had forced back part of the Parliament's main battle, now, in the moment of success, found foes in his own rear, and had to surrender with his men.

Broken and routed, the Royalists on all sides fled, and were chased with terrible slaughter to within a mile of York. By ten o'clock, the battle was over, and after scarce three hours' fighting, more than 3000 Royalists lay dead upon the field. The Parliamentarians lost, it was said, only some 300 men; they made 1500 prisoners, and took all the enemy's artillery, ammunition, and baggage. "The Earl of Manchester," says his chaplain, "about eleven o'clock that night, did ride about to the soldiers both horse and foot, giving them many thanks for the exceeding good service they had done for the kingdom; and he often earnestly

entreated them to give the honour of the victory unto God alone.
The soldiers unanimously gave God the glory of their great deliverance and victory, and told his lordship with much cheerfulness that, though they had long fasted and were faint, yet they would willingly want three days longer, rather than to give up the service or leave his lordship." It was not, however, till noon the next day, that the joyful news reached Leven, who had fled in the belief that the battle was irrecoverably lost. Upon hearing of this, he knocks upon his breast, and says, " I would to God I had died upon the plain."* Leven bewails his flight.

Newcastle, in disgust at seeing his army destroyed and power gone through Rupert's rashness, went beyond seas, accompanied by more than eighty gentlemen. The prince returned to Chester, with the remnants of a broken army. York surrendered to the Parliament, and the king lost all hold in the north. Such was one result of the battle; but there was a second hardly less momentous. The Independents had triumphed not only over the Royalists, but over the Presbyterians. In London, it was told how " Cromwell, with his unspeakable valorous regiments, had done all the service; the Presbyterians, the Scots, had fled."† As though to render the triumph of the Ironsides the more complete, a terrible misfortune befell the army in which the Presbyterians placed their trust. Results of battle.

The Royalist leader, Sir Richard Grenville, on hearing of the presence of Essex in the west, raised the siege of Plymouth, and marched for refuge into Cornwall. Essex had already advanced as far as Exeter, when the news reached him that the king had defeated Waller, and was now following in pursuit of himself. Some of his officers, who had estates in Cornwall which they wished to visit, persuaded him to march after Grenville, instead of turning at once to meet the royal forces. He soon found that he had taken a fatal step. The country people were Royalists, and gave him no support. The country itself is enough to embarrass a general, with its bare back-bone of mountain, moor, or marsh, while the southern coast, which is the least desolate, is split up into a succession of deep valleys running to the sea.

* Rushworth; Ormond Pap., i. 56; Fairfax' Mem.; Cromwelliana; Sir H. Slingsby's Mem.; Letters and Accounts of Ash, Watson, and Steward, in King's Pamphlets, 164, 166; Memorials touching the battle of York, in Clarendon Papers in Bodleian.    † Baillie, ii. 40.

Essex had his head-quarters at Lostwithiel, in the valley of the Fowey, then spelt, as it is still pronounced, Foy, when the king, advancing from Liskeard, pitched his camp and standard on Broadoak or Braddoc Downs, near Boconnoc. Hoping to profit by the enmity existing between the Presbyterian and Independent commanders, he wrote Essex a letter, calling on him to end the war by uniting the two armies, and promising on the word of a king that he would ever prove a faithful friend to both him and his army. The Royalist officers afterwards set their names to a letter, in which they undertook to see carried out all that his Majesty might promise. But Essex' honesty stood the test. In answer to their overtures he declared his inability to treat, and referred the king to the Parliament. His generalship, however, did not prove equal to his honesty. Though he was in possession of the valley of the Foy, from the haven itself to Lanhydrock, a house belonging to the Parliamentarian Lord Robartes, so that supplies could be brought into his army, both by sea and land, from all sides, excepting the east; yet with little opposition, he suffered the king to draw the toils so closely round him, that starvation or surrender were the only alternatives left. Grenville, at the head of 1400 men, advanced from Bodmin, gained possession of Lanhydrock, and thus opened communication with Charles on Broadoak Downs, and shut in the army of the enemy on the north (12th August). Essex had neglected to occupy View Hall, a house on the east bank of the river opposite Foy, and Pernon Fort, standing on the same side and commanding the entrance of the harbour. These important positions were now seized and occupied by the Royalists, so that the Parliamentarians were prevented any longer from bringing provisions into Fowey by sea (13th August). Their position at Lostwithiel soon became still more circumscribed. Sir Richard Grenville advanced from Lanhydrock and drove Essex out of Lestormel Castle, which commands the Fowey valley scarce a mile above Lostwithiel (21st August). The same day the king, advancing from enclosures which bounded the south side of Boconnoc Park, forced the Parliamentarians to quit their quarters on a beacon hill, which stands about a mile east of Lostwithiel. Here the following night, he raised a battery, whence he shot right into their camp. The west was now the only side still open to

Essex, and even from this he was shortly to be cut off. Goring and the horse seized possession of St. Austell, and thus commanded all the country round Tywardreath Bay, whence provisions had still reached Lostwithiel by sea (25th August). Essex had now no choice left but to surrender.

The horse escaped by riding off about three o'clock one misty morning, between the armies of the king and Prince Maurice, which were encamped a small distance apart (31st August).

Essex and the foot marched from Lostwithiel for Foy, hoping as a last resource to escape across the river and sail from Lanteglos to Plymouth. Before leaving Lostwithiel, they tried to break down the bridge over the river, but were prevented by the enemy's infantry, who followed them through the town and down the valley, forcing them to a hasty retreat. On the march they came to some high ground and enclosures, which they occupied, and succeeded for the time in making a successful stand and driving the enemy back. The next day, Essex sailed from

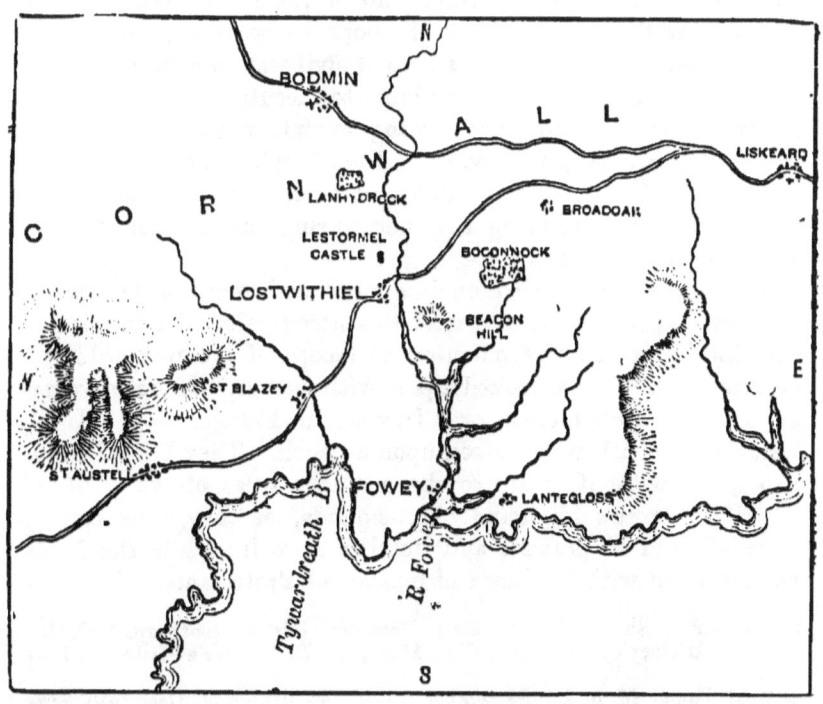

Foy, in company with his principal officers. As he left the harbour, he narrowly escaped being taken prisoner by the garrison of Pernon Fort. The infantry, about 6000 in number, surrendered their ammunition, artillery, and arms, on condition that they should be allowed their liberty and conducted to the nearest quarters of their friends. The terms, however, were not kept; the men were maltreated and plundered all the way on their march through the enemy's country, and so many were the deaths and desertions, that only some 1000 arrived at Poole in safety. Thus the two Presbyterian generals in the west were crushed in a single campaign. "Mr. Sheriff," said Charles, on his departure from Cornwall, "I leave the country entirely at peace in your hands."*

At this time the flames of civil war had spread from England into Scotland. Before the cessation of arms had been concluded with the Irish, and before the Scots had declared themselves for the Parliament, the Marquis of Montrose had formed with Charles a secret plan of raising the Highlanders and uniting them with a body of troops to be transported from Ireland, and thus beginning a second civil war in Scotland. An attempt was made to carry this plan into execution during the present summer; and Montrose, coming down from the Highlands at the head of a brave, but savage and undisciplined, army of Highlanders and Irishmen, twice defeated such forces as the Covenanters were able to bring together during the absence of their best troops in England.†

*Civil war in Scotland.*

Hostilities were carried on in a more and more brutal spirit. This was especially the case after the introduction of Irish troops into England. The introduction of troops of a lower order of civilization is always looked upon with horror. If not savages as Indians in America, or 'Turcos' in France, both Highlanders and Irish were looked upon as such. They both fought without regard to the ordinary rules of war. Montrose's Highland 'hell hounds,' as they were called, were allowed to plunder and butcher at will; while the Irish came stained with the blood of massacred Protestants. An ordi-

*Irish and Highlanders*

---

* Letter of Sir F. Basset; Hals' Parochial History (both *apud* Davies Gilbert's History of Cornwall); Clar. Hist.; Sir E. Walker's Historical Discourses.

† At Tipper Muir, 1st September, 1644. At Bridge of Dee, 14th September, 1644.

nance passed by the Parliament forbidding quarter to be given to any Irishmen or Papists taken in arms (Oct. 3rd), was in their case literally enforced. Irish soldiers seized on their way to English ports were tied back to back and cast into the sea; those made prisoners in England were shot by hundreds. The more moderate of the Royalists had objected to the introduction of the Irish; but the less scrupulous, not to be behind in acts of cruelty, would retaliate by hanging English prisoners, taken in arms, twelve at a time, on a tree, or by putting members of garrisons to death on slight excuses, contrary to articles of capitulation. Thus the war was more and more embittered as it went on.

Charles, on hearing of Montrose's victories, regarded, the disastrous day of Marston Moor as already retrieved. He expected either that the Scotch army would return to defend their homes, or else that Montrose would march into England, fight the Scots, and recover his lost ascendancy in the north. But his wishes made him overlook the character of Montrose's army. After a raid on the Lowlands, the Highlanders' custom was to return to the mountains, and enjoy their spoil. The present expedition was nothing to them but a raid on a larger scale than usual; and no sooner did the winter set in, than they melted away from their leader, who found his Irish troops insufficient to protect him, and was fain to follow his Highlanders and take refuge in their mountains.

Charles, meantime, was marching back from Cornwall to Oxfordshire. He had passed through Wiltshire, and reached Newbury, when he heard that the armies of Waller, Essex, and Manchester were advancing from London to meet him. The Independents, content with the proved superiority of their army, had not pressed their victory over the fallen Essex and Waller. Waller's army had been recruited once more; and Essex' men had been re-furnished with arms on returning from their catastrophe in the west. Essex himself pleaded sickness, and remained absent from his army, feeling that since the relief of Gloucester, the day of his triumphs was over.

As the united armies of the enemy were 16,000 strong, and his own forces not above 8000, Charles, not venturing to risk a battle in the open field, took up a strong defensive position in Newbury, between the rivers Kennet and Lamborne. On the south the town was protected by the Kennet. On the north-east troops were quartered in Shaw village, which was strengthened with a breastwork, and in a large house, called Doleman's, still standing, as the map shows (p. 144), a little in advance of the village on the northern bank of the Lamborne. Bodies of horse occupied a gentle eminence rising immediately east of Doleman's House, and a few neighbouring hedges were lined with musketeers. On the west Prince Maurice's infantry was quartered in the village of Speen; and in two large fields, lying north of Newbury, between the rivers Kennet and Lamborne, was stationed a large body of horse together with a train of artillery.' Approach to this quarter was rendered the more difficult by the neighbourhood of Donnington Castle, which was held by a strong garrison for the king.

The Parliament's generals took possession of Clay Hill, lying to the north-east of Newbury, and agreed to make a combined attack upon Shaw and Speen. For this purpose, the greater part of Manchester's horse, all Essex' horse and foot, and almost all the forces under Waller, separated from Manchester, and making a detour beyond Donnington Castle, surprised the Royalists in their quarters on the north-west. Many of the king's guards being absent from their posts, the Lamborne was crossed without opposition, and Prince Maurice's infantry quickly dislodged from Speen. A fierce three-hours' contest followed in the fields lying between Donnington and Newbury. The king, who was present in person, could not prevent some of his troops from flying under the walls of the castle for protection. Essex' men, crying out "that they would be revenged for the business of Cornwall," carried off in triumph the very cannon they had before surrendered. The Royalists, however, succeeded in retaining possession of the field, and when night caused the battle to end, Waller retired into Speen. Meanwhile, on the other side of the town, a still fiercer struggle had been maintained. Manchester had agreed with Waller that as soon as the sound of cannon should be heard from Speen, he would advance with his forces upon the Royalist quarters at Shaw. During the morning he "rode about from regiment to regiment to encourage the soldiers, and to keep them in due order fit for that service which every hour almost was expected." It was about four o'clock in the afternoon when, says an eye-witness, "we saw the firing of the muskets in Speen, which discovered the service to be very hot, and with joy and thankfulness beheld the hasty disorderly retreat of the enemy towards Newbury." On this encouraging sight 3000 of Manchester's foot burst down Clay Hill singing a psalm as they came, intending to storm the defences of the Royalists, and meet their friends in the fields lying between Newbury and Donnington. Charging furiously, the Parliamentarians forced the king's horse back into the garden of Doleman's House, and made their way right up to the breastworks. Here, however, they were exposed to a murderous fire, and fell in numbers, while they were able to do little execution upon enemies sheltered by walls and earthworks. As was not seldom the case in this war, with the approach of night, friends were mistaken for foes; so that after one company of Manchester's foot had possessed themselves of one of the enemy's outworks, a second beat them out again with great loss of life to both. After four hours' hard fighting, the Parliamentarians gave up the attack and drew off, while sheltered from pursuit by their own horse, which had stayed all the time barely beyond range of the enemy's pistols. It was now ten o'clock, and a clear, moonlight night. Charles, seeing that he had lost ground upon the western side of the town, forsook his quarters, and, without meeting any opposition, withdrew by Donnington Castle to Wallingford, passing between Waller's and Manchester's armies.*

It was a victory, but not a victory to break the king's power in the south, as Marston Moor had broken it in the north. When the generals returned to London, Cromwell laid a heavy charge against the Presbyterian earl in the House of Commons; how Manchester had always been for such a peace as a victory would be a disadvantage to; how he had often acted as if he thought the king too low and the Parliament too high, but especially at Donnington Castle: "Though," said Cromwell, "I showed him evidently how this success might be obtained, and only desired leave with my own brigade of horse, to charge the king's army in their retreat, leaving it to the earl's choice, if he thought proper to remain neutral with the rest of his forces. But he positively refused his consent, and gave no other reason but that, if we met with a defeat, there was an end of our pretensions—we should all be rebels and traitors, and be executed and forfeited by law."

*Dissensions in London.*

---

* Ludlow Mem.; Clar. Hist.; E. Walker's Hist. Discourses; A true relation of the most chief occurrences at and since the Battle at Newbury, (by Simeon Ash, chaplain to Manchester) in King's Pamphlets.

Manchester, in turn, retorted on his lieutenant-general charges of insubordination, and of deep dark designs; of having said, "that it would never be well in England till I were plain Mr. Montague, and there was never a peer nor a lord in the land." Indeed, it was reported that Cromwell said to his soldiers, "if he met the king in battle, he would fire his pistol at the king as at another." The charges were not pressed on either side, and no judgment was passed. But the Presbyterians from this time feared Cromwell as the ablest and most determined of their opponents. Pym was dead nearly a year now, and there had risen up in his place a man they owned to be "of a very wise and active head, universally well-beloved as religious and stout, being a known Independent, and loved by the soldiers." Their fears made them the more eager to effect a peace, which would secure their own ascendancy, and crush the hated Independents. Peace propositions were accordingly brought forward, and passed both Houses of Parliament after meeting much opposition from the Independent party (9th Nov.). Charles agreed to send seventeen commissioners to Uxbridge, to discuss the terms proposed, with thirty-five members of Parliament and the Scottish commissioners.

But while the Presbyterians were intending peace, the Independents were preparing to re-model the army, and place it in the hands of men who knew how to conquer; for it was evident that the war would never be brought to a successful close while the command of the forces of the Parliament was divided between rival generals of different principles, some of whom did not wish to push matters to an extreme. To effect their purpose, they proposed to deprive of office, civil and military, all members of Parliament. The House was considering the sad condition of the kingdom, when Cromwell rose and spoke to the following effect : " It is now time to speak, or for ever hold the tongue. The important occasion now is no less than to save a nation out of a bleeding, nay almost out of a dying condition. . . . For what do the enemy say? Nay, what do men say that were friends at the beginning of the Parliament? Even this, that the members of both Houses have got great places, and commands, and the sword into their hands, and will not permit the war speedily to end, lest their own power should determine with it." " Whatever is the matter," continued another member ; " two summers are passed over, and we are not

*Self-denying ordinance.*

saved. A summer's victory has proved but a winter's story; the game has shut up with autumn, to be new played again next spring, as if the blood that has been shed were only to manure the field of war. I determine nothing, but it is apparent that the forces being under several great commanders has oftentimes hindered the public service." "There is but one way of ending so many evils," said a third member. "I move that no member of either house shall, during this war, execute any office or command, civil or military" (9th Dec.).

The motion was acted upon, and a 'self-denying ordinance' to the effect proposed was ordered to be brought into the House. Though the Presbyterians fully understood that this measure was intended to place the army under the sole control of the Independents, they were not inclined to relax in their opposition. But they had now been three years at the head of affairs and not yet brought the war to an end. Public opinion was strong against them and turned the waverers, so that the ordinance was carried by a small majority of seven votes (19th Dec.).

In the Upper House, the opposition was even stronger than in the Commons. The peers of England had always held the highest command in the state, and were now unwilling to make way for the rise of their inferiors in rank, by yielding up honours that they regarded as their hereditary right. They accordingly rejected the ordinance, saying, that they did not know what shape the army would take (15th Jan., 1645). The Independents answered the objection by introducing into the Commons a second ordinance for the re-modelling of the army. There was only to be one army, to consist of 21,000 men. Sir Thomas Fairfax was named commander-in-chief; Skippon, major-general; and a blank was left for the name of the new lieutenant-general. This ordinance also passed the Commons, and was sent up to the Lords (28th Jan.). *Ordinance for re-modelling army.*

Meanwhile, commissioners from king and Parliament met, as agreed, at Uxbridge. The question of religion was first discussed. The Parliament demanded that Episcopacy should be abolished, the Presbyterian Church established, and the king himself take the covenant. The king's commissioners offered so far to reduce the power of bishops that, in most points, they should be incapable of acting without the consent of the ministers of their respective dioceses. *Uxbridge negotiations.*

This concession might have been accepted at the beginning of the war, before the hopes of the Presbyterians had soared so high. But the two nations were now bound together by their solemn league and covenant, and nothing would satisfy Scotch or English Presbyterians but the entire abolition of the order of bishops. Next came the question of the militia. The king offered to resign the command to Parliament for seven years, on condition it should then revert to the crown. Two years ago, this concession also might have given satisfaction, but the strength of the Independent party was now far too great to allow of its acceptance by the Commons. Thirdly it was required that the cessation of arms, made by Charles with the Irish, should be declared void, and, hardest of all, that all his friends, even his very nephews, should be excepted from receiving the benefit of the royal prerogative of pardon. It was through the Independents that the stringency of the terms had been increased. The offer of peace was genuine on the part of the Presbyterians, who were most anxious that the king should accept terms before the army passed out of their hands. It was certainly a time for Charles to consider the question seriously. If he accepted, the Presbyterians would restore him—at least, in a manner—to his throne; the army of the Scots, the armies of Essex and Waller, united with the Cavaliers, would present a force more than enough to meet any opposition the Independents might offer. On the other hand, if he refused, the Independents would gain the sole control of the forces of the Parliament, and the result was sure to be some crushing defeat to himself.

This was the sober truth; but Charles' eyes were dazzled by a far more brilliant prospect, as he sat over letters and despatches in his rooms at Oxford. The queen, who had fled from Exeter to France, when Essex marched into the west, constantly sent her husband advice, much in the shape of command, bidding him be careful of making any peace that should not restore him to his full rights, and ensure her own safety. Montrose, who had gained a third victory in Scotland, at Inverlochy (2nd Feb.), wrote to implore him not to make himself 'a king of straw,' promising, before the end of the next summer, to be in England at the head of a gallant army. Charles, however, did not need to be dissuaded from accepting the terms offered by the Parliament, for he still believed in the final success of his arms.

*Charles opposed to peace.*

He was soliciting both France and Denmark for assistance, and, through the queen, was carrying on a negotiation with the Duke of Lorraine for the transportation of 10,000 soldiers into England. He was writing to Ormond that if the Irish Catholics should assist him, and he be restored to his throne by their means, he would consent to repeal all the penal statutes made against them.* He was trusting for success to the divisions of his enemies, and believed that, if he failed in the field, he could still play off one against the other, and that either section must be glad to bid high for his support against the other. Buoyed up by such hopes, Charles wrote to the queen, that he would never quit Episcopacy, nor the sword which God had put into his hands, and that she need not doubt the issue of the negotiations, for there was "no probability of a peace." He forbade the commissioners to make any further concessions, and the negotiations at Uxbridge were accordingly broken off (21st Feb.).

The king's rejection of the propositions was a terrible blow to the Presbyterians. The Lords, of whom only five or six had any sympathy with the Independents, had now to pass the ordinance for the re-modelling of the army (15th Feb.), and a second self-denying ordinance, depriving members of any office conferred on them since the election of the Parliament (3rd April). Any further opposition on their part would only have accelerated the speed of the revolution, by causing the Commons to declare their ordinance good at law without the consent of the House of Lords. For, in times of revolution, when the real powers in the State are the sword and the people, an upper chamber is useless and weak. The Commons, now acting as the executive, commanded the sword, the people supported the Commons, and the Lords were powerless to guide or stay the march of events. *Lords pass self-denying ordinance.*

The self-denying ordinance, which now passed the Upper House, differed in an important point from the one before rejected. By this, members were not precluded from taking office on any future occasion. Its only effect was, in fact, to make, as it were, a fresh start. The existing Presbyterian generals were practically cashiered, but new nominees could be generals as well as members. But the Presbyterians, though foiled in these matters through their political half-heartedness, could still console them-

* Ludlow, iii. 232, Letter to Ormond.

selves with their ecclesiastical supremacy. In that sphere they never pretended to be tolerant. Their victim now was Laud. He had been impeached of high treason at the same time as Strafford, but the charge in his case was not pressed to an issue, and Pym and his party had contented themselves with leaving him to die a natural death in the Tower. Now, however, through the bigotry of Scotch and English Presbyterians, these proceedings were revived against the old man, already a four years' prisoner. His innovations in religion, the cruel sentences of the Star Chamber, and his interference with the judges, were charged against him, as an endeavour to subvert the laws and overthrow the Protestant religion. The judges, on being asked their opinion by the Lords, replied that the charges did not fall within the legal definition of high treason. The Lords would doubtless have followed the opinions of the judges. The Presbyterians, however, being determined on his death, voted him guilty by an ordinance of Parliament, which the House of Lords wanted spirit to reject. The verdict of the judges marked this as far more unjustifiable than Strafford's case. The fact that the chief prosecutor was Prynne, whose body showed the marks of the cruel judgments of the Star Chamber, roused, no doubt, a strong feeling against the archbishop. But a Parliament cannot plead the excuses of a mob, and cruelty did not constitute high treason. The conviction shows how little the securities that fence justice round are likely to be regarded when a popular assembly usurps the functions of the judicature. It shows, also, the evil of the precedent which was set when Strafford's conviction was secured by a Bill of Attainder instead of the legal process of an impeachment. The ordinance was simply a Bill of Attainder without the king's consent. The Presbyterians desired the blood of their former persecutor; and the Independents, in return for the passing of the self-denying ordinance, refrained from offering opposition to the gratification of their rivals' vengeance.

# CHAPTER VIII.

## NASEBY.—END OF WAR (1645—1646).

Fellows in arms, and my most loving friends,
Bruised underneath the yoke of tyranny,
* * * *
In God's name cheerly on, courageous friends,
To reap the harvest of perpetual peace
By this one bloody trial of sharp war.—RICH. III., v. 2, 1—16.

THE army, re-modelled at Windsor, was reduced, according to the ordinance, to a body of 21,000 men—14,000 foot, 6000 horse, 1000 dragoons. Though a smaller, it was a far more formidable force than it had ever been before, its ranks being now almost entirely composed of sectarians, and these either freeholders' sons or artisans. A clause introduced into the self-denying ordinance allowed religious men to serve without first taking the covenant, so that the new army was in no way bound to the Presbyterians.

These men had taken up arms, not to earn pay, but to win the victory of liberty of conscience. They proved no ordinary soldiers. A severe but popular discipline banished profane language and drunkenness from their camp. They would pass hours with their officers reading and expounding the Bible, and were able and ready to win converts for their doctrine by argument. A Presbyterian, appointed chaplain to one of these regiments, found his life a 'daily misery,' from abhorrence of the new views of these zealots. One soldier would argue against set forms of prayer; another against the baptism of infants; a third would maintain the thesis that there was no need of ordained ministers at all, since any man might be moved by the Spirit of God to preach and pray—a doctrine as horrible to the Presbyterian as making priests of the lowest of the people to the Levite; while all alike would contend for liberty of conscience, including the right of every sect to worship with its own forms, and promulgate its own doctrines.

*Re-modelled army.*

In Oxford the new army was rather despised than feared. The Cavaliers scoffed at "Noll Cromwell" going forth "in the might of his spirit, with his swords and his Bibles, and all the train of his disciples, every one of whom is as David, a man of war and a prophet." Yet such confidence was singularly ill founded. It was Cromwell's men who had overthrown the Cavaliers on Marston Moor, and now a whole army was coming against them, fired by the same fierce enthusiasm as the Ironsides. Fanatical as these might be in their zeal, their courage was undoubtedly steeled by the conviction that, like the Israelites of old, they were fighting in God's cause, and that in such a cause victory must come, and death was better than delaying it.*

Obedience—the first step to victory—was rigidly enforced. Soon after the army left Windsor, a council of war was held upon several soldiers for disobeying regulations, and the body of one was left hanging upon a tree, as a warning to his comrades. The following day a proclamation was made that it was 'death for any to plunder.' The man whom Charles described as the "rebels' new brutish general," was Fairfax. He had been the chief framer of the new model army. He was no self-seeker, but a simple and straightforward patriot. Too refined to be a fanatic, he was deeply religious. His family had fought for the Protestant cause in the Low Countries, and he had himself seen service there as a lad. Fearless as a lion, fire and daring were his chief characteristics at first, but he soon showed power as an organizer, and was as vigilant as he was collected in the field. His wife was a general's daughter, and cheered his soldiers by her presence in the camp. Though of delicate health, he was as ready to face discomfort and hardships as peril. Once, when his own regiment grumbled at being ordered to bring up the rear instead of leading the column, he dismounted from his horse, and himself marched on foot that whole day at its head. Lessons like these have not to be read twice. By the self-denying ordinance Crom-

* The spirit of the Ironsides is not wholly extinct. In 1856 the question whether Kansas was to be a free or slave state gave rise to a border war. John Brown, a descendant of one of the English pilgrims who sailed to America in the "Mayflower" in 1620, formed a camp of God-fearing Puritans, who were "earnestness incarnate." Six of them were his own sons. Twenty-eight of these defeated fifty-six pro-slave borderers, and once 2000 Missourians retreated before 250 of his men. John Brown was taken and hanged in 1859, but his story became the marching-song in the great war of abolition (1861—1865).

well had been displaced. But Cromwell's name had become a talisman of victory, and instructions were soon sent him by the committee of the two nations to take command of a body of horse in the west (23rd April). Fairfax and his officers not long afterwards petitioned the Lower House for Cromwell's appointment as lieutenant-general of the horse (6th June); and though the appointment was nominally temporary, it was always renewed, and his position, both as officer and member, soon became unassailable. *Cromwell lieutenant-general of new army.*

On the other hand some of the best of the king's officers had been killed, others displaced to make way for worse men than themselves. Goring and Grenville, two unprincipled adventurers, commanded in the west, and were ruining the king's cause by their conduct towards one another and the people. Hyde and Colepepper were sent with the Prince of Wales, now a boy of fourteen, to bring them to obedience; but the prince's presence only added new fuel to the fire, and between the jealousy of the generals, the insubordination of the officers, and the marauding habits of the soldiers, the king's interest declined rapidly in those parts. *Royalist decline in west.*

Early in May the king himself left Oxford for the north, and joined Rupert near Chester, intending to take the enemy in detail, and attack the Scots before he met the re-modelled army of Fairfax. This plan was changed on the news that the re-modelled army was itself investing Oxford. He now determined to march east towards the associated counties, expecting that Fairfax would draw off his forces from Oxford for their protection. The line of march led the army by Leicester, which was held for the Parliament. Rupert erected a battery, and sent a summons to the garrison to surrender. Not receiving an answer at once, he opened fire. For three days " both sides plied each other with cannon and musket-shot as fast as they could charge and discharge, and so continued all day and all night." On the morning of the fourth day a general assault was ordered on six or seven different points, and, after a terrible struggle, the Cavaliers forced their way into the town, falling three to one, according to their own calculation. The garrison, about 1000 in number, threw down their arms and became prisoners of war; but the townspeople suffered dreadfully, the Royalists at their first entrance putting many to the sword, and *Storming of Leicester.*

plundering churches, hospitals, Royalists and Roundheads indiscriminately.* Charles was so much elated by this success that, a few days after the storming of Leicester, he wrote to the queen: "I may, without being too much sanguine, affirm that since the rebellion my affairs were never in so fair and hopeful a way."

Rupert was still in favour of one of the bolder courses, of marching either east against the associated counties, or northwards on the Scots; but Charles was persuaded to turn south and relieve Oxford, which he believed was still closely invested. He was grievously misinformed. On hearing of the fate of Leicester, Fairfax had raised the siege, and was now marching north to offer the king battle. On reaching Kislingbury, within five miles of the Royalist quarters, which were on Borough Hill, outside Daventry (12th June), he learnt from some stragglers that the enemy were in complete ignorance of his movements, the king out hunting, the soldiers in no order, the horses at grass. Yet all that night the careful general rode round his outposts in the rain, half expecting the Royalists would attempt a surprise on hearing of his presence. But at three in the morning he saw a blaze on Borough Hill; the Royalists had fired the huts they had made of the furze then covering the hill, and could be seen riding fast away to the north. The unexpected arrival of the enemy had, in fact, determined Charles to return to Leicester, and there recruit his army before risking a battle. Fairfax was holding a council of war at six in the morning, when Cromwell, just made lieutenant-general of the horse, came in from the associated counties, bringing with him a troop of six hundred horse and dragoons. The soldiers greeted Cromwell's arrival with huzzas; the generals soon settled their plans; the king was pursued; and that same evening (13th June) a body of horse under Ireton beat up the Royalist rear at Naseby, taking several prisoners. The fugitives carried the news that night to the main body, who had advanced some seven miles to Harborough. The

*Charles holds a council of war.* king himself was lodged at Lubenham Hall, a mile or two west of Harborough, to which town he rode at once, and summoned a council of war, 'resting in a chair in a low room,' till his officers were roused from their beds, and collected from their various quarters. Of the council, some proposed

* Sprigge, Anglia Rediviva; King's Pamp., 212.

to wait for reinforcements expected from the west, but the majority agreed with Rupert that the insult was too much to be endured; that, as the Roundheads pleased to follow, they would turn and fight, not doubting they would defeat the psalm-singing saints, who had cast off their natural leaders.

Between Sibbertoft and Naseby the country rises and falls in a succession of rounded undulating hills. Both villages stand high; the lowest depression between the two is a piece of marshy land, now called Broad Moor. From Broad Moor the ground rises rapidly at first to the south; it is then broken by smaller hollows, and then continues to rise more gradually to the village of Naseby. This country, now covered with trees, hedges, cornfields, and meadows, on that morning of the 14th of June lay still in nature's keeping, for the most part an open pasture-ground, scattered over with furze-bushes. Patches of corn-land were discernible here and there, but the ground was mainly unenclosed, as in fact it remained till within the last half-century.

Fairfax, who early in the morning saw large bodies of horse moving on a hill a little south of Harborough, drew up his army on the brow of Mill Hill, which immediately slopes down into Broad Moor. Cromwell and the Ironsides occupied the ground on the right, flanked by Naseby rabbit-warren. Fairfax himself commanded the main body. The left wing, led by Ireton, was composed of horse, with some dragoons on foot, who were set to line the one hedge on the field which then, as now, marked the boundary line of the parishes of Naseby and Sulby. The baggage was left behind at Naseby, nearly two miles in the rear. The word for the day was passed along the ranks as "God is our strength."

About ten o'clock the Royalists were seen advancing over the Sibbertoft Hills in order of battle. The two armies were both between 10,000 and 11,000 strong, there not being "five hundred odds in number." The king's force consisted of about 5520 horse and 5300 foot. The Parliamentarians were stronger in infantry than in horse. Fairfax, wishing to conceal from the advancing enemy the exact form of his battle, ordered his soldiers to fall back a hundred paces in a hollow behind the brow of Mill Hill. Rupert, who, as usual, commanded the Royalist right wing, gathered from this movement that the enemy was in full retreat, and thought the day already his own.

*Battle of Naseby, 14th June, 1645.*

## MAP OF NASEBY.

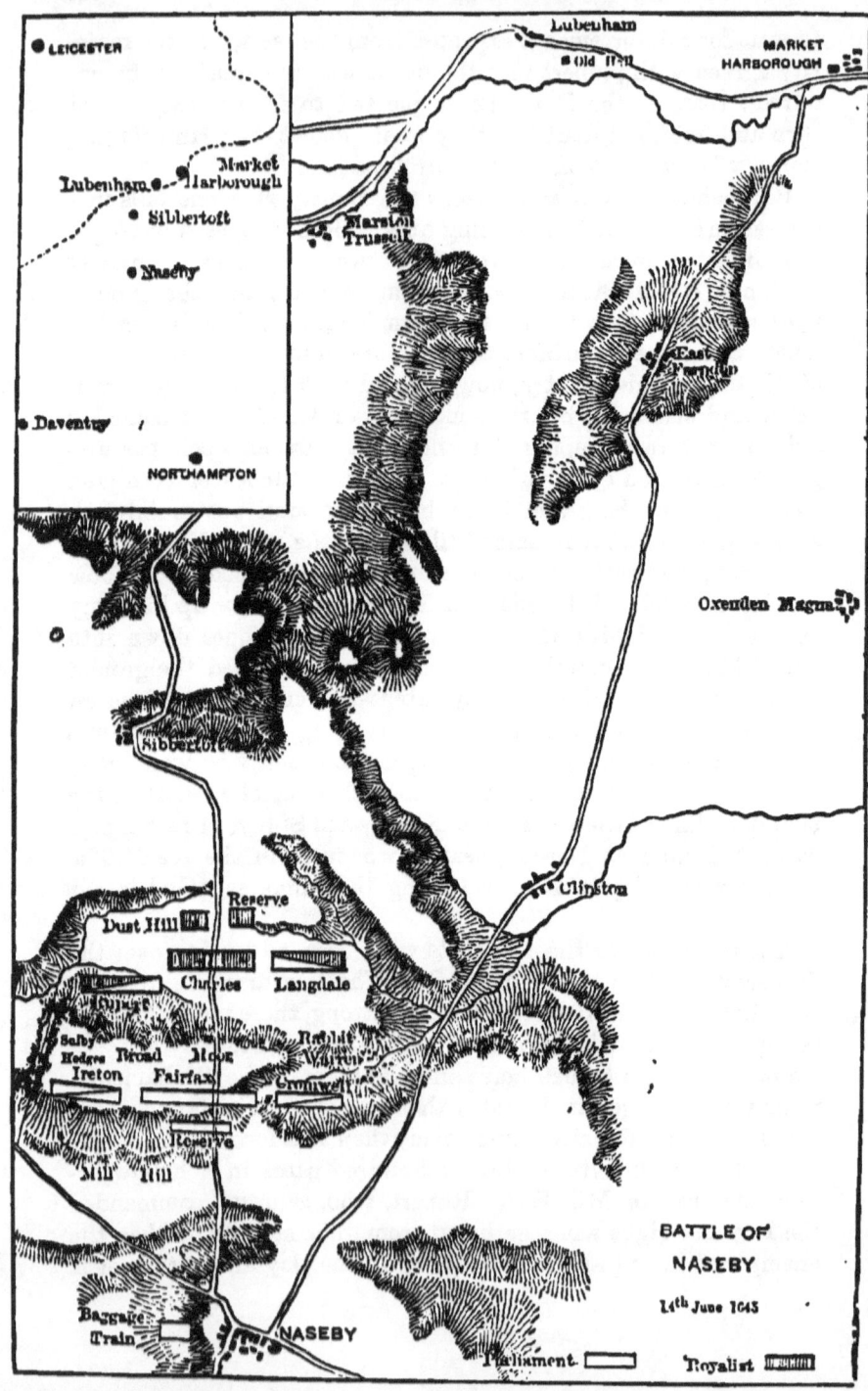

It was the work of a moment to send word back and bid Charles come on with all speed, and then he and his Cavaliers, shouting their word, "Queen Mary!" dashed down Dust Hill, over Broad Moor, and up Mill Hill. The dragoons who lined Sulby hedges on his right fired hotly on him as he passed, but he charged till he drove into Ireton's horse, sent them fly- ing before him, and in headlong course galloped away hard up to Naseby hamlet. There he spied the baggage-train, and made for it; the commander, hardly thinking the Cavaliers could be there already, seeing, as he thought, his own general officer approaching, asked, hat in hand, "How goes the day?" "Will you have quarter?" was Rupert's curt rejoinder, for it was he. The commander declined, and Rupert, still nothing doubting his friends were as successful as himself, wasted much precious time in an attack on the baggage, which the guard successfully repelled. <sub>Charge of Rupert.</sub>

The other divisions of the king's army hurried on after the right wing, in slight disorder and too quickly to bring up all their artillery with them. Their left wing was ordered to charge up the hill against Cromwell, who commanded the Parliament's right wing. But before they had time to charge home, the Ironsides came on over rabbit-burrows and furze-bushes, swinging down upon Broad Moor with all the impetus of the hill, broke the Royalist horse, and sent them flying fast and far behind their foot. Leaving some horse to prevent their rallying again, Cromwell turned round with the remaining troops to assist his friends. The infantry in the Parliament's centre was in difficulties; on the first charge of the king's foot all, except Fairfax' own regiment, "gave back in disorder," but their officers snatched the colours, and, with the help of the reserve, soon rallied and brought them on again. Fairfax, with animation in voice and eye, looking even taller than his wont, rode about in the thick of the danger, cheering on his troops. His helmet was beaten off by a sword, and the colonel of his guards, seeing him riding bareheaded amid showering bullets, begged him to take his own in its place. "'Tis well enough," shortly replied the general. Skippon behaved as bravely; though dangerously shot in the side, he refused to leave the field—"As long as one man will stand, I will not stir." It was at this critical moment, when the Royalist left wing was broken, Rupert and the right wing nowhere to be seen, that Cromwell's horse rode up and charged the king's main <sub>Ironsides break Royalist left.</sub>

body in flank. This decided the day. The Royalist lines turned and fled. One regiment of Bluecoats, indeed, rivalled the gallantry of Newcastle's Whitecoats on Marston Moor in resisting the efforts of the enemy to break them. Leaving their greater number lying wounded or dead upon the ground, they too at last were scattered before the combined charge of Cromwell and Fairfax. The Royalist reserves of horse and foot now alone remained undisordered. Rupert, as usual, brought back some of his Cavaliers to the field in time to see the battle lost. His return awoke a gleam of hope in Charles' breast, who, placing himself at the head of his horse-guards, prepared for a last desperate charge upon the Ironsides. "Face about once!" he cried, "give one charge more, and recover the day!" But a Scotchman, the Earl of Carnwath, seized his bridle and turned his horse's head, swearing and saying, "Will you go upon your death?" Some one at the same moment cried out, "March to the right!" an order which caused the whole troop to turn their backs on the enemy, thinking they were intended to shift for themselves. In an instant all were in full flight, and had ridden a quarter of a mile before they could be rallied again. And then, indeed, the day was lost, for the Royalist foot were flying, hopelessly broken by the final charge of Cromwell and Fairfax. "They ran away," says a Parliamentarian, "both fronts and reserves, without standing one stroke more." Off went the beaten Cavaliers after the foot, leaving for the enemy their cannon, carriages, arms, jewels, clothes, and a cabinet of letters belonging to the king, "supposed to be of great consequence." The battle had lasted only three hours when the day was won. The chase was carried for twenty miles, through Harborough, to within sight of Leicester; 5000 prisoners were taken; 2000 Royalists said to be left dead on the ground.*

*King's letters taken.*

The victory was complete, but it was not the Royalists only who were depressed by it. The Presbyterians felt their sun had set to the Independents, and became more desirous than ever to conclude a peace with the king. This was the king's chance, but the cabinet of letters foiled it. The Independents agreed the Presbyterians should have their way if this prize proved the king was not the deceiver they had painted him. A trial of the

* Rushworth; Whitelock; Clar. Hist. v., 175; Sprigge, Anglia Rediviva; King's Pamphlets, 212; Markham, Life of Lord Fairfax; Carlyle, Letters and Speeches of Cromwell.

king's capacity for keeping treaties was then held before a crowd of citizens at Guildhall. The letters were read, and amongst other passages the following, addressed to the queen :—" I give thee power to promise in my name, to whom thou thinkest most fit, that I will take away all the Penal Laws against Roman Catholics in England, as soon as God shall make me able to do it ; so as by their means I have so powerful assistance as may deserve so great a favour, and enable me to do it" (5th March, 1645).— "I must again tell thee that most assuredly France will be the best way for transporting the Duke of Lorraine's army, there being divers fit and safe places of landing for them upon the western coasts" (Oxford, 30th March, 1645). These letters were then published by order of Parliament, who were bound to make known to the nation the dangers that menaced it. A cry of indignation rose on all sides against the king. Men said there could be no doubt of his bad faith. Though he had so often declared his intention of maintaining the Protestant religion, he was allowing his wife to make promises to the Catholics in his name ; and then, while his commissioners were negotiating peace at Uxbridge, he had been intriguing to bring over foreign soldiers into England. The questions of peace, war, and religion were all to be settled by the Catholic queen ; she was to have the disposal of the destinies of England, and the concessions at Uxbridge had been only a blind—no peace was ever intended. To offer the repeal of the law as a price for the aid of the English Papists was either a mockery, or a proof of the intention to rule without Parliaments.

The war now entered on its last stage. Charles' army was gone ; all that was left were small forces, scattered about in the west, or engaged in garrison duty. The Scots, who had been besieging the towns near the Border, now marched right down through the country and laid siege to Hereford, while Fairfax and Cromwell marched west, driving before them Goring and Grenville's beggarly troops, with their knavish leaders—as Clarendon himself described them—and forcing the garrison of one town to surrender after another. The king, meanwhile, with a body of 1000 horse, was in Wales and the western counties, flitting about from place to place in a purposeless way, and sometimes hardly knowing where to betake himself for safety. "Whatever you do," writes Colepepper, still with the

*Last stage of war.*

Prince of Wales, to Lord Digby, "take care of the king's person. I assure you these skipping jaunts make my heart ache."

Though the war had now reached its lowest ebb, the country suffered more than ever. The adherents of the Parliament, whose estates lay in districts hitherto Royalist, now came down upon their tenants for rents already paid to the king's friends. Excisemen, sent by the Parliament into the country, compelled the people to pay taxes for sheep, money, or provisions of which they had been robbed by the plundering Royalists. In some cases so much suffering ensued, that the very soldiers said "they would starve before they would be employed in forcing the tax, or take any of it for their pay." In the north the Scots lived at free quarters, and their conduct made the people look on them as freebooters rather than as friends. In the west the king's soldiers became mere marauders; men were captured with as much as £20 in their pockets; while their leaders cast innocent men into prison, merely to exact a ransom.

*Clubmen in west.* When Fairfax and Cromwell marched into the west, they found that in these counties the country-people had begun to assemble in bodies, sometimes 5000 strong, to resist their oppressors, whether they fought in the name of King or Parliament. They were called clubmen from their arms, and carried banners, with the motto—

> "If you offer to plunder our cattle,
> Be assured we will give you battle."

The clubmen, however, could not hope to control the movements of the disciplined troops who now appeared against them. After a few fruitless attempts at resistance they dispersed, leaving the new army to do their work more effectually by completely suppressing the Royalists.

Charles himself, in the midst of his wanderings and reverses, was too proud to think of leaving England or deserting his throne, or even as yet of humbling himself to purchase peace from Presbyterians or Independents. But his friends began to despair.

*Rupert surrenders Bristol.* Rupert himself wrote to counsel peace, and soon afterwards surrendered Bristol, the most important town in the west. The defences had been stormed and partially carried by Cromwell and Fairfax; and though Rupert was severely criticized by men who believed the town might still have held out, there seems no just ground for attributing the capture

## 1645.] DEFEAT OF MONTROSE. 189

to any pusillanimity in the prince. Charles, however, who had understood from Rupert that, if no mutiny happened in the garrison, he would keep the place for four months, felt deeply wounded at this apparent desertion of his cause. He sent the prince an indignant letter, with a pass to take him beyond seas.

The surrender of Bristol was soon followed by a second blow. Montrose had come down from the Highlands for another summer's raid, in which he gained three victories over the Covenanters (Aulderne, 4th May; Alford, 2nd July; Kilsyth, 15th August); gentlemen of the Lowlands had been induced by his success to declare for the king; Edinburgh had opened its gates; and the army of the Covenanters in England had been obliged to raise the siege of Hereford, and march back northwards to meet this new enemy. Charles, on hearing of the surrender of Bristol, started to join Montrose, now, as he believed, about to fulfil his promises, and enter England at the head of a Royalist army. But at Chester his own troops were defeated and dispersed by Poyntz, a commander of the Parliament, and, after he had escaped himself to Wales, he heard the disastrous news that the army he sought to join no longer existed. Montrose, surprised by Lesley at Philiphaugh, on the border, not far north of Carlisle, had been entirely routed, and had again become a fugitive in the Highlands. *Montrose defeated at Philiphaugh (13th Sept., 1645).* The king with difficulty now made his way first to Newark, and afterwards to Oxford, where he was thankful to find himself once again in safety for a time (6th Nov.). But it was evident that Oxford would not be safe for long. Fairfax was completing his victorious career in the west; that over, the siege of Oxford would follow at once, and then it would not be long before the king was a prisoner of war. Overtures of peace were the only hope, and Charles sent one message upon the heels of another, offering to come to London and treat in person with the Parliament (Dec. and Jan., 1645-6). But his messages met with no friendly reception at Westminster. The Presbyterians, no doubt, would before have been glad to treat, preferring even the Royalists to the Independents; but they had now lost alike the power and the will to treat. Two causes had weakened their power. During the autumn months 130 new members were elected to fill the vacancies five years had caused by death, desertion, or expulsion. Though Presbyterians were returned in larger numbers, *Presbyterian decline. —Causes: I. New elections.*

yet through want of experience, or want of ability, they did not carry half so much weight with them as the new Independent members, many of whom had already won distinction in politics or in war. Such were Hutchinson, Ludlow, Blake the admiral of the future, Fleetwood, Ireton who soon afterwards became Cromwell's son-in-law,* and Algernon Sidney son of the Earl of Leicester. The officers who got their seats by these new elections did not come under the provisions of the self-denying ordinance, so that, while the Presbyterians had lost their commissions, the newer party won their seats and kept their commissions as well.

The second cause that weakened the influence of the Presbyte-

II. Conduct of Scots.

rians was the oppressive conduct of their friends the Scots while quartered in the northern counties. But, supposing the Presbyterian party had had the power to make peace of themselves, at this time they had no longer the will. This was in consequence of a new disclosure. A year before this Charles had authorized Ormond to make promises to the Irish Catholics in his name.† The Catholics, however, were wary, and refused to hear of a peace, or of rendering the king any assistance, without first obtaining his consent to the establishment of their own religion in Ireland. If Charles granted these conditions, he knew the affection of his own party in England would be cooled, while the hate of the Puritans would be increased ten-thousand-fold against him. The problem that had been occupying his mind for the last twelve months was how to obtain aid from the Irish, and yet keep concealed from the English the terms on which it was granted, until victory should enable him to set public opinion at defiance. He had solved it by entrusting to Lord Herbert, Earl of Glamorgan, the most loyal of Catholics, a secret warrant, signed by his own hand, and sealed with his private seal, giving him power to make terms with the Council of Kilkenny, without

III. Glamorgan's secret treaty with Irish.

the privity of the Earl of Ormond. Accordingly Glamorgan concluded a secret treaty, in which it was agreed that, all penal laws being repealed, the Roman Catholics were to be allowed the public exercise of their religion, and to hold the revenues of all churches of which they had gained possession since the war first broke out. As they held far more than half the churches, this amounted to the establishment of their religion. They, on their side, were to send 20,000 men to assist his Majesty in England (12th Aug., 1645). After the defeat

. * Married Bridget Cromwell, 15th June, 1646.   † See p. 176.

at Naseby, Charles also wrote to the pope, engaging his royal word to fulfil whatever conditions should be agreed upon by Glamorgan. But this treaty came to light, like Charles' other secret plots. In a skirmish fought in Ireland, duplicates of the whole transaction were taken in the carriage of a Catholic archbishop, and sent to London to the committee of the two nations (Oct., 1645). After having reserved this secret for three months, the Independents caused the papers to be read in Parliament and published, at the very time when Charles was sending one message after another for a treaty of peace (Jan.). The country was in a ferment of indignation. The establishment of the Roman Catholic religion in a Catholic country seems an innocent proposition, if not a just concession. To understand the ferment it raised, it is necessary to recall the circumstances of the time. The Thirty Years' War was still in progress. The fire of the Reformation was still burning in men's hearts. They had come out of a great struggle, in which Europe had been split into two camps. Protestant nations had preserved their religious independence only by resisting the armed assaults of Catholicism. The gain was worth the struggle, but there is no struggle without some bitterness remaining, and the Catholics were the victims of this bitterness. The hate felt by Protestants towards Catholics was, in fact, one of the characteristics of the age. The Protestants regarded the Catholic religion as at once idolatrous and subversive of all good government. The gorgeous and imposing ceremonies, standing in such striking contrast to the simplicity of Puritan worship; the blind obedience to the pope; the doctrine that the end justifies the means, illustrated as this had been by the massacre of St. Bartholomew, the Gunpowder Plot, and the late butchery in Ireland—all this had raised up in the nation's mind such a wall of prejudice that the Catholics, regarded as a class, were shut out of all sympathy whatsoever. For a people with these feelings to see, as it seemed, the fruits of the victory over Spain bartered away by the king in return for the loan of savage and Popish troops, to be used against the liberty of Protestant subjects, was more than could be borne. The Royalist Hyde, in the history he wrote of the rebellion, omitted all mention of this business with Glamorgan, which he could not palliate. In his private correspondence he calls it "inexcusable to justice, piety, and prudence."

While Charles' friends were disgusted with the treaty, his enemies looked upon it as another proof of the unfathomable deceitfulness of his nature: for, "while he was protesting before God to the Parliament, saying, 'I will never abrogate the laws against the Papists,' he was underhand dealing with the Irish rebels, and promising to repeal the laws against them; and while he said, 'I abhor to think of bringing foreign soldiers into the kingdom,' he was soliciting the Duke of Lorraine, the French, the Danes, the very Irish, for assistance." The newspapers had their scathing criticisms. "We are experienced," wrote a weekly Intelligencer, "that kings often deal like watermen: look one way and row another. What else mean those overtures of a treaty with us, when those bloodthirsty rebels are proffered the enjoyment of Popery! Now judge whether the king hath any real intention of peace, when he labours to bring over 10,000 of the Irish rebels to cut our throats here, as they have done to divers of our brethren there!" Meantime, to save the king's character, the Earl of Ormond put Glamorgan at once into prison, as though he had acted without authority. Charles again offered to come to London for a personal treaty, declaring to the Parliament that, until Glamorgan's arrest, he had never heard of the negotiations (January 29th). His words, however, found no credit at Westminster, and his warrant to Glamorgan still remains to give the lie to his statement. Glamorgan, who had been devoted enough not to reveal his secret instructions, was released after a month's imprisonment (February 1st), and continued the negotiation. The landing of a body of Irish troops was, it seems, only prevented by the war coming to an end before they were ready to sail.

*Indignation felt in the country.*

Whether or no such a treaty would have been politic at any time in the war, it was certainly impolitic now. The one chance now was to divide the two parties; the arrival of Irish soldiers on such terms would have thrown Presbyterians and Independents into one another's arms as brothers, while the troops themselves would have been taken at sea, or crushed on landing, where there would have been no force to join them.

By the end of March, the royal forces, scattered over the west, were all defeated and dispersed, or forced to take refuge in garrison towns. Hyde and the Prince of Wales were driven down to the very extremity of Cornwall, and had to sail from the coast (March 1st). Sir Jacob Astley, an old gray-headed Cavalier, was the last to resist in the open field. "Now, gentlemen," he said, to the officers of the Parliament, on surrendering, "you have done your work, and may go play, unless you choose to fall out amongst yourselves" (March 22nd).

It was on the belief that his enemies would still fall out among themselves, that Charles now grounded his hopes of restoration to his throne. At the same time that he was courting the Presbyterians, and proposing to come to London and treat with them in person, he was making secret offers to the Independents to root out the Presbyterians, offering them freedom of conscience, if they would ensure the same to the Royalists. "I am not without hope," he wrote about this time, "that I shall be able to draw either the Presbyterians or Independents to side with me for extirpating the one or the other—that I shall be really king again." But the distrust he had engendered was too deep: his advances were not met, and he soon found that, unless he made haste to get out of Oxford before it was invested, he should fall into his enemies' hands, without having bound them to any conditions at all.

After much consultation, it was agreed that his best plan would be to seek a refuge in the Scottish army. M. de Montreuil, the French ambassador, had been authorized by Cardinal Mazarin, the chief minister of Louis XIV., to negotiate an agreement between Charles and the Scots, and engage the faith of France for the performance of whatever promises either side should make. Though Charles refused to agree to take the covenant, Montreuil at first obtained a written engagement from the Scots' commissioners in London, to the effect that if the king came to them, they would receive him as their natural king, offer no violence to his person or conscience, and endeavour to procure a happy and well-grounded peace. But the London commissioners soon drew back, thinking they had gone too far; while the commissioners at the Scottish camp refused to make any such agreement, only promising to receive the king, and demanding that he should give them satisfaction in the question of religion, by which they meant, take the covenant, as soon as possible. Upon this poor security, Charles, accompanied by two companions, left Oxford in the guise of a servant (27th April), and after nine days' wanderings, arrived in safety at Kelham, near Newark, the head-quarters of the Scots. Montreuil brought him some

*Charles with Scots.*

verbal promise of safety and introduced him into the camp (5th May). The chief officers affected extreme surprise at his appearance, but at the same time great gratitude for the trust he had placed in them. "I shall be well satisfied," replied the king, "if you perform the conditions upon which I have come to you." But they corrected him when he used the word "conditions," saying, 'they had never been privy to anything of that nature; and if the king had made any treaty, it must be with the Scottish commissioners in London, which was no concern of theirs.' Charles' spirits fell, and he already wished himself out of their power.

When the news reached London, the Independents were furious. They thought the king would never have taken the step without having made up his mind to consent to the covenant, establish the Presbyterian Church, and in return be allowed to rule subject to Presbyterian guidance ; while they, the true conquerors, would be persecuted by Presbyterians and Royalists, their noble army be disbanded, their noble cause—freedom of conscience—be stifled at its birth. To stave off such an end as this, they might, no doubt, have used their army, and appealed to force. But the Independents still aimed at a victory within the lines of the constitution. Parliament, and not the army, was the supreme authority ; it was in the sacred name of Parliament that they had won their victories, and they still wished to lead the Parliament, and not to fight it. Although, therefore, inclined in the first flush of anger to have followed the Scots and taken possession of the king's person by force, they contented themselves with doing all in their power to produce a rupture between the two nations, in order that the Commons might vote war, and they, in obedience to the supreme authority of the nation, might lead the Ironsides to fight the hated allies. In the newspapers, in pamphlets, in Parliament, at all times, in all places, the Independents attacked the Scots as traitors, the cruel oppressors of the northern counties, who designed to betray and ruin England. The national hatred was readily excited, and, after many debates, the Commons voted that the Scotch army was no longer required, that it should be asked what was owing to it, and be requested to withdraw (11th June).

But the Scots, who had already retreated in fear as far as Newcastle, were willing to bear any amount of reproach rather than draw down upon themselves the Independent army. On their side, the English Presbyterians, still the majority in the Commons, were far more anxious to disband the dangerous sectarian army, than to batten it on the blood of their own northern allies. The Independents could not bring about a war, when so many were determined not to quarrel. Charles outwardly did what he could to effect an agreement. He sent messages to the two Houses, urging them to draw up peace propositions; ordered the commanders of all towns and castles still held for him to surrender (10th June); bade Montrose, who was then a wanderer in the Highlands, to lay down his arms; and made a parade of sending orders to Ormond to make no peace with the Irish rebels—orders which Ormond had secret instructions to disobey (11th June).

Charles' outward submission aided the efforts of the Presbyterians, and he finally received peace propositions from Parliament (23rd July). By these, he was required to take the covenant, to establish the Presbyterian Church, to surrender to Parliament, for twenty years, the command of the army, navy, and militia; to consent that seventy-seven of his friends should be excluded from amnesty, and that all his party should be shut out from public employment during the pleasure of Parliament. Anxiously was Charles' answer looked for on both sides. If he consented, the Independents would either be obliged to submit to Presbyterian tyranny, or begin a second civil war against Scots, English Presbyterians, and Royalists united. If he refused, the Presbyterians were checkmated; they could make no concession on the Church question; on the militia question they could not get easier terms for him against the opposition of the Independents, and dared not offer easier terms if they got them, because they had no confidence in his word. The possible prospect of his refusal revealed darkly looming before them a thousand difficulties in retaining their own supremacy over the sectarians. "The great God," was their prayer, "soften that man's heart, or else he will fall in tragic miseries, and bring ruin upon himself and us together."

The king endured a bitter trial for the next six months. He would have made some concessions about the militia, had not his wife forbidden him; but he could not bring himself to establish a new Presbyterian Church in England. Some trace his reluctance on this point to a belief that the support of the Church was even more essential to monarchical power than the command of the militia; but this view seems to do injustice both to his sense and his sincerity. He had too much ability to believe the pen of the bishop could guard his throne as well as the sword of the army. The 'command of the militia' had been the stake of the war, and there was now not a militia, but an army, to command. Secondly, a careful study of his letters induces the belief that his religious convictions were deeper and stronger than his political views. His political views may have been taught to him by his father and his ministers; his religious views were taught by his father, his ministers, and his heart. Yet it was on this very point that his friends, both at home and abroad, most urgently pressed him to yield. They thought that if this concession by itself did not win over the Parliament, it would certainly win over the Scots. To keep the militia, to yield the Church, was the command, rather than the advice, of his wife. "By granting the militia," she wrote, "you cut your own throat, for then there is nothing you can refuse, no not my life even, if they ask it; but I will take care not to fall into their hands."* Her letters were always written in the same heartless tone. She was far less tender of her husband's happiness, conscience, or life, than she was of his power. If he regained his old authority, she was ready to return and share it with him; if he lost it, she would sooner he stayed a prisoner in England than trouble her with the presence of a crownless fugitive. Charles, however, wrote doleful letters, pointing out that if he did not quit the kingdom now, he might lose his last chance of escape. These she only answered by forbidding him to think of escape, until the Scots should have declared in plain language they would not protect him. Poor Charles! there were two acts for which he felt real regret, and to both of which he had been urged by his queen; the first was, in his own words, "that base, unworthy concession about Strafford;" the second, "that great wrong and injustice to the Church, of taking away bishops' votes in Parliament." Though he sacrificed his personal safety to her wishes, he refused to load his conscience a third time for her

* "Vous vous êtes coupé la gorge; car vous ne leur pouvez rien refuser, pas même ma vie, s'ils vous la demandent. Mais je ne me mettrai pas entre leurs mains."

## HIS SCRUPLES.

satisfaction. It was one of the few occasions on which Charles resisted Henrietta's wishes. The result was that he came off with more honour than he usually did out of such negotiations. He had, in fact, asked advice of a worthier counsellor than either his weak self or his worldly wife. The policy which he was himself tempted to adopt, though seemingly aware it was wrong, is expressed in a letter to Juxon, from which it appears that he had a scruple about breaking the letter of the formal contract he had made in his coronation oath, even with the consent of the party with whom he had made it, but had none about making a new oath to his people and breaking it as soon as he had got all he could by making it. Like other kings he considered that the sanctity of an oath only attached to one which bound him to do what he himself approved. He had, in fact, the casuistical conscience, which instead of shrinking from what it condemns, only asks, 'How can I do it without guilt?' Juxon's answer is not recorded, but as on the memorable occasion of Strafford's trial so now he doubtless bade Charles 'follow his conscience,' and this time apparently with more effect. The issue, at all events, was that Charles only gave the commissioners a letter to Parliament, proposing he should come to London to treat in person (1st Aug.).

Though the Presbyterians were disappointed with his answer, which was tantamount to a refusal, they still believed that, once in their hands, they could wring the concessions from him, and then disband the Independent army. After some haggling, the Scots secured a written promise for £400,000, as the charge to which they had been put by the war. A treaty was signed accordingly (Dec.). Though no mention was made of the king, it was fully understood that the Scots were to deliver him up, when their army evacuated Newcastle. As Charles had come to his enemies' camp, uninvited, after refusing the covenant, Scots surrender king. the only terms on which they offered to protect him, they were not bound to let him go, still less to fight for him ; though they would have done even that, if he would now have agreed to their offer. It was understood that if he was given up, the English Presbyterians would restore him to the throne, on their own terms, and disband the 'evil army'* of the Independents. It would have been perfectly justifiable in the Scots to give him up

* Baillie.

on these terms. Not content with this they made a canny bargain. No doubt, had they given him up without a money treaty, they would never have been paid their arrears, and this was much to poor men. As it was, they got their money, but more than their money's worth of abuse. They earned the abuse by making the terms of surrender mercenary, and not political. The distinction may seem fine, and the judgment hard. But there are cases where a high sense of honour can alone save men from deep dishonour. They were now called 'the traitor Scots,' 'the Jews who sold their king,' and as they marched out of Newcastle, which was always Royalist in feeling, the very women were all but stoning them (30th Jan.). Meantime, the Presbyterian commissioners escorted the king from Newcastle to the residence assigned him at Holmby House in Northamptonshire. On the road crowds flocked to see him. The country people everywhere hoped that their troubles were over, that an agreement would be made on which the army would be disbanded, and the king return to London with honour and safety.* Near Nottingham Charles met Sir Thomas Fairfax, who dismounted to kiss his hand, and afterwards rode through the town by his side. At Holmby he received a hearty welcome from a large concourse of gentlemen, ladies, and yeomen (Feb. 13th). Well content with his reception, his spirits rose, and he made no doubt he should yet get either Presbyterians or Independents to unite with him, "to extirpate the other and make him really a king again!"

* Ludlow, i. 162.

www.ingramcontent.com/pod-product-compliance
Lightning Source LLC
Chambersburg PA
CBHW020925230426
43666CB00008B/1571